Boys Don't Cry

Boys Don't Cry

*The Struggle for Justice and Healing
in Canada's Biggest Sex Abuse Scandal*

Darcy Henton
with David McCann

Canadian Cataloguing in Publication Data

Henton, Darcy, 1957–
  Boys don't cry: the struggle for justice and healing in Canada's biggest sex abuse scandal

Includes index.
ISBN 0-7710-4066-0

1. Child sexual abuse – Ontario – Alfred. 2. Child sexual abuse – Ontario – Uxbridge. 3. Child abuse – Ontario – Alfred. 4. Child abuse – Ontario – Uxbridge. 5. St. Joseph's Training School (Alfred, Ont.). 6. St. John's Training School (Uxbridge, Ont.). 7. Christian Brothers. 8. Adult child abuse victims – Canada. I. McCann, David, 1946–   . II. Title.

HV6570.4.C3H45 1995   364.1'536   C95-930138-0

The publisher acknowledges the support of the Canada Council and the Ontario Arts Council for their publishing program.

Typesetting by M&S, Toronto

Printed and bound in Canada on acid-free paper

McClelland & Stewart Inc.
The Canadian Publishers
481 University Avenue
Toronto, Ontario
M5G 2E9

1 2 3 4 5   99 98 97 96 95

To the boys of St. Joseph's and St. John's training schools and to the families and friends who stood beside them. Their courage in voluntarily disclosing the abuse they suffered at the hands of some of the Christian Brothers and staff in whose care they were entrusted has enabled the healing of these old wounds to start and has fundamentally altered the way we, as a society, deal with the survivors of male child abuse.

Contents

Foreword by Judge David Cole

In 1848, a royal commission, known as the Brown Commission, was appointed to investigate complaints that the warden and staff of Kingston Penitentiary had watched over a cruel, indiscriminate, and ineffective disciplinary regime. The commission found that children, who at the time were kept in the same institutions as adults, suffered disproportionately under this administration. The commission reported that

> an eleven-year-old whose offences were talking, laughing and idling was flogged, over a three year period, thirty eight times with the rawhide and six times with the cat [o' nine tails]; another boy whose "offences were of the most trifling description − such as were to be expected from a child of 10 or 11 . . . was stripped to the shirt, and publicly lashed thirty seven times in eight and a half months."[1]

Beyond these individual examples of "barbarity, disgraceful to humanity," the commission found that the provision for outside inspection "had proved inadequate to the task of controlling the abuses and excesses of the warden." Despite the existence of a local board of inspectors, the commission "pointed out how likely the unrestricted and continued exercise of arbitrary power is to degenerate into apathy or tyranny."[2]

Since the publication of the Brown Commission Report, some fifteen other royal commissions in Ontario have substantiated allegations of mistreatment of children in training schools, orphanages, children's mental health centres, residential schools, and prisons. Most recently, the Commission on Systemic Racism in the Ontario Criminal Justice System has released an interim report which concludes that overt and systemic racism are rife in both adult and young offender facilities.

And these reports deal only with Ontario. To get a true sense of the scale of the problem, we must add federal and provincial royal commissions that have examined conditions in aboriginal schools and penitentiaries in other parts of the country, including the Hughes Inquiry into the incidents at Mount Cashel, elements of the Aboriginal Justice Inquiry in Manitoba, the Linn Inquiries into Aboriginal and Métis Justice in Saskatchewan, and the Cawsey Report in Alberta, to name a few. And then there are the departmental and other "in-house" inquiries (such as the Sinclair reports referred to in this book) as well as court cases and newspaper exposés.

Despite all these reports, with their constant recommendations for testing and better training of staff, and despite increased public scrutiny and accountability of officials who run these facilities, the difficult questions remain: Has anything changed since 1848? Could what happened at St. Joseph's and St. John's be repeated today? Though partly accurate, it is little comfort to answer yes to the first question and no to the second.

To my mind, one of the most telling vignettes in *Boys Don't Cry* is the story of the retired police officer who finally admitted publicly that he had heard and seen some of what was going on at St. Joseph's Training School, but carried his concerns no further because a senior officer told him that the wards "were bad bastards and probably deserved everything they got." I do not think that would be as likely to happen today.

Physical torture such as the boys and girls in these schools endured would probably be more easily detected and rapidly investigated today. Changes in the laws and practices relating to the detection and prosecution of sexual abuse have made it easier to bring accusations into the courts. Public scrutiny in the form of open visits, the availability of communications technology, the establishment of child and other advocacy offices, and official encouragement of "whistle blowing," combined with some (not many) mechanisms for community involvement, have done much to change the climate in which our penal and reform institutions operate. Above all, staff are better selected and trained.

Nevertheless, when one reads any of the historical or contemporary reports I have referred to, the stench of corruption seems to permeate everything, as it does the pages of *Boys Don't Cry*. And corruption continues to infect almost every element of the institutions in which we incarcerate those who have transgressed against our laws or who have become, for one reason or another, a charge upon the state.

Darcy Henton, a journalist with a proven nose for sniffing through official bafflegab, and David McCann, a man with a mission to make out of his troubled life some good for others even less fortunate than himself, have combined in a superb piece of reporting to provide us with a troubling picture of the evolution and persistence of cycles of physical, sexual, and emotional abuse in two training schools. Almost 150 years after the Brown Commission, *Boys Don't Cry*, a searing indictment of indifference and paternalism, reminds us that if we continue to incarcerate vulnerable people in "caring institutions," we must constantly scrutinize the bona fides of those charged with looking after them. If we are at all serious about equality and equity, we owe them no less.

---

1. M. Jackson, *Prisoners of Isolation: Solitary Confinement in Canada* (Toronto: University of Toronto Press, 1983) p. 28.
2. Ibid., pp. 30-1.

Come with Me

•

"This boy has had a difficult life and I feel that
if we cannot help him soon, it may be too late."
— Marie McCann, in a letter to
St. Joseph's Training School for Boys, August 24, 1961

THEY ALWAYS came at night. He would lie in bed trembling with fear, praying that the approaching black-robed figure would stop beside another bed. Anybody's but his. It was like a bad dream and he was able to cope only by separating his mind from his body. They could do what they wanted with his body; he had long since fled to another place, a place where little boys were safe.

The abuse began the night David Richard McCann arrived at St. Joseph's Training School for Boys in December 1958. St. Joseph's was operated by the Brothers of the Christian Schools in the small Ontario village of Alfred, a cluster of buildings on the Trans-Canada Highway about seventy kilometres east of Ottawa. Arriving at night from Kingston, the freckle-faced twelve-year-old had long since missed dinner, and the dormitories were dark and quiet, except for the creaking and hissing of the old steam radiators. He was led past the rows of steel-frame beds and sleeping children in the junior dormitory to what would be his bed.

Close to fifty children were sleeping head-to-toe in a room that reeked of urine and dirty socks, of too many bodies and not enough soap. Alone, homesick, and frightened, McCann pulled a green bedspread up over his head and quietly cried himself to sleep.

He was awakened some time later by a hand tapping on his shoulder. The Christian Brother who had been supervising the dormitory from a chair near the doorway when McCann arrived was at his side, speaking to him in French.

"*Viens avec moi,*" said the tall, balding man. Come with me.

Without waiting for a response, he pulled the sleepy boy up and led him to a small room near the entrance of the dormitory. The Brother pushed the boy roughly onto a bed and closed the door.

Over the next few months, this Brother frequently pulled McCann from his bed. At first the child could not comprehend what the man was doing to him. All he knew was that it hurt. God, it hurt.

Soon another Brother came calling at his bedside. This one was tall, with wavy brown hair and a deformed left hand, and he would drag McCann into the showers at the end of the dormitory and sexually assault him. The encounters were over quickly, with the monk barely uttering a word. But McCann would always remember that hand.

In the daylight, it was safer. McCann quickly learned to avoid being caught alone at any time with certain Brothers. There was one who would try to fondle his genitals through holes in the pockets of the jeans he had issued McCann, all the while pretending he was frisking him for contraband. Another would grab at his buttocks whenever they were in the room where the Brothers kept an electric toy train, and still another tried to remove McCann's pants once when he was placed in the school's solitary confinement cell. As the days and nights passed, McCann identified five Brothers who had to be given a wide berth.

The only Brother he came to trust was Brother Ernest, a teacher whose real name was Paul Bisson, who encouraged his reading and smuggled him books to read in solitary confinement. A learned man, Brother Ernest recognized something special in the timid child and always greeted him with a smile. There were other friendly faces. The gardener and the placement officer were pleasant men, but they were elderly and had little contact with the students.

McCann was terrified of all the others. He saw Brothers beat the children. He saw them kick them. He saw them punch them in the face so hard that blood spattered the school's cinderblock walls. He had never before seen such violence. To escape the brutality, he withdrew into himself and his books. The other kids called him a bookworm.

David McCann had been sentenced to St. Joseph's for an indefinite period after being found guilty of a string of break-ins. In one night, in the fall of 1958, he and two acquaintances had broken into eight Kingston businesses, including a flower shop, a photo studio, a coal company, and a construction company. The young thieves made off with about $300 in cash and stolen property, including a $50 watch and several sticks of dynamite.

The boys were arrested and brought before Judge James Garvin on November 27, 1958. McCann's two partners were released on probation after agreeing to make restitution, but Garvin wanted to make an example out of McCann as this wasn't his first visit to a courtroom. One month earlier he had been placed on probation for theft from a parked car. David's father, Thomas McCann, offered to make restitution for his son's most recent crime, but Garvin was not interested in giving the boy another chance.

"We just cannot carry on successfully if I let your boy go today," the judge explained. "I mean, what effect is it going to have as a deterrent? This boy was here just a month ago today, and then within two weeks, he is out on these things again. It just won't work. And it won't be good for your boy unless there is some discipline other than what's been given to him. It's as plain as that."

Garvin told Thomas McCann that he had decided to send his son to the training school at Alfred.

"I believe that at St. Joseph's Training School there will be the discipline and the instruction given to him that will try and correct his ways. We hope so anyway."

The next day, McCann was referred to a psychologist by his probation officer. In a report he completed a week later, Dr. Oscar Karabanow noted that David McCann was a boy struggling to find acceptance from his parents and stature among his peers.

Dogged by ill health and accidents throughout infancy and early childhood, McCann had always been one step behind other boys. First it was rickets, then, at age two, he underwent surgery for a strangulated hernia. At age four, his arm got caught in the wringer of his mother's washing machine. When the hernia problem resurfaced at age seven and again at age eight, he was ordered by his doctor to abstain from sports.

His father was a cook. In 1956, when McCann was ten, his father moved the family from Perth, Ontario, to Kingston where he had landed a job with the Department of National Defence in Barriefield, a Canadian Forces base at the mouth of the St. Lawrence River. His mother, Marie, was a war bride, who had met her husband while he was with the Royal Canadian Army Service Corps in England during the Second World War. Their first child, Kathleen, was born in England, and Marie was pregnant with David when she and Kathleen joined Thomas in Canada in April 1946. David was born three months later, on July 31, in Ottawa, and two other girls, Anne Marie and Valerie, followed respectively three and five years later.

McCann felt ignored by his father, disliked by his teachers, and hurt by his lack of close friends. Although he did well academically, he often skipped classes to sit and read in the Kingston Public Library, across the street from the truant office. From his vantage point, near a window, he could watch the comings and goings of the truant officer, whose job it was to catch boys like him.

Dr. Karabanow did not believe a boy with David's problems would benefit from the harsh environment of a training school, and he said so in his report to McCann's probation officer.

"Punishment is not likely to increase his usefulness in the community," he stated. "Basically, the boy is good material for therapy. The value of the training school appears doubtful owing to its rigorous discipline, and in the fact that it might precipitate further anti-social behaviour – again to gain approval from the other children. The forcing of interpersonal contacts until basic insecurity is relieved could, in my opinion, be severely damaging."

Dr. Karabanow's recommendation came too late; McCann had already been sent to St. Joseph's.

David McCann discovered that life in St. Joseph's was a contradictory world of compassion and corruption. To frightened boys away from home for the first time, it was a bewildering, unstable universe, where an act of kindness could be a prelude to sexual abuse or violence.

Officially at least, corporal punishment was forbidden at the school. The Brothers were not permitted to strike, cuff, or kick boys. In 1957 and again in 1958, the Ontario Department of Reform Institutions, which oversaw St. Joseph's and St. John's, another boys' training school run by the Brothers near Toronto, ordered staff at both institutions to read and sign directives banning strapping boys on their bare buttocks. Two years after McCann's arrival at the school, the ban was extended to prohibit strapping boys on the hands.

In truth, however, banned or not, physical violence was a staple of life at the Brothers' two schools. If a boy tried to escape, he could expect the worst corporal punishment imaginable. He would be beaten on the bare buttocks with a razor strop, often until his entire backside, from his knees to the small of his back, was bruised and bleeding. Or he might be whacked, again on the bare buttocks, with a large wooden paddle or a sawed-off goalie's hockey stick, which caused the flesh to swell and the skin to split. After this, he could expect to be handcuffed and shackled, then thrown into solitary confinement for two weeks and fed only bread and water. Sometimes the handcuffs would be kept on for days or weeks after his release from solitary confinement. Habitual runaways were handcuffed to their beds at night.

Even the most minor of offences were punished with punches, kicks, and judo chops. Some Brothers liked to give boys "the knee" as punishment – driving their knees into the boys' thighs, hobbling them for days. Often entire dormitories of boys were punished when the perpetrator of some misdeed refused to come forward. Boys were frequently forced to run until they collapsed from exhaustion or made to stand outside, almost naked, shivering in the cold until they nearly succumbed to hypothermia.

Occasionally a boy would be punished even if he had broken no rule. A hockey player could expect a punch in the face for missing a goal on a breakaway. A goalie who turned in a shoddy performance during a game could be forced to face a barrage of pucks while wearing only his underwear and skates.

David McCann's teachers at St. Joseph's noted that he was a sullen lad, but they spoke glowingly of his academic ability. Intelligent, polite, one of the best, they would say. He was scoring 90s in literature every term, and he was one of only a few boys who made it into the "excellent" and "honour" categories.

By the spring of 1959, McCann had seemingly adapted to the school regimen: roll calls that were held several times a day, the constant lining up, the lack of privacy, and the bad food. Life was a ceaseless routine of "hurry up and wait" – wait for a turn in the shower, wait for lunch, wait to go to class, wait to go outside. It was the only way twenty-three Christian Brothers could manage 160 boys twenty-four hours a day, seven days a week. At the same time, a provincial training school at Cobourg had nearly four times the staff to supervise the same number of boys.

The boys at St. Joseph's usually wore dirty clothes and shoes in need of mending – a condition which puzzled inspectors from the Department of Reform Institutions since the school had both a tailorshop and a shoe repair shop. The school kitchens, dining rooms, dormitories, washrooms, even the rooms in which the Brothers lived were unkempt and smelly. The floors were unswept, the tables covered with crumbs. In the summer there were flies everywhere.

The boys' meals were usually of poor quality and insufficient quantity, but the Brothers ate well. If the Brothers had tender-loin for dinner, the boys had fried luncheon meat. The Brothers ate bacon and eggs or pancakes every morning; the boys had por-ridge or cream of wheat.

Although there was a farming operation attached to the school, which included vegetable gardens, 22 cows, 1,000 poultry, and 400 hogs, the boys seldom got fresh meat, milk, eggs, or vegetables. Most of the produce was sold locally.

Despite pressure from the Department of Reform Institutions, until 1960 the school lacked both adequate recreational facilities and technical shops with qualified instructors to teach the boys trades. Most of St. Joseph's industrial and vocational shop was taken up by the miniature electric railway, which was surrounded by a mock city, complete with illuminated skyscrapers. One department inspector ordered that it be thrown out so the space could be put to better use. "This is a cleverly constructed piece of eye-wash and no doubt provides the Brethren with long hours of entertainment," he complained.

Meanwhile, boys either worked on the school farm or were hired out to local farmers. Children as young as twelve were forced to work twelve-hour days in the fields or to operate heavy machinery. Few ever saw the money they earned.

Whatever peace David McCann found at St. Joseph's was in the books his parents sent him and in the projection room of the theatre where, as projectionist, he was in a world of his own, safe and happy.

By the fall of 1959, even the Brothers realized that McCann was not benefiting from the program at St. Joseph's. Rather than send him home, they placed him in a foster home where he lived with an honest, hardworking farm family.

Those were good days for McCann. This family welcomed him as one of their own, making him feel like the son they didn't have. He got along well with the daughter, who was about his age, and he took delight in flaunting his grades over hers. The Brothers who visited him periodically marvelled at his progress. "David gives good co-operation both at school and at home," his placement officer reported.

In the summer of 1960, after McCann finished second highest in his Grade 7 class, his placement officer recommended he be returned to his parents' custody. McCann was ecstatic, but his joy did not last long.

McCann did well at his new school for the first term, but he soon fell into his old habits. By Christmas he was staying out late, much to the consternation of his parents. Tom and Marie McCann tried to keep David under close supervision, but on Saturday afternoons, when he was supposed to be at the movies, he was relaunching his life of crime. He began to pilfer coins from parking meters and was planning to steal a church's "poor box" when, in March 1961, the law caught up with him again and he was sent back to St. Joseph's.

This time he wound up in the school's senior division with Brother Léo, the monk the boys called "Puss Eyes." Although he was not a big man – about five-foot-eight and 160 pounds – he had a nasty disposition. Black robe or no black robe, he was a mean man who terrified all the boys. Few ever stood up to Brother Léo.

Léopold Monette had been an athletic young man in the years before he became a Christian Brother. After he joined the order in 1938, he relived those days by coaching the school hockey and gymnastics teams. But with no post-secondary education to take him to other missions around the world, Brother Léo was stuck as a supervisor of the boys' dormitories at St. Joseph's.

His cruelty was legendary. Once he smashed a fifteen-year-old boy's nose and practically bit off his finger when the teen tried to defend himself.

Brother Léo had been the prefect of the senior boys at

St. Joseph's for a dozen years before David McCann's arrival. He would roust them in the morning, hustle them into the showers, make sure they made their beds, line them up for breakfast, march them to the dining hall, and supervise their meals. He watched them in the recreation room, or outside at the end of the school day, and he made sure they were safely tucked in bed at night. He ate with them, slept with them, beat them, and sometimes at night, he performed oral sex on them behind the closed door of his office.

McCann tried to keep his distance from Brother Léo, but it was impossible. One day, after a visit home, McCann decided he wasn't going back to St. Joseph's. He had boarded the bus, but got off at the first stop, turned in his ticket for a refund, and fled. He was convinced the Brothers were going to keep him at St. Joseph's until he was eighteen. The thought of spending another two years in the place was unbearable.

One week later, two Kingston City police officers caught up to McCann at the Kingston fair. He had been working as a farm-hand and had come into town to tend the farmer's cows at the agricultural exhibition.

McCann's mother begged the Brothers not to punish him when he returned because he had already spent two days in the city jail, but they ignored her plea. Back at St. Joseph's, McCann was kicked, punched in the face and chest, and thrown into solitary confinement. Forcing McCann face down on a cot, Brother Léo beat the boy's bare backside with a leather strap, dipping it into a pail of water between each of the ten strokes.

Upon his release from the cell, McCann was required to wear handcuffs and leg-irons for two days. The Brothers said it was a precaution against his running away again, but the boys all knew it was an additional punishment. McCann also had to eat his meals standing, handcuffed to a heating pipe in a corner of the dining room. At night, before being permitted to go to bed, he was kept standing for two hours after the other boys had gone to sleep.

David McCann never did try another escape. Instead, he withdrew deeper into himself, adopting a studied aloofness. He would do his time at St. Joseph's, then he would leave and never have anything to do with the accursed training school again.

Saintly Beginnings

•

*"These Brothers are well trained, well disciplined, and
the sorrow is that we have not sufficient numbers of them."*
— James C. Cardinal McGuigan,
Archbishop of Toronto, April 29, 1958

ON NOVEMBER 7, 1837, after a stormy twenty-four-day Atlantic
crossing marked by bouts of seasickness and terror among
the passengers, four Brothers of the Christian Schools arrived in
Lower Canada (now Quebec) from France, via New York. They
were the first Christian Brothers to visit the northern half of the
North American continent.

They might have arrived in what was then New France more
than a century earlier, but the order's founder, Jean Baptiste de la
Salle, had been reluctant to send the Brothers so far from the Old
World. Only long after his death, in 1719, did members of the
order venture so far abroad.

Jean Baptiste de la Salle was born in 1651, the eldest of seven
in an aristocratic Rheims family. Educated in the country's best
schools, he decided when he was eleven years old that he would
enter the priesthood. He was ordained in 1678 and subsequently
made canon of the cathedral of Rheims.

He became involved in education reluctantly, as a favour to a wealthy relative who wanted to hire schoolmasters to instruct the children of the poor. De la Salle rented a house for them and established there a regimen of daily prayer and study. Over time, he became so captivated by the enterprise that he eventually gave up his canonship, assumed control of the school, and dedicated his life to educating the poor.

With this end in view, de la Salle set up a novitiate in 1684 to train willing men to be teaching Brothers. The Brothers took vows of poverty, chastity, and obedience. Although they constituted an independent lay order of the Catholic Church, they maintained contacts both with the Vatican and the bishop of the dioceses in which they served. They were not, as members of a lay order, permitted to perform such sacraments as marriage, baptism, or communion.

The Christian Brothers were governed by a Superior-General, who was elected for life, and twelve assistants who formed the administrative council of the institute. The order was separated into districts or provinces. Each province was governed by a Provincial or Visitor, and each community of Brothers was gov- erned by a Brother Director.

De la Salle's educational philosophy was, in its day, relatively forward-looking. The Brothers taught in French rather than the customary Latin. And they divided their pupils into groups according to their ability – a relatively new concept at the time.

Just the same, the order's schools were depressing. Classes were run in near silence and neither play nor fun was permitted. Teachers relied on hand signals and whispers to deliver their lessons. They were permitted to use corporal punishment, but not without restraint. "Let them do everything for all their pupils to win them all to Our Lord Jesus Christ," de la Salle wrote, "for they should all be convinced that authority is acquired and maintained in a school more by firmness, gravity, and silence than by blows and harshness."

The four Brothers who arrived in Lower Canada 120 years after de la Salle's death were put to work almost immediately teaching French Canadian children in Montreal parishes. Within four years they were teaching English-speaking Irish Canadians as well. By 1848, the Montreal community of Christian Brothers had grown to fifty-six men. The order had expanded into the United States and was making plans to establish institutions in Kingston and Toronto.

The Brothers recruited initially from the large families of Quebec. Thirteen-year-old candidates were trained in novitiates where they underwent five years of theological and secular training. (The entrance age for novitiate training today is eighteen.) Acceptance into the order became permanent only after a candidate reached age twenty-five and had held his vows for at least five years. A council in each province, called the Chapter of Vows, voted annually to accept or reject eligible members. Perpetual vows had to be ratified by the Superior-General.

The qualifications that made a Brother a teacher under the rules of the order did not necessarily jibe with those of the gradually emerging public school system. Legislation passed in 1907 required the Brothers to acquire Ontario teaching certificates. Pressure exerted by the bishops, however, resulted in a ruling by which members of religious communities who had more than five years of experience received certification provided they took summer courses and, in some cases, examinations.

Five Brothers arrived in Toronto in 1851 and soon began teaching in St. Paul's Church. They opened St. Michael's School in 1852 and went on to open St. Patrick's School and St. Mary's School. In 1863, they set up the De La Salle Academy to teach

commercial subjects and to prepare students for studies in philosophy and theology. The order continued to grow and thrive
in the last years of the nineteenth century. By the early part of
the twentieth century, the Brothers had expanded to the western
reaches of Ontario and to the Prairies.

(A separate order of Irish Christian Brothers, founded by
Waterford merchant Edmund Ignatius Rice in 1802, arrived in
Newfoundland to establish the now infamous Mount Cashel
Orphanage in St. John's. But the two orders, although both
Catholic lay orders, were not connected in any way.)

Towards the end of the eighteenth century, the Church hierarchy petitioned the Ontario government for permission to establish a school for delinquent Catholic boys, to be run by the
Christian Brothers. It was in the interest of the Church to have
Catholic children raised in a Catholic environment, and it was in
the interest of the government, at the time, to permit it if there
was a cost saving involved. If salaries did not have to be paid for
teachers, obviously the cost of housing the delinquents would be
substantially cheaper than housing them in provincially run institutions staffed by civil servants.

The Archbishop of Toronto, John Walsh, appealed to Roman
Catholics for $20,000 to erect a building to house forty boys and
their teachers on a sixty-five-acre property on the shore of Lake
Ontario, east of Toronto. "For years," Walsh told members of
his diocese, "our poor Catholic boys have been sent to [the]
industrial school at Mimico, which is a thoroughly Protestant
institution. It would be folly to expect that a boy detained for
considerable time in such an institution could leave it without
having made a shipwreck out of his Catholic faith – the most
precious gift of God."

St. John's Industrial School opened its doors in 1895. Over the
course of the next five decades, 4,200 boys would pass through
the school. They worked in the carpentry shop and made their

own shoes, tended fields of vegetables, prayed, and expended a great deal of energy in sports: hockey, skating, lacrosse, softball, handball, rugby, football, and soccer.

By 1952, eighteen Brothers and seven civilians were taking care of 145 boys in a complex of three buildings at Victoria Park Avenue and Kingston Road in Scarborough. "We are not here to punish the boys," a Brother told a Toronto newspaper reporter in 1952. "Occasionally we have to change their view about some things, but once they realize why they are here, they try to co-operate."

St. Joseph's Training School in Alfred was nominally the francophone version of St. John's, but Catholic boys were sent there from all across northern Ontario, whether they spoke French or English. A total of $360,000 was raised for the school by Les Frères des Écoles Chrétiennes, the three-hundred-member Montreal-based branch of the Order of the Brothers of the Christian Schools. It's not known why, in the depths of the Great Depression, the government agreed to let the Brothers build the training school in the village of Alfred, population eight hundred. In winter, the village was accessible only by train and although it was just seventy kilometres east of Ottawa, it was a long way from the more westerly regions of the province. Sudbury, for instance, was more than eight hundred kilometres away, Kenora, two thousand — yet it was from towns like these that delinquent boys would be sent.

The Ontario premier, George Stewart Henry, and several cabinet ministers, including William George Martin, the minister of public welfare, were in attendance when the school was opened in 1933.

"I am not uttering words of idle flattery when I say that St. Joseph's Industrial School is the equal of any institution of its kind in the Dominion," Martin told the audience. "This magnificent structure will be a lasting monument to the work of the noble order which has carried the torch of religious faith and Christian virtue in many lands of the earth."

The hopes of the government and the Church were summed up in the words of St. Luke, etched in concrete above the school's main entrance: "*Jeune Homme Lève-Toi* — Young Man, Arise." The biblical passage from which the phrase was taken referred to the miracle of Nain, in which Jesus raised the only son of a widow from the dead.

The first 36 wards were sent to St. Joseph's from St. John's on August 6, 1933. Over the succeeding weeks and months, a stream of boys followed, boosting the population to the maximum capacity of 160 in just three years. Almost from the day the school opened, it was understaffed, with only ten Brothers to teach the originally anticipated population of 100 wards. Thirty years later, the situation was only marginally better, with 6.4 wards per staff member. In province-run training schools, the ratio was 3 wards per staff member.

The boys were issued lockers and a number that was inscribed in India ink on all assigned institutional clothing. They ate their meals in a refectory in the basement of the building, where they were watched over by the prefects who sat at a table on a raised dais. A Brother would whistle to signal the start of the meal; the boys would say a prayer and dig in. After the meal, the Brother would whistle again and one boy would be chosen to receive the scraps from the Brothers' table.

For every boy in residence at the school, another two or three were "on placement." They were still under the legal guardianship of the Brothers, who were paid by the province for their upkeep, but the boys lived with foster parents or their own families.

For the boys placed in foster homes, the school received $3.50 per day per ward from the provincial government. Only a small portion of that sum was passed on to the foster parents. St. Joseph's and St. John's paid them "what the traffic would bear," sometimes as little as $1.25 a day, and pocketed the rest. The schools could earn more than $50,000 each year by placing just seventy boys in foster homes. The system invited abuse. One year, St. Joseph's placed four times as many children in foster homes as St. John's, and twenty-six times as many as the province-run Bowmanville training school, east of Toronto.

The original St. John's training school was condemned as a firetrap by a York County grand jury in 1944, but it survived two fires in the years that followed before, finally, the Brothers raised money for a new facility. Construction began in 1956 on the 150-acre Cedar Brook Farm, near Uxbridge, sixty-five kilometres north-east of Toronto.

The new school was filled to its intended capacity of 150 almost immediately; by 1960, it housed more than 200 boys. In 1962, six new classrooms and a gymnasium were added. Ontario taxpayers – Catholic and non-Catholic alike – provided half the cost of the $2-million expansion.

The main building was a two-and-a-half-storey structure shaped in what the Brothers called a triple cruciform – a long rectangular building intersected at right angles by three arms that, viewed from above, resembled a three-armed crucifix. The light, airy limestone complex contained a school for junior wards and another for senior wards. Each had its own classrooms, dormi-tories, dining rooms, and recreational facilities. The complex also contained administrative offices, staff living quarters, and a central chapel.

The wards at St. John's had to be at least seven years of age (it was later changed to nine) and no older than seventeen. Many were sent to the school by their school principals, priests, and parents, who thought it would be beneficial to their development. Some were pulled from their homes for their own protection and were wards of the Children's Aid Society. Some had been abandoned by their parents. Those who had broken the law (mainly by stealing) were sentenced, usually to indefinite terms, by family court judges, who often had no legal training.

About 5 per cent of the school population had been convicted of no specific crime. They had merely been deemed incorrigible or unmanageable by a family court judge, usually because they habitually stayed out late, skipped school, or disobeyed their parents. Some came from other boys' group homes where they had behaved badly. Boys stayed at St. John's an average of fourteen months; a few were sent home sooner, and some stayed for years.

As before, when the school was located in Scarborough, the boys of St. John's spent the mornings in classrooms and the afternoons in the shops or the fields. Those with little aptitude or interest in academics were often excused from classes altogether and given full-time jobs on the farm, in the greenhouse, or elsewhere in the institution. The extensive sports program was also carried over from Scarborough and expanded with the addition of a swimming pool and facilities for volleyball, basketball, and gymnastics.

Boys were required to write home once a week to their immediate families and were allowed to receive food parcels once a month. Visiting was restricted to three hours in the afternoon of every first and third Sunday of the month. Phone calls were not permitted – either in or out – except in emergencies.

Every three months the institution was required to file a placement report with the Department of Reform Institutions Training School Advisory Board. But by and large the board merely rubber-stamped the recommendations of the training school superintendent. Boys who displeased the Brothers had no way out.

The Catholic-run training schools – St. John's, St. Joseph's, and the Toronto girls' school, St. Mary's – operating under the auspices of the Ontario Training Schools Act, were the only privately run training schools in the province. Initially, the Catholic organizations and the municipal and provincial governments shared the cost of running the institutions, but over time the province assumed the total burden.

By 1958, Toronto Archbishop James C. Cardinal McGuigan was lobbying the province for a $1 increase in the per diem paid for each ward, claiming that St. John's, in particular, was foundering in debt. The province reluctantly agreed. Between 1952 and 1960, the provincial government's per diem payments to the Catholic institutions more than tripled, rising from $160,000 to more than $540,000.

To the outside world, at least, the Christian Brothers' schools at Alfred and Uxbridge offered delinquent youths a chance to redeem themselves. The Brothers, with their 250-year-old history, were supposedly providing firm, disciplined, but caring, instruction in a nurturing environment far from the temptations of the city.

The reality was vastly different. Many wards came to see themselves not as wards but as inmates. Instead of straightening out their delinquent charges, the schools often had the opposite effect. They took children and created disturbed, angry young men.

When Archie Villeneuvre first arrived at the new St. Joseph's training school, he was astonished by what he saw. "I walked in the front door and I saw this beautiful chapel and this beautiful parlour and this shiny, new terrazzo floor and I thought, 'This must be heaven,'" he said. "But it was hell."

St. Joseph's Training School for Boys in Alfred, Ontario, opened its doors in 1934.

David McCann was a freckle-faced boy of twelve when he was sent to St. Joseph's in 1958.

Known as a bookworm by the other wards, McCann (front row, centre) excelled in classes at St. Joseph's.

The present-day St. John's school was built on a farm property northeast of Toronto in 1956.

Accordion-playing St. John's wards perform for visiting dignitaries at the opening of the school's new wing in 1963.

St. John's wards beam with delight as hockey star Eddie Shack attends a school awards banquet in 1967.

St. Joseph's superintendent Brother George (left) accompanies Ottawa Archbishop M. Joseph Lemieux during a 1960 visit to the school.

Donald Sinclair (front row, centre) poses with St. John's superintendent Brother Adrian (front row, right) at a meeting of wardens of the school.

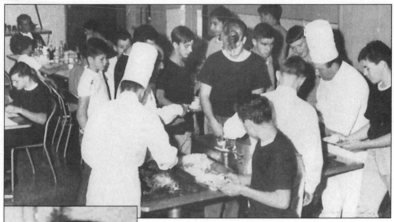

St. Joseph's wards line up for meals in the school's senior boys dining hall. The boys helped to prepare the meals.

Claude Larocque, shown in photograph when he was about ten years old, spent six years at St. Joseph's, from 1963 to 1969.

Armand Jobin, Jr., was raped on his first night at St. Joseph's in 1966. He revisited the school in 1990.

Jobin and Larocque, boyhood chums at St. Joseph's, were reunited in 1990, but the friendship turned sour.

Sent to St. Joseph's when he was fifteen, Patrick Healey was whacked across the head with a wooden crutch by Brother Léo.

Healey, shown here with his wife, Dora, took over the leadership of the victims' group Helpline after David McCann's departure in 1992.

Michael Watters, sent to St. John's for being incorrigible, prompted a provincial investigation into abuse at the school in 1958.

At a 1994 press conference, Watters announced the launching of a $40-million lawsuit against the Toronto Christian Brothers.

Grant Hartley was repeatedly physically and sexually assaulted during his stay at St. Joseph's in the early 1950s.

Hartley teamed up with McCann to found Helpline and was actively involved in negotiating the $23-million reconciliation deal.

Former St. Joseph's wards Gerry Sirois (right) and Norman Godin visited the school in 1992 during the trial of Lucien Dagenais, (Brother Joseph, the Hook).

DARCY HENTON

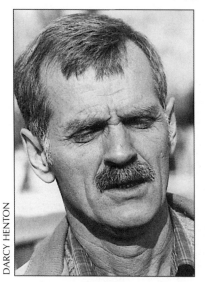

DARCY HENTON

Albert Daigneault was one among many St. Joseph's wards terrorized by the Hook. He complained at the time but was ignored by police.

Helpline director Gerry Belecque, who was sexually assaulted by Brother Gabriel, has been haunted by the incident all his life.

FRED SHERWIN/TORONTO STAR

Armand Jobin, Jr., squares off with an usher at St. Michael's Cathedral in Toronto in a demonstration intended to force the archbishop to meet the victims.

3

For Crying Out Loud

•

"The Brothers are a closely knit organization, and
the boys are reluctant to squeal.
It is — and always has been — very difficult to obtain
information in this institution."
— Gerry Wright, chief inspector, Department of Reform
Institutions, in a memo to the deputy minister, August 8, 1960

EARLY ON the morning of July 20, 1948, a flatbed truck pulled out of the schoolyard in Alfred and headed east towards Montreal. At the wheel was fifty-eight-year-old Brother Philip, a greying twenty-five-year veteran of the order who ran the institution's farm. Brother Philip was accompanied in the cab by a local farm implement dealer, Gerald Landriault, who had arranged for the Brothers to pick up a new hay baler in Terrebonne, Quebec, northeast of Montreal.

Four St. Joseph's wards were riding in the back of the truck. The trip was a reward for their hard work on the school farm. The wards were: Joseph Henry Muskerelle, Bernard Lajoie, Clifford Ethier, and Albert Bruneau. The fourteen-year-old Bruneau was a ward of the Children's Aid Society. His mother, a native of Sault Ste. Marie, was in the Brockville Psychiatric

Hospital. He had no father, but there was a sister who was also mentally ill.

Although Montreal was just 160 kilometres from Alfred, it took most of the morning to get there. Brother Philip and Landriault made repeated stops at taverns along the way.

When the truck finally reached Montreal, around lunchtime, Brother Philip dropped the boys off at a restaurant while he and Landriault went to another bar. When they resumed the trip to Terrebonne, the two men began to pass a flask between them in the cab.

Eventually they arrived in Terrebonne. The baler was a huge steel contraption weighing nearly two tons, which, when loaded, stuck two feet over the truck bed. When it was secured by chains, the boys climbed in alongside it and settled down for the ride back to Alfred. It was getting late.

Brother Philip and Landriault continued to sip from the flask and stopped at another tavern before reaching Montreal. The boys waited in the truck, hoping their chaperones would not be long. Around suppertime, Brother Philip emerged alone from the pub. He invited Muskerelle and Ethier to join him in the cab while Lajoie and Bruneau remained in the back with the baler.

They drove on towards Montreal. Despite his earlier dawdling, Brother Philip now seemed anxious to get back to Alfred before dark. He drove quickly through the city's streets and the big truck groaned under its heavy load. It soon became apparent to the boys in the cab that, without Landriault, the monk had no idea how to get home. He finally had to stop at a service station to ask for directions.

No sooner were they again on their way than Brother Philip took another wrong turn. Confused and frustrated, he drove even faster. Rounding a corner, he narrowly avoided a streetcar and several other vehicles. In the back, the heavy baler began to move in its moorings, frightening Lajoie and Bruneau, who clung on for dear life.

The truck veered wildly around a sharp curve in Montreal's Westmount residential district. It passed an intersection, lurched over the curb, and careened across the sidewalk. It climbed halfway across a lawn before finally flipping over, sending its two-ton cargo and the two boys in the back hurtling through the air. The baler landed upside down with a dull thud, at the base of a tree.

A local resident raced to the scene, but recoiled in horror when he saw Bruneau pinned between the baler and the tree. The top of the boy's head had been shorn away above the eyebrows.

Lajoie and Muskerelle were taken away in an ambulance, but Ethier remained trapped inside the cab. Brother Philip, in the meantime, wandered around in a daze. He was holding one hand against an ear that was bleeding profusely. He reeked of alcohol, was unsteady on his feet, and, when asked for it by a police officer, had difficulty producing his driver's licence.

Ian Barclay, a lawyer who had been driving home when he witnessed the mishap, stopped to help rescue Ethier. When he pulled the dazed boy out of the cab, Ethier told him that Brother Philip had been speeding and drinking. Barclay passed the information along to the police officer on the scene, Sgt. Peter Morgan, and accompanied him when he interviewed the other boys, separately, in hospital. They all told the same story about a hair-raising ride through the streets of Montreal with a drunken monk.

Bernard Lajoie told Dr. Sidney Barza, who had accompanied the boys in the ambulance from the accident scene to Montreal's Western Hospital, that Brother Philip had been drinking heavily. "Why didn't you tell him to slow down?" asked Barza.

"I told him to, but he wouldn't listen to me."

"Why didn't you get out of the truck?" asked the doctor.

Lajoie snorted derisively. The doctor obviously didn't understand the nature of the boys' relationship with the Brother.

"We weren't allowed to leave," he said.

Barza went back to check on Brother Philip, who was sitting
in a waiting room holding a bandage over his ear. The doctor
could smell liquor on the monk's breath and noticed that his
speech was slurred. He stitched up the injured ear, and then
watched the monk lurch unsteadily into the hallway. Brother
Philip walked with his feet wide apart, swaying from side to side.
It made the doctor wonder why the police had not requested a
blood test.

Muskerelle and Lajoie were kept in hospital overnight for
observation. Ethier, who had a broken leg, was kept longer at
another hospital. When Brother George, the superintendent of
St. Joseph's, arrived the next day to pick up the two boys and
their driver, Brother Philip was morose. "What can you do?" he
asked his superior. "It's unfortunate – an accident."

The circumstances in which the mishap occurred meant that
there would be a coroner's inquest.

Back at the school, the wards pressed the survivors for details
of the accident. One told them that Brother Philip had been
drinking. Another Brother overheard and struck him on the side
of the head.

Brother George drove the two boys and Brother Philip back
to Montreal early on the morning of July 22 for the coroner's
inquest. Ethier, who was still in hospital, would not be called to
testify. Neither would another key witness, Gerald Landriault,
whose whereabouts were apparently unknown.

Both Sergeant Morgan and a lieutenant who had been at the
scene of the accident told the coroner of conversations in which
the boys had said that Brother Philip had been drinking. Neither
officer was in a position to corroborate their claims. They could

report only that the monk appeared to be dazed after the accident and that his breath smelled of alcohol.

The coroner called the two boys. A nervous Joseph Muskerelle took the stand first. Brother George stared at him intently from the back of the room.

"How was the driver, Brother Philip, driving before the accident?" the coroner asked.

"Oh, he was driving pretty good," answered Muskerelle.

"Was he driving slowly or fast?"

"A steady gait."

"Did you noticed anything unusual about his way of driving the truck?"

"No."

"You did not?"

"No."

"Can you tell us whether he was driving fast or slowly before the accident?"

"It did not feel fast."

"Did you tell anyone after the accident, either at the hospital or at the scene, that the driver had been driving fast?"

"Oh, I said he was driving a good gait."

"You said he was driving what?"

"Pretty fast."

"Do you know why he was driving so fast?"

"No."

"Did you know whether he had been drinking before the accident?"

"No, I didn't take notice."

Lajoie was next.

"Could you tell us what happened just before the accident?" asked the coroner. "How was the truck driven?"

"It was driven pretty fast before the accident."

"Can you tell us what speed the truck was being driven?"

"About thirty."

"Thirty!" exclaimed the exasperated coroner. "You call that fast?"

"Yes."

"Had you seen the driver taking any drinks?"

"No."

"Did you tell anyone after the accident that the truck was being driven fast because the driver had been drinking?"

"Sure."

"Why did you say that?"

"I could smell it off his breath."

Brother Philip declined to testify on the grounds that he might incriminate himself.

After deliberating for twenty-five minutes, the six jurors announced their verdict. By a vote of 4-2, they determined that there had been no criminal negligence.

The body of Albert Bruneau was buried in an unmarked grave in a small cemetery beside the school. Only his schoolmates were present to mourn his death.

From about the mid-1940s until the early 1960s, wards consigned to the Catholic boys' training schools in Ontario endured a regime in which institutionalized neglect, inadequate supervision, random and frequently excessive violence, and incidents of sexual molestation and homosexual rape were endemic. A handful of people, including neighbours and government officials, were aware that there were problems at the school. A few were even in a position to gauge their seriousness. But, despite occasional revelations, investigations, reprimands, and warnings, the full extent of the depravity remained unknown to the public, and nothing really changed.

The prevailing atmosphere was different in those years. What is now recognized as abuse, the Brothers who ran the schools could call discipline, and usually get away with it. The public at large was not inclined to be indulgent towards children who had been identified as delinquent. This was a time when images of rebellion, such as Marlon Brando's portrayal of a biker in the film *The Wild One* made people nervous. The spectre of an international communist conspiracy, flaunted before Americans by Senator Joe McCarthy, induced a kind of continental paranoia. It was a time when respectability counted for a lot. The Christian Brothers were, to all appearances, the guardians of respectability. What they could keep out of sight, they could also be keep out of the public mind.

The inquest into the death of Albert Bruneau was one of relatively few occasions when the conduct of the Brothers was the object of public scrutiny. Just occasionally, in those years, an angry parent was also able to draw attention to the plight of a son.

One such stubborn parent was Doris Watters. There was a rule at St. John's that boys could have visitors only once every two weeks, but twelve-year-old Michael Watters was an exception. His mother, despite the objections of the Brothers, visited every Sunday.

Doris Watters had worked hard to provide for her son and daughter. When her marriage ended in 1951, she initially moved in with her parents in Oakville, a small community just west of Toronto. When she opened a restaurant in the town, she and the children moved into an apartment that was closer to her work. On weekends, when she couldn't look after them, she sent the children to stay with their grandparents. However, when Michael began getting into trouble, the Children's Aid Society took a dim view of the arrangement.

The matter came to a head in the fall of 1957 when Michael was accused of stealing two pigeons. Although the boy was acquitted of the charges in juvenile court, Judge K. M. Langdon committed him to an indefinite sentence at St. John's Training School, asserting that the youth was incorrigible.

An angry Doris Watters stormed out of court, but not before buttonholing the police officer who had arrested her son and telling him there was no way Michael was staying in the training school. Michael's grandmother, a former teacher, launched a letter-writing campaign to the Department of Reform Institutions and the local newspapers, but to no avail.

On her first visit to Michael at St. John's, Doris discovered that a cut on his foot he had suffered before being sent to the school had become terribly infected. The boy had cut himself badly enough to need stitches, and at the time of his committal, the stitches still had not been removed. Incensed by the neglect, Doris demanded that she be allowed to take her son to a doctor. When she was refused permission by Brother Francis, the school's superintendent, she took Michael to the doctor anyway. And she kept the boy at home until he could walk again.

A few months later, Michael was given permission to telephone his mother, who had arranged with Brother Francis to meet her son at a Toronto medical clinic where some of the wards were being taken for a routine chest X-ray. Michael sounded troubled, but refused to discuss what was bothering him over the phone.

He was quiet while Doris drove him to his grandmother's house for lunch, and Doris became alarmed when she noticed a tear rolling down her son's cheek. Still, he volunteered nothing.

Once they arrived, the cause of Michael's distress immediately became apparent. When his grandmother patted his backside affectionately as he came through her door, he let out an involuntary yelp. The boy then explained to his astonished family that he was recovering from two severe beatings. The bruising from the first beating had not healed, he said, before he had been strapped a second time. His buttocks were a mass of red welts and bruises. Michael told his mother he had been strapped with a two-foot-long wooden-handled leather strap as punishment for trying to run away from the school.

Doris Watters took her son to her doctor to be examined. The doctor was appalled. "If you want to press charges and take it to court, I'll be a witness for you," he told her.

At the local police station, Chief Fred Oliver also expressed astonishment when he saw the extent of the boy's injuries. "Jesus!" he exclaimed. "What bastard did this?"

Oliver, a squat fireplug of a man, had recently charged an Oakville school principal for strapping a student in similar fashion. The man had been convicted. But St. John's was outside his jurisdiction. He advised Doris to see a lawyer. He also recommended that she return her son to the school.

"You know they can arrest you?" he warned. "Put you in jail?"

"I don't care what they do," she snapped. "I am not taking him back to get more beatings like that." But as a precaution, she checked Michael and his grandmother into a local motel.

Before she could meet with her lawyer, Brother Francis phoned her and began, patiently but firmly, to negotiate Michael's return to St. John's.

Anxious not to have the police brought into the matter, Brother Francis promised her that the boy would not be strapped again if she brought him back immediately. "You know, Mrs. Watters, even if you lay charges against us, Mike will still have to go back to training school – whether it is this one or another one."

He told her that if she brought Michael back, he was prepared to forget the fact that she had twice taken him from custody without permission. He hadn't forgotten the stitches incident.

"If you bring him back here, this is never going to go on the record at all," he told her. "If you bring him back, I'll give you my word that he will not get beaten again. Would you agree that would save us both problems? I give you my word, he will be out right after the Christmas holidays."

Doris Watters relented. She couldn't keep Michael hidden forever. And there was little point in charging the Brothers if Michael was, indeed, released soon.

Unknown to both Brother Francis and Doris Watters, however, the case was not being swept under the carpet. Chief Oliver had contacted Halton County Crown attorney Lloyd Dingle, in Burlington, who wrote to the Department of Reform Institutions on November 11, 1957. "I have discussed the matter with Chief Oliver," Dingle wrote, "and he tells me that the marks on the boy's back were evidence, in his opinion, of a very severe beating."

Several weeks passed before Gerry Wright, the Department of Reform Institutions' chief inspector, visited the school. By then Michael's bruises were nearly healed. Wright did, however, note that the boy's first absence, when he sought treatment for his foot, had not been recorded in the school's log book. Nor were his two beatings. Wright also discovered that corporal punishment had been administered without a ruling by the superintendent stating that it was justified. In contravention of the department's policy, there had been no witness present at either beating and the number of strokes had not been recorded. The chief inspector also discovered that boys at St. John's were being hit with a sawed-off goalie's hockey stick.

Brother Francis did not deny that corporal punishment was being inflicted on the wards. He explained that staff members used the stick to curtail horseplay among the boys in the shower. He called the blows administered to the children "friendly taps." The hockey stick, the monk said, was also used to give each boy his customary "whacks" on his birthday.

Later, Albert Virgin, the director of Ontario training schools, wrote a stinging letter to the St. John's Brothers, pointing out both the "serious lack of method in recording important items" and the disregard for the department's policies regarding corporal punishment. "It is very necessary that strict control of punishments be instituted immediately, particularly corporal punishments," he wrote. "Where this is lacking, pupils can easily be subjected to assaultive treatment, resulting in serious bodily injury. 'Friendly taps' with sticks or other similar weapons are dangerous and should not at any time be used, even though accepted in good part by the students. It should be the policy that any staff who resort to slapping, punching, shaking, roughing and so on, should be dealt with severely."

Virgin sent a follow-up letter a week later – a letter he also sent to St. Joseph's – all but banning corporal punishment. The directive permitted staff in training schools to strap misbehaving boys only on the palms of their hands. No more, he decreed, were boys to be strapped on their bare buttocks or cuffed, kicked, poked, or punched. Yes, he agreed, there would be cases in which wards might display rebellion, violence, disobedience, or insolence, but the staff must not respond in kind.

These directives, however, were ignored. For nearly two decades, boys at the schools continued to be paddled with a sawed-off hockey stick, strapped on the buttocks, and manhandled as before.

Brother Francis kept his end of the deal he had struck with Doris Watters. Michael left the school early in 1958, not quite as early as promised, but his indefinite sentence ended up lasting about six months. His grandfather, a lumberjack, found him a job cutting logs.

When a child died at St. Joseph's, it was often the result of poor medical treatment, either in diagnosis or treatment, or of inadequate supervision. Although inquests were, at the time,

mandatory when inmates died in prisons, they were seldom called
when children died in custody. It was not until three boys died
in the space of three years that the province took a long, hard
look at the medical treatment being provided by the Brothers at
St. Joseph's.

Jeffrey Hudson was a nervous, intelligent boy whose father,
John Hudson, was killed in a railway accident in the Maritimes
when the boy was just six years old. His mother moved to
Kingston after his father's death. By the time he was nine years
old, Hudson was getting into trouble.

He arrived at St. Joseph's on October 19, 1955, the day after his
appearance in family court for stealing cigarettes from a truck.
Five months later, he developed a high fever and his joints swelled.
Although the swelling eventually subsided after a stay in hospital, Hudson never fully recovered.

A year later, Hudson, now fourteen, was still exhausted. He
was depressed, pale, and couldn't keep any food or liquid down.
When the local doctor visited him, however, he could detect no
fever. Suspecting peritonitis – an inflammation of the membrane
covering the intestinal tract – the doctor gave the boy a needle
for pain, and prescribed some antibiotics.

Two days later, the doctor transferred the teenager to Ottawa
General Hospital. By then, the boy's condition was critical. He
complained of abdominal pain. He was extremely pale and the
veins in his neck stuck out noticeably. He died on March 2, 1957.

The autopsy showed that Hudson died of rheumatic heart
disease and pneumonia. Rheumatic fever, which is an inflammation of the joints and heart, can permanently damage the
valves of the heart, leading to congestive heart failure. But it
could not have struck him on February 29 and killed him three
days later. He would have to have had the condition longer –
much longer – to have suffered such lethal damage.

John Bennett, the chairman of the training schools advisory

board, told Albert Virgin, the director of training schools, that the boy's condition should have been detected when he first entered St. Joseph's, eighteen months earlier. All boys were required to undergo a medical examination upon admission, Bennett noted. Why wasn't it detected then? "Rheumatic fever, as a rule, causes death slowly and there was almost certainly evidence that this boy's heart had been affected a considerable period of time before his death."

When Virgin investigated, he discovered that Hudson had been confined to bed at St. Joseph's on and off for a year with symptoms of rheumatic fever. "In spite of this, there is no record on file here that the boy was ill or that anyone examined his heart." Indeed, reports of his illness at St. Joseph's only reached Ottawa General Hospital after his death, and the information was provided by his mother.

Virgin ordered the school's superintendent, Brother George, to ensure that full medical examinations were carried out upon boys upon admission to the school and that all their illnesses be recorded. He also directed that all serious cases of illness be reported to his office.

Subsequent events would show that these recommendations were not acted on.

On June 16, 1957, twelve-year-old Claude Deschamps went for a swim in the dugout – a dammed area of a creek that the school used for swimming – with about forty children under the age of thirteen. Deschamps, who had been sent to Alfred for theft just three months earlier, was hanging around with a friend. Since neither of them could swim very well, they both were ordered to stay in the shallow end of the dugout.

But, as the afternoon wore on, the pair became more adventurous. They both climbed the highest of the two diving boards, but when Deschamps reached the top he froze. Other boys shouted at him to get off the board.

"Come on, let's jump!" said the friend. He gave Deschamps a push and jumped in behind him.

Deschamps' friend swam safely to the ladder. When he clambered out, he went to join a group of boys playing in the shallow end and failed to notice that Deschamps was no longer with him.

It wasn't until the whistle blew to end the swim that he noticed Deschamps was missing and raised the alarm. Several boys immediately dove into the water to probe the muddy bottom for Deschamps. Within moments, the boy was located. But it was too late. Deschamps was dead.

No one ever questioned Deschamps' friend about the death, and it was never discussed among the boys at the school. But a department inspector who probed the drowning made five recommendations to improve safety at the dugout. In the course of his investigation, he had also discovered and reported back to the department that the Brothers were still not heeding the earlier order that boys receive thorough medical examinations upon admission to the school.

Gerry Champagne, a pint-sized, fleet-footed Ottawa boy, was sent to St. Joseph's in December 1958, as punishment for breaking into a service station. The fifteen-year-old made his first escape attempt moments after he was delivered to the junior dormitory on his first day at St. Joseph's. He was caught and soundly thumped by a Brother before he made it out the door.

Champagne's second escape attempt was only marginally more successful. This time he made it halfway to the railway tracks, nearly two kilometres south of the school, before he was observed and headed off by a squad of boys picked from the senior division. The subsequent strapping was so terrifying and brutal that it caused him to soil the bed upon which he was punished.

Five weeks later, he was off again. This time he made it back to his home in Ottawa. Hiding beneath a neighbour's veranda, he kept a watch on his parent's place until nightfall. Only when he was convinced that all was clear did he scoot across the street and into the house. His parents weren't surprised to see him. In the kitchen, he found a Brother chatting amiably with his father. He had been there all along. The monk slipped a pair of handcuffs on the sobbing boy and dragged him past his tearful mother to the car. Back in Alfred, Champagne was again strapped and thrown into solitary confinement. This time he had to fend off a sexual assault from the infamous Brother Joseph. The monk, whose hand had been mutilated in a carpentry-shop accident leaving him with only a finger and thumb, was known among the boys as "the Hook." Brother Joseph attempted to insert his finger in the boy's anus under the guise of examining the welts on his buttocks. Champagne spun around and pushed him away.

On his next escape attempt Champagne headed away from home. Brother George, the school's superintendent, found him in a restaurant in L'Orignal, fifteen kilometres up the road. Champagne was getting used to getting caught, but there was no getting used to the strap.

When he took off again, accompanied by three other wards, the break-out was much better planned. Unfortunately, it happened during one of the worst blizzards of the winter.

The escape was set for midnight, February 19, 1960. At the appointed hour, the quartet crept between the rows of beds and gathered underneath the open window above the locked washroom door. Champagne, the smallest of the four, was hoisted up through the window and, once inside, let his buddies in.

Clad only in boxer shorts, they wrapped towels around their

feet and leapt from the second-floor window onto the snow-covered lawn. Shivering in the sub-zero temperatures, they scurried around the corner of the building to a side door they knew was always left unlocked.

The door opened into the recreation room where there were lockers with clothes, overcoats, and boots. They dressed quickly and then ran west along the nearby highway, towards a darkened service station. Inside the service bay of the garage was a car. One of the boys smashed a window in the garage door, reached in, and flipped the handle. The car, amazingly, had the keys in the ignition. Champagne, the oldest at age sixteen, slipped behind the wheel and started the car. In his excitement, he neglected to check the fuel gauge before swinging the car out onto the dark, empty highway and stomping on the accelerator. His only previous driving experience had been motoring Brother George's Buick around the schoolyard after the boys had washed it one day.

They ran out of gas about an hour later near the village of Apple Hill, some forty kilometres south of Alfred. By now the snow was blowing so fiercely it was barely safe to travel. The boys knew they would freeze if they didn't get out of the storm.

On the edge of town, they came across a private garage. Again, luck seemed on their side when they discovered the owner had left the keys inside the car, a big Mercury Monarch. This time, one of the other boys slid behind the wheel. Snow drifts were beginning to accumulate on the road and they hadn't gone more than nine kilometres when the car ploughed into a ditch.

They were still in the car arguing about what to do next when a farmer came along in a tractor. They managed to squeeze inside for the short ride to the farmer's house, where they huddled around a wood stove eating crackers until dawn.

The next day, the farmer dropped them off on the edge of Apple Hill. They had just bid him goodbye when a police officer, investigating a rash of vehicle thefts, approached them in his patrol car. He had little doubt that he had found the culprits when he saw them scatter into the snow-filled ditch. They tried to make it into the nearby bush, but the snow was nearly waist deep. They soon realized that flight was hopeless and plodded wearily back to the road.

The officer drove them to nearby Martintown to a juvenile detention home where they would wait for the Brothers to retrieve them. The woman who operated the home invited the boys to join herself and her daughters for breakfast.

The boys told their hosts the story of their escape and about life in general at St. Joseph's. They told them about the beatings and the mistreatment they suffered there and they begged not to be sent back. When the Brothers arrived, they seemed by their actions to confirm what the boys had said. As the boys were led, in handcuffs, to the car by one Brother, another charged into Champagne with fists flying and pummelled the boy to the ground. As Champagne struggled to get up out of the snow, his assailant kicked him in the ribs and groin before, finally, the other Brother pulled him off.

Champagne lay in the driveway, writhing in pain, his hands clasped over his testicles. As he was helped into the vehicle, he struggled to remain conscious. On the ride back to St. Joseph's, his attacker glared at him from the front seat.

Back at St. Joseph's, the boys were thrown into the solitary confinement cells. Then, one at a time, they were taken out, lashed to a metal bed frame, and strapped.

But their impassioned pleas to the family at the detention home had not been ignored. The woman there contacted Ralph Ross, president of the eight-member Cornwall Juvenile Court Committee, a civilian group that worked closely with young offenders. For some time, Ross had been troubled by reports and rumours of abuse at the training school. Indeed, he and a probation officer had visited St. Joseph's just a few months earlier and had heard complaints from several children. Ross contacted the same probation officer now.

The officer, Maurice Egan, suggested they ask the minister responsible for Reform Institutions, George Wardrope, to investigate the matter personally. Wardrope, a nine-year veteran of provincial politics, had assumed the portfolio a year previously. Wardrope saw himself as a reformer. He often drew cheers from prisoners when he walked, unescorted, through their midst, largely because he had moved to abolish the lash in adult prisons. "If an official can't handle a prisoner without beating him into insensibility, he's not good enough to be on the staff of my reform institutions," he had said in May 1959. Egan drafted a letter to Wardrope, dated February 26, which Ross signed and posted.

The letter expressed Ross's deep concern about the treatment of boys at St. Joseph's. "I feel that these allegations are sufficiently serious to warrant a personal investigation, either by yourself or a very responsible delegate of your department," the letter stated. "I also think the confidential nature of any such inquiry is of prime importance. Other members of our committee have limited knowledge of this situation, but the problem has never been openly discussed at any of our meetings. Those of us who do know are concerned with two things: the correction of these conditions, should they in fact exist, and the suppression of unfavourable publicity, should the stories that have reached us become more widespread."

Wardrope responded promptly by launching a formal investigation.

4

Lifting the Veil

•

"We know that you will appreciate our desire to take the necessary action before the growing number of complaints received by us from parents, welfare workers and others reaches such a magnitude that the matter becomes public knowledge, in which event the school, this department, and the Church can only suffer."
— Archie Graham, deputy minister of the Department of Reform Institutions, in a letter to M. J. Lemieux, Archbishop of Ottawa, August 11, 1960

THE MAN sent to investigate the allegations made by Egan and Ross was Donald Sinclair. Sinclair had been just three years with the department which he had come to regard as hidebound and authoritarian. It was run by extremely conservative retired British military officers, and he often felt that he was just a glorified assistant to the advisory board's high-profile chairman, Martin Pinker. Still, Sinclair was an optimist, confident that time would bring change.

It was Sinclair's job to co-ordinate the activities of the advisory board that oversaw the province's training schools. The board met weekly to deal with the quarterly reports submitted on the progress of each child in the schools. It determined how long a child would remain a ward, when a ward would be discharged, and when he or she could be placed in a foster home. Usually the board, whose members included a retired businessman, a librarian, a priest, and a Health Department official, rubber-stamped the recommendations of the training school staff. Actual visits to the schools were rare.

Sinclair's first destination that March morning was Cornwall, Ontario, where he met Ralph Ross and Maurice Egan. In the course of their meeting, Ross told Sinclair that the allegations conveyed by Gerry Champagne and the other boys were similar to complaints he had heard before. In fact, Egan said, he had heard rumours of mistreatment of boys at St. Joseph's for more than a year. "I discounted much of what I heard," said Egan, "until January when Ross and I visited the school to take presents to a dozen or so boys from the Cornwall area. We spoke at length to some of the boys and these conversations gave us further cause for concern."

Egan said these boys told him that a staff member was attempting to force them to participate in sexual acts. The boys also claimed that they were being beaten across the buttocks with a leather strap and were sometimes forced to carry weights around the institution while handcuffed.

"The boys complained that staff members cuff, kick, and shove boys," continued Egan. "They reported that one boy was so beaten by a staff member that he had to be hospitalized."

Sinclair proceeded from Cornwall to St. Joseph's, where he spoke with a total of seven boys, one on one, in the visitors' parlour. He made a valiant effort to put them at ease, but soon understood that they had no more reason to trust him than they did the Brothers.

Gerry Champagne told Sinclair that since his escape on February 19, he and his cohorts had been handcuffed and beaten with a leather strap. One of his fellow escapees was still in handcuffs when Sinclair summoned him. This boy told Sinclair he had been forced to carry weightlifter's barbells around the school and outdoor rink as punishment for the escape. "They become heavy after a time," he told Sinclair.

Another ward told Sinclair about a boy who was involved in sexual activity with a Brother, but this boy denied it. "All that ever happened is that once he draped his arm around me," he told the inspector.

Sinclair believed the stories the boys told him. Their claims, remarkably, were supported by the school's superintendent. Yes, said Brother George, boys who ran away often were subjected to up to seven strokes of the strap on the buttocks while they lay spread-eagled on their stomachs on a bed.

Brother George admitted he had received a letter from the former minister of the department informing him that only strapping on the hands was permitted. He said the school outlawed strapping on the buttocks, but reintroduced it because staff felt that strapping on the hands was completely ineffective.

Yes, Brother George acknowledged, boys were forced to carry a barbell or other weight for periods as long as two hours – sometimes while handcuffed – but surely this was no worse punishment than scrubbing floors. And as for those boys who were locked in solitary confinement for days at a time and occasionally struck by staff, well, this was the only way the Brothers could get them to behave. "It is impossible for my small staff, who work very long hours, to keep control in any other fashion," he asserted.

Back in Toronto the following week, Sinclair told his superiors that if corporal punishment continued to be used at the training school, it would be just a matter of time before a boy was injured. "This cuffing and striking could well terminate in a broken jaw or an ear perforation, which, though never intended, would be none the less disastrous. There is, in fact, no justification for such practices as handcuffing boys, not permitting them to sit down, forcing them to carry weights around, and cuffing and striking them," he said.

He suggested that some of the Brothers lacked the training to deal properly with disturbed and insecure adolescents. Yes, the Brothers worked long hours and could be tired and irritated, but surely the boys at St. Joseph's had a right not to be abused. Sinclair doubted that simply ordering Brother George to stop the practices would be enough. "It would seem that an approach to the superintendent's superior in his religious order is indicated."

His recommendation was supported two days later by the advisory board. It suggested that a copy of Sinclair's report be sent to the head of the order or the bishop of the Ottawa Catholic diocese requesting appropriate action "to remedy a situation that is fraught with danger and could bring grave discredit upon the School and the Department."

The deputy minister of Reform Institutions, Archie Graham, chose to ignore the board's suggestion and instead advised George Wardrope to summon Brother George to Toronto to discuss the treatment of boys at his school.

The monk arrived at the department's headquarters on April 5, 1960. Brother George tried to downplay the boys' allegations, but Graham pointed out that he had already admitted most of the practices to Sinclair. "These methods of punishment remind me of the Dark Ages," he snapped. In the meantime, Wardrope read over the list of punishments Sinclair had noted in his report and insisted that they cease immediately. "When these stories become public," he said, "they are inclined to be exaggerated and can bring a great deal of concern to the department."

As the weeks passed, Ralph Ross waited impatiently in Cornwall for news from the department that something was happening.

Both he and Maurice Egan were concerned that their complaints would be swept under the carpet. After taking a new job in Ottawa, Egan decided to raise the matter with a highly placed priest he knew there. Father John A. Macdonald, director of charities for Catholic Family Services, took Egan's concerns directly to Ottawa Archbishop M. Joseph Lemieux. The archbishop called in Brother George for an interview.

Macdonald, meanwhile, contacted Wardrope with an offer from the archbishop to assist in rectifying the problems at St. Joseph's. "As this institution is in the Diocese of Ottawa, the Archbishop is deeply concerned and has asked me to tell you that he will do everything possible to have corrected whatever situations may be found to substantiate these complaints," Macdonald wrote.

The intervention by the archbishop infuriated Brother George, who complained to the advisory board chairman, Martin Pinker, that Egan was "stirring up trouble." Brother George also lamented that the complaints had reached the ears of James C. Cardinal McGuigan, the Archbishop of Toronto, "who has nothing to do with it since it was outside of his area."

He warned Pinker that the scandal was likely to become public. He had learned that a Cornwall newspaper reporter was working on a story critical of the school and of the province's failure to adequately investigate the allegations.

This news alarmed Archie Graham, and on June 24, 1960, he phoned Ralph Ross in Cornwall. In a telephone discussion that was recorded and later transcribed for the file, Ross told him that the problems hadn't been corrected at the training school and that, in his opinion, the situation was getting worse.

"Have you heard anything more about punishments?" asked Graham.

"No," replied Ross. "They told me all this had been stopped. No more punishment. No more solitary confinement. No more beatings. They told me this only last night, but I have only their word and I am not satisfied with their word. We have to make sure these things are not going to happen in the future."

"Anything more about sexual perversion?" asked Graham.

"That happened five years ago," said Ross. "I know the man. He is still there. I do not know of it happening recently."

Graham assured Ross that the investigation was continuing and that a board of inquiry was being established to probe the complaints. After the call, the deputy minister began planning for the inquiry. In a letter to the Archbishop of Ottawa, he wrote, "Apparently, conditions have not improved and there are still rumours in the community that certain practices are still going on. Whether these stories are exaggerated I am not prepared to say at this time."

The inquiry finally got underway in July when three members of the advisory board, including Martin Pinker, met Ralph Ross and members of the Cornwall Juvenile Court Committee in Ross's home.

Ross expressed concern that many of the practices that Sinclair had documented in his report were still employed at St. Joseph's. He had grave doubts about the integrity of the Christian Brothers. He said the Brothers advised him that the solitary confinement cells had been closed, but that when Egan visited the school recently, they were still being used. Moreover, a Brother widely considered to be a sexual "pervert" within the school — Brother Étienne, whose secular name was Lionel Vezeau — was still at the school.

"The boys say he is the one who really abuses them."

Then Reverend Harold Burgess, a member of the Cornwall committee, called for decisive action. "Something must be corrected or else these children must be moved," he argued. "If these people were responsible to your department, they would no longer be there."

Pinker explained that while the ultimate responsibility for the boys lay with his department, the school was run by the order. Section 11 of the Ontario Training Schools Act stated that a Roman Catholic boy or girl must go to a Roman Catholic institution.

"We have responsibility, but in the exercise of that responsibility we must take note of the fact that this school must be run by the Brothers," he told Burgess. "Either they must conform or grants will be withdrawn, a course to be taken in the last resort and with regret."

Burgess shifted the discussion to Brother Étienne. "Would it be possible, for the good of the school, to have the Brother who had already been investigated moved to some place where he does not have contact with boys?"

This prompted Pinker to ask if there were any other Brothers at the school who were cause for concern.

"Get rid of them all," Ross declared. "It's my opinion that the Brothers who have been in the school for some years and who put up with this type of treatment of boys should not be in a school where boys are at all."

Pinker let the comment pass. His chief concern was, apparently, to keep the investigation out of the newspapers. As he told the Christian Brothers, "It is always a pity when something of this nature happens that can stir up a lot of controversy in the press and bring discredit on all the training schools. It is the sort of criticism that could be so construed and magnified that it would take a generation to live down."

The Brothers, meanwhile, assured Pinker and the committee that reforms were being carried out with dispatch. "I told the Brothers from now on the strap must be stopped," Brother George announced. "We may say quite frankly today there is no strap here."

He went on to note that handcuffs were no longer used because the school now had proper detention cells. Furthermore, wards would not be required to carry weights as punishment.

"What about cuffing and hitting the boys?" asked Pinker.

"It is quite diminished," answered Brother George. "We can say nearly stopped."

"So if Mr. Ross and Mr. Egan were under the impression that these practices have been continued, they have been misinformed?"

"You listen to the boys," one angry Brother snapped. "How is it you do not invite us to explain the situation?"

Pinker refused to be drawn into that argument. He pressed on to other matters. Did the Brothers still employ "fox hunts" to catch runaway boys?

"We do not," retorted Brother George. "It was never a policy to harm boys. One boy tried to escape from their hands and the other boys tried to punish him."

Pinker raised the issue of sexual activity. "Something came up a few years ago and now crops up again," he said, obliquely. "These matters are always difficult to prove unless the culprits are caught in the act. One of the points that has been raised is that the Brother who was accused of this a few years ago is still here and the boys are not happy about that. Do you feel happy about this situation?"

"It is a surprise to me," shrugged Brother George. "I would like you to interview our Brother Provincial. I think, myself, we have cleared up this matter."

Pinker went on to discuss staffing. More than once the Brothers had complained about being short-staffed. Was this part of the problem? Was this why Brothers might be assaulting the boys? "If you are short-staffed, it means the Brothers in turn are over-worked," he noted. "In the end, the Brothers are going to get irritated and nervous."

"I disagree with you," said Brother George. "I may say that the best supervisor here rarely touched a boy."

That evening, the board members went to Ottawa to meet with the Brother Provincial, Brother Arsene, head of the Ottawa Brothers of the Christian Schools.

"What I don't like about the whole situation is that the people of Cornwall have accepted the children's version," Brother Arsene complained. "It seems that the whole thing has been blown out of proportion."

Pinker responded by reading Sinclair's report aloud, and the discussion quickly shifted to other issues. Brother Arsene explained the school was badly in debt as a result of a fire in the workshops and the construction, budgeted at $700,000, of new wings, a gymnasium, and a swimming pool.

What he did not mention, however, was that the Department of Reform Institutions had repeatedly urged the order not to go ahead with its construction plans until it had adequate staffing and classroom space. Now he was saying there was no money for new staff. "I can change one or two Brothers this coming August, but when it comes to increasing staff, I cannot. We should increase our staff by six Brothers or six laymen, but it is impossible. I have not got the Brothers. We cannot afford laymen."

Brother Arsene informed Pinker that in August Brother George would become principal of an Ottawa separate school. In the meantime, while Brother George attended conferences in France and Rome, Brother Giles, Brother George's former assistant, would assume the superintendency of St. Joseph's. As further evidence of the order's dedication to housecleaning, Brother Arsene said Brother Étienne would be transferred in the early fall.

Pleased with these indications of progress, the board packed up and returned to Toronto. On July 8, 1960, George Wardrope congratulated Brother Giles on his appointment as new superintendent of St. Joseph's. He indicated an additional grant likely would be forthcoming to assist the school with its construction program and advised him that Donald Sinclair would be returning the following week "to spend a few days and share his experiences with you.

"Always look on us as friends," he told Brother Giles.

At the time he wrote the letter to Brother Giles, George Wardrope was not aware of the outcome of his department's most recent inspection of the training school. A department inspector who visited the school July 7 had found its farm in a mess. The barn was filthy, and carcasses of livestock were rotting in the barnyard: "a sign of sheer neglect and carelessness to the Nth degree."

The inspector also noted that the school's lone placement officer now had a horrendous caseload of 118 boys and that 3 boys had recently escaped, taking with them a shotgun from one of the farm sheds.

Additional criticism came from Sinclair when he returned to the school the following week. In a nine-page July 15 memo to Martin Pinker, Sinclair blasted the school's decision to spend $700,000 on capital projects when it could not afford to hire teachers. The ratio of staff to wards at Alfred was lower than any other training school in Ontario. "It is totally inadequate, and thorough supervision – particularly of the type which can prevent trouble by means of purposeful programs rather than attempt to cure it by punitive methods – is impossible when there are so few staff," he wrote.

Respect for rules and regulations could not be taught by punishment alone, Sinclair stressed. Effective treatment was impossible without wholesome relationships between staff and wards, and these relationships could not exist in an atmosphere of hostility. "Skilled workers with children need to use punishment rarely while the inadequate worker depends on it habitually and uses it as a crutch on which to lean."

Sinclair was also concerned about the length of time boys

were being kept in the school. He noted that little if anything was done to assess their behavioural progress.

"Alfred has, not unfairly, been criticized in the past for keeping some boys for an inordinate length of time," he wrote. "It should be apparent that if the training school has not succeeded in accomplishing its task in about two years, it is very unlikely it will succeed in four years."

Sinclair suggested the establishment of a school advisory committee, composed of prominent people from nearby communities, to help both the staff in doing its job and the boys in finding jobs when they left the school. In the meantime, he wrote, the school should be visited by a board member or himself at least once every two months until "the Board can rest assured not only that punitive practices have ceased, but that a more humane and progressive era is on the way."

Another case, similar to that of Jeffrey Hudson, pointed out the continuing inadequacies of health care as managed by the Brothers. Real Forget, a twelve-year-old boy who had been at St. Joseph's for three years, was playing baseball one hot July afternoon. While standing near the third base line, he was struck in the head with a bat that had slipped out of a batter's hands. Blood oozed from his right ear. He ran in circles, holding his hand to his head and waving off teammates who wanted to help. Eventually he collapsed and was carried by two boys to the infirmary.

By the time a doctor arrived, Forget had apparently recovered from his initial dizziness. The doctor found that his temperature and pulse were normal. Forget was cheerful and did not complain of either pain or distress. The doctor did notice a small, mastoid-like lump behind Forget's right ear, but he did not consider it serious.

The next day, Forget's condition deteriorated. He grew
extremely restless and reported that his head was throbbing.
Eventually, the doctor advised the Brothers to take the boy to a
small hospital in nearby Eastview. There, a neurologist, suspecting Forget had suffered a brain haemorrhage, made a lumbar
puncture of the boy's spine to check the spinal fluid for signs of
bleeding. He didn't find blood, but he did find signs of meningitis, an often fatal infection of the thin membranes that cover
the brain and spinal cord. The doctor prescribed antibiotics to
combat the infection, but they had no effect. Forget died three
days later.

The province sent Gerry Wright, the Department of Reform
Institution's chief inspector, to investigate the fatality. Wright
made it his first task to convince the local coroner to call an inquest. Brother Giles, the new superintendent, argued that an
inquest was unnecessary because the death had not occurred in
the institution. An inquest was subsequently held.

Wright noted that Forget's doctors were initially puzzled that
antibiotics had failed to arrest the boy's infection. It was only when
they discovered that Forget had suffered from a chronic ear infection that had been treated by antibiotics before he was sent to
St. Joseph's that the explanation became clear. Forget's body had
built up a resistance to the antibiotics used in the treatment of
his ear problem.

The Brothers claimed not to be aware that the boy had suffered
from an ear infection. Despite the department's explicit directive
following the death of Jeffrey Hudson, the school had kept no
medical records on Forget, other than the initial examination he
underwent when he arrived at the school.

"It is reasonable to assume that if Forget's eyes, ears, nose and
throat had been properly examined, the old mastoid condition
would have been discovered and could have been kept under

observation," Wright reported to his superiors. "This condition is apt to frequently recur."

Wright complained that the Brother who ran the infirmary was not a qualified nurse and had very limited medical knowledge. "His only record [of illnesses] is a scribbler in which he keeps the names of boys who have asked to see the doctor or dentist. The scribblers are destroyed as they are filled."

The chief inspector found no records of examinations, diagnoses, treatments, or complaints. Although there were blank dental cards in a desk drawer in the dentist's office, Wright was advised that they weren't used because regular dental examinations weren't conducted.

Wright was appalled by the condition of the infirmary. The bed linen was dirty and it was apparent that it wasn't changed from one patient to the next.

He recommended that a younger doctor with some training in psychiatry be hired by the school to assist the elderly local doctor, and that a registered nurse be hired to establish and maintain the infirmary and medical records. Convinced that a more thorough examination of Forget would have detected his ear problem, Wright also recommended that new medical forms be provided that would require the doctor to report the condition of every area of the body. He also called for regular dental check-ups.

Wright also believed that the baseball accident that led to Forget's hospitalization might have been avoided had there been stricter supervision. No staff member had even witnessed the incident. Either more staff should be hired, said Wright, or fewer wards be placed in the school.

In the aftermath of Forget's death, the Christian Brothers hired a nurse and a younger doctor, Dr. Germain L. Houle, to assist the elderly doctor. But there was no major increase in staff.

Following the coroner's inquest, a jury ruled that Forget died of cerebral spinal meningitis. The baseball incident, it said, did not contribute to his death.

Wright's investigations also showed that boys at St. Joseph's were still being strapped on the buttocks despite all protestations that the practice had been stopped.

When apprised of this, the advisory board urged the minister to cut off funding to the school. George Wardrope fired off a four-page missive to Brother Giles, full of thunder, fire, and smoke: "The school is far below the standard set by the Training School Advisory Board in regard to supervision, discipline, methods of treatment and in its provisions for the overall physical, mental and emotional welfare of the boys," he wrote. "Parents, welfare workers and members of the community are, with some justification, making complaints as to the manner in which the school is catering to the needs of its wards. It is evident that, in spite of the minister's directive, corporal punishment has since been resorted to and that, in spite of assurances by your predecessor that this would not occur again, it is still being used. This constitutes final warning that, if proof is ever obtained in the future that corporal punishment is still in effect, every step will be taken under Section 4 of the Ontario Training Schools Act to cancel the authority of your school to be maintained as a training school."

The deputy minister, Archie Graham, sent off his own letter to Brother Arsene with a copy of the minister's letter to St. Joseph's. "The minister is very disturbed to find that despite repeated assurance from the school to the effect that corporal punishment would no longer be resorted to, as late as two weeks ago it was still being administered," he wrote. "The situation calls for far-reaching changes."

Pointing out yet again that St. Joseph's had a ward-to-staff ratio nearly twice that of St. John's, he urged the Brother Provincial to increase staff to forty, and, if necessary, halt its $1-million construction program. A similar letter was sent to Archbishop Lemieux of Ottawa.

"St. Joseph's has been the subject of three separate investigations within the past four months," Graham noted. "The reports which resulted from these investigations clearly indicate that corporal punishment is still in effect at the school in spite of a ministerial directive that it must be abolished."

If the changes weren't made, the department would have to suspend the school's authority to operate as a training school, Graham wrote. "We know that you will appreciate our desire to take the necessary action before the growing number of complaints received by us from parents, welfare workers, and others reaches such a magnitude that the matter becomes public knowledge, in which event the school, this department, and the Church can only suffer."

And still the incidents kept occurring.

On August 14, 1960, Ruth Jenkins visited her thirteen-year-old son, Bobbie, at St. Joseph's. From the moment she saw him, she knew something was wrong. When they were alone, he told her what it was: one of the Brothers had done "something" to him. Ruth didn't understand all of it, but she understood enough. Grabbing Bobbie by the arm, she hustled him to the bus station where, without so much as a word to Brother Giles or anyone else, they hopped the next bus back to her home in Ottawa.

That afternoon, Ruth had the boy examined at Ottawa Civic Hospital's free clinic. She also made an appointment to see her lawyer, Ted Mettrick, the next day.

That night at home, a calmer Bobbie was able to tell his mother the full story. He had been in the school's stamp collection room on the main floor when Brother Sylvio entered the room and put his arm around him. Instead of just hugging the boy affectionately, as he often did, the monk slid his hand down the boy's pants and caressed his penis. Bobbie was stunned. For a moment he didn't know what to do, then he howled in anger. Brother Sylvio quickly retreated.

The next day, Ted Mettrick interviewed Bobbie and was soon satisfied that he was telling the truth. Mettrick then called Archie Graham to demand an investigation. "Take whatever action is necessary to remove this problem from the school and stop these practices."

Graham assured Mettrick the matter would be investigated. He also advised the lawyer that the boy must be returned to the school. Officially, he was unlawfully at large. It was no easy matter persuading Ruth Jenkins to send Bobbie back, but, in the end, she reluctantly complied with the order.

Graham called on Donald Sinclair to undertake yet another investigation at St. Joseph's. It was to be the fourth in six months.

By the time Sinclair arrived on the scene a week later, Bobbie had been placed in the same foster home as his older brother, who had just been released from St. Joseph's. Sinclair interviewed the two boys separately, but received no co-operation from the eldest, who kept repeating "I've had enough of that place and now I just want to forget it."

At St. Joseph's, Brother Giles told Sinclair that he had heard "rumours" about Brother Sylvio's behaviour with the boys and had confronted him about it. The Brother had confessed, and was transferred out of the school on August 19, just five days after Ruth Jenkins got the story from Bobbie.

The following day, when Sinclair met with the Brother Provincial in Ottawa, he was officially informed that Brother Sylvio was being released from the order and that Brother Étienne

(Lionel Vezeau), who had been the subject of previous allegations of sexual abuse, would also be removed from St. Joseph's within two to three days.

On his returning to Toronto, Sinclair told his superiors, "In view of the fact that the Brother Provincial has taken immediate and positive action, there seems little point in obtaining further statements from the boys."

With four investigations coming one after another in a single year, the Christian Brothers may have felt that some action was required, as a matter of self-preservation. But still, nothing really changed. And it would soon become evident that St. John's was afflicted with similar problems regarding both corporal punishment and sexual abuse.

Early in the morning of September 24, 1962, fifteen-year-old Steve Lamb (not his real name) arrived unannounced at his sister's apartment in east Toronto. He had run away from St. John's the day before. Exhausted, he fell asleep on a bed in his sister's bedroom. When she entered the room to check on her baby, who was sleeping in a crib in the same room, she noticed some marks on her brother's lower back. Lifting the bedsheets, she discovered several raw, ugly red welts, stretching from his lower thighs and across his buttocks up his back. She asked Lamb about the marks when he woke up and he explained that he had been beaten with an eighteen-inch long razor strop for attempting to run away.

"But that's nothing," he informed his horrified sister. "One night one of the Brothers wandered into the dormitory drunk and was feeling up the boys."

Lamb left his sister's home before she could get a doctor to see his injuries, but her parents reported her observations to the Department of Reform Institutions. They also met with their parish priest, who suggested they obtain a written statement from their son. They next heard from Lamb in a letter from the Sault St. Marie jail. He had been recaptured and was being sent directly to the maximum-security Ontario Training School for Boys (Hillcrest) in Guelph. They wrote back to him immediately, urging him to report his allegations.

On October 22, G. E. Jacobs, a department inspector, visited St. John's. It was immediately apparent to him that Lamb had, indeed, been beaten. Although the boy's injuries had healed, Brother David, the dormitory senior prefect, admitted giving him ten strokes across the buttocks with a razor strop. Jacobs also quickly established that a Brother Ernest (not the same Brother who befriended David McCann at St. Joseph's) had entered a boys' dormitory after a drinking session one night and had gone from bed to bed fondling the genitals of the boys.

One boy told Jacobs, under oath, that Brother Ernest stopped at his bed to fondle his genitals three times during the night. The story was confirmed by Brother David, who had steered the drunken Brother back to his bed after one startled boy woke up, shouting, "What's going on here?"

"There had been quite a party the night before and he had had quite a bit to drink and did not remember anything," Brother David explained. "I asked the boys what happened. One said that he had come over to his bed and rubbed his face against his. Another said that Brother Ernest came over to his bed and patted him. He did not say where. Another said that Brother Ernest had touched him on his private organs."

The boys told Jacobs that Brother Ernest had blamed the incident on the fact that he had a cold and had been taking pills for it and drinking brandy. They said Brother Ernest had apologized to them the next day after breakfast. Brother David said that when he met with Brother Ernest and four boys in his room that morning, Brother Ernest was extremely contrite. "Brother Ernest sat in my room and cried, saying he could not believe he could do anything like this."

Jacobs learned that Brother Ernest had come to St. John's for the summer from Quebec as temporary relief help and had since returned to Quebec. Although Jacobs didn't have an opportunity to interview him, he had a long discussion with Brother David about the use of corporal punishment at St. John's.

Brother David conceded that he knew the strap was prohibited, but claimed he was just carrying out the orders of the school's superintendent, Brother Adrian, when he strapped Lamb. He disputed the Lamb family's allegations that Lamb's buttocks were cut and blistered after the beating, but he admitted striking him on the face with his hands or fists. "I know I hit him," he was quoted saying in a report Jacobs sent to the department. "I am not sure whether I slapped or punched him."

Brother David told Jacobs that boys were often struck for "trivial" reasons and that he sometimes punished boys by making them run to the point of exhaustion. When asked to produce the punishment log, he couldn't. He did, however, produce the strap, which Jacobs promptly seized.

In a report, dated October 23, 1962, Jacobs wrote, "From the evidence taken, there would appear to be little doubt that Brother Ernest did, on more than one occasion, molest the boys as they slept at night. Brother David testifies as to this man's show of emotion on the morning following the episode. Whether this reaction was the result of pills or brandy taken during the evening, such an incident establishes beyond any doubt that Brother Ernest is anything but a suitable or fit person to supervise pupils in their quarters and should be denied the opportunity to ever repeat such actions."

He recommended that the department re-emphasize the prohibition of corporal punishment and the requirement that the

school superintendent keep a punishment log. He also recommended that Brother Ernest be denied, "for all time," the opportunity to work at any Ontario training school and that he be
required to attend the department offices to "explain his actions."
Jacobs also recommended that the practice of forcing children
to run as punishment be stopped.

Archie Graham called Brother Adrian into his office for the
now-familiar expressions of outrage. Later he consulted Martin
Pinker, who expressed confidence that Brother Adrian was on top
of the situation. Although Brother Adrian had approved the use
of the strap, the sexual assaults by Brother Ernest had occurred
while he had been away on vacation.

"Without minimizing the seriousness of the situation that has
come to light, I think we must not lose sight of the many good
things that can be said about this school," Pinker advised Graham.
"I am satisfied that we shall receive the fullest measure of co-
operation from Brother Adrian in doing his utmost to safeguard
against such incidents in the future."

Years later, Brother Ernest would return to Ontario and resume
his teaching career. Today he teaches at a public school within
an hour's drive of Toronto.

One thirteen-year-old St. Joseph's ward, an anglophone awash in
a sea of francophones, wanted out of Alfred so badly he was prepared to claim he was Baptist rather than Roman Catholic. In
April 1963, he wrote a letter to the Supreme Court of Canada
demanding to be transferred. Alfred was too violent, he complained. "Here I am hit so often, I feel like I might send one of
them to hospital if I am not careful. I have developed such a
temper here, I hardly recognize myself. This is a training school,
but what does it train you to do? When someone lays a hand on
you, you turn around and hit them in the mouth."

The ward got an immediate transfer to the training school in Guelph, but not because of his request. When the department's deputy minister discovered he had a record for arson, he quickly moved him to a more secure setting. St. Joseph's had already lost its barn and workshops to fire.

The Brothers, meanwhile, did not deny hitting the boy. "It was not a vicious blow," explained Brother Andrew, who had punched the boy in the mouth when he caught him fooling around in a meal line-up. "The boy had been troublesome, talking and generally acting like a fool. I had no trouble after that."

Brother Giles, the superintendent, explained that the actions of his young prefect were perfectly reasonable. "He was no doubt riled by the boy's behaviour."

Archie Graham issued yet another stern warning and received the following perfunctory reply: "We still are against corporal punishment." In what would be his last words on the matter, Graham issued a harshly worded letter to all training school staff in October 1964 reiterating the department policy prohibiting corporal punishment. He demanded that staff read it and sign their names to show that they understood the directive. "I want to make it abundantly clear that no corporal punishment of any type is to be awarded a student of our schools." The penalty, he warned, was immediate dismissal.

In all essentials, the situation that existed in the mid-1940s remained unchanged in the mid-1960s. While presiding over the most corrupt regime imaginable, the Christian Brothers at St. John's and St. Joseph's successfully fended off every investigation with empty promises and minor acts of contrition. While the attitude of the public was to become more sceptical towards authority in the years that followed, many years would pass before significant reforms were put into effect.

The Untouchables

•

"I suggest that the safe cloak of the clergy can provide
a shield such as to make persons involved untouchables."
— father of abused St. John's ward in a letter to
Ontario Attorney General Dalton Bales, January 1973

GEORGE WARDROPE had initiated some significant reforms after he took over the department in 1958, but it was still considered a backwater when Allan Grossman moved into the minister's office six years later. "I wondered why I was being asked to take over a department that was at the bottom of the barrel," Peter Oliver quoted him as saying in the book, *Unlikely Tory: The Life and Politics of Allan Grossman.*

At the time, according to University of Toronto criminologist Tadeusz Grygier, the department was grossly underfunded and had few qualified professional staff. Most staff members were ashamed to tell anyone where they worked. Grygier told Oliver the department was "a joke. People knew it was a dead-end department."

Those who challenged the status quo eventually got tired of butting their heads against a wall and left. Albert Virgin, the director of training schools, was followed out the door by Donald

Sinclair and, presently, by Archie Graham. Graham's successor, Leo Hackl, had come up through the ranks, having started out with the department as a teacher. He fired his first salvo in November 1965, reissuing Graham's warning with respect to corporal punishment, again demanding that staff read it and sign it.

With the arrival of Grossman, there was, for once, some money available to fund many of the reforms that had been recommended by previous administrations whose ministers had been unable, because of their lack of political clout, to act on them.

Both St. Joseph's and St. John's were expanded. New secular training schools were opened in Lindsay and Simcoe. A forestry camp for delinquent boys was opened northeast of Bowmanville. By January 1966, the department had added two more training schools in Hagersville. The province attributed the increased need for training schools to a burgeoning juvenile population – the baby boom.

Grossman gave the department a new name – the Ministry of Correctional Services – and he began bringing in people with the expertise to deal with troubled children. He also made it mandatory for police to be contacted when ministry inspectors were investigating allegations of a criminal nature. Hackl brought in new people, too. Tad Grygier, long a ministry critic, was appointed to head research and develop policy. And Donald Sinclair, who had quit in 1963 to head the Canadian Mental Health Association in Ontario, assumed responsibility for the province's eighty-two correctional institutions, including the training schools.

Changes at the political level reflected changes in the attitude of the general public. Occasionally, the voices of critics were to be heard in public forums. A major legislative initiative by Grossman was the occasion for informed complaint.

In November 1965, the province proclaimed a new Training Schools Act, which dropped the labelling of children. No longer were they "delinquent," "neglected," or "incorrigible." The revisions ensured that only the courts could order a child into custody in a training school, wiping out a provision that permitted the minister, and thus his bureaucracy, to make such an order. The revised act, however, continued to allow juvenile court judges to send children to training schools for behaviour that would not be considered criminal if committed by an adult. Children who stayed out too late and disobeyed their parents were being sent to the equivalent of a children's prison.

The reforms to the act were undertaken without any public consultation. Even senior officials in the department were excluded from the process. Bernard Green, a University of Toronto law professor, argued in an October 1966 article in the *Canadian Journal of Corrections* that the new act represented a serious threat to civil liberties. Seen through a child's eyes, it made no difference that he was being sent to a training school for his own protection: it would seem like punishment regardless. Green believed strongly that locking up a child, even for his own good, was inherently wrong.

Although the new act required judges to hold hearings in open court and state their reasons for committing a child to a training school, it contained no provision for children to be represented or advised by a lawyer. The act even empowered judges to hear evidence against the child when the child was absent. The very notion made Green and other civil rights advocates seethe.

"These reforms are minuscule compared to the grave errors of commission and omission perpetrated by those responsible for the legislation," Green wrote.

For his criticisms, Green was branded a misguided idealist. Although he was seen as "a reformer, whose heart is in the protection of children," ministry officials lamented that the professor saw only the shortcomings of the legislation and was "unable to appreciate the progress made."

In 1968, two Ontario politicians picked up where Green left off. New Democratic Party members of the provincial parliament John Brown and Stephen Lewis launched a vociferous campaign against the act. They called for "the emergency rescue" of children from training schools.

Describing the schools as "inhumane, archaic and 40 years behind the times," Brown demanded they be closed. He declared that children at the new Grandview School in Galt were being treated "like rats in a maze." Innocent children, he charged at an NDP meeting, were being forced to submit to inhumane practices in these schools. "These kids never committed a single anti-social act. They were just kids that someone wants put out of the way."

Complaints from the children and some of the people who worked with them continued to find their way to the ministry. In early 1969, Margaret Milne, a civilian teacher who had just been fired from St. Joseph's, informed Harry Garraway, the training school administrator, that the school was a mess. Three supervisors punched out a boy for stealing cigarette butts, she said. Another boy had been strapped; sick boys were not receiving adequate medical treatment; textbooks were in short supply; and staff used foul language.

In a follow-up letter to Allan Grossman, Milne noted that there was an undercurrent of sexual deviancy in the institution. "One boy in my class was habitually called a homosexual by all the boys with whom I came in contact," she wrote. "I asked the principal about this and he gave a smirk and said that this was found in all institutions. I said I still thought something should be done about it. This same boy was punched out by two adult supervisors one evening, much to the delight of all boys who witnessed it."

Garraway sent the Brothers another warning. "While the department does not have the authority to dismiss staff in the private training schools, we do however feel that you would wish us to bring this matter to your attention. We would appreciate being advised as soon as possible what action you intend to take." No action was taken.

A number of boys complained in July 1969 that they had been struck on the bare backsides by a Brother using a sawed-off goalie's hockey stick. Garraway went to the school to investigate. He seized the stick and confronted the offending Brother, Gilles Nadeau. Nadeau told Garraway he had, in fact, used the "gizmo," but did not see any harm in it, Garraway reported. Brother Gilles also conceded that, on occasion, he had been frustrated to the point of slapping or shaking a boy.

Garraway was flabbergasted. "I spent a considerable amount of time with him in explaining the consequences of his actions and the unfavourable criticism of himself and the administration of the school which could follow," he later told Donald Sinclair.

Sinclair experienced an uneasy feeling that he had seen it all before. He wrote to the school's superintendent, Brother Maurice-Jacques, warning him to guard against this flagrant disregard of ministry directives.

But Garraway was back at St. Joseph's before the year was out to investigate a complaint that a boy was made to stand for hours in handcuffs and then forced, while still wearing the cuffs, to sweep the dormitory floor. Soon after this incident, the ministry received a complaint that a boy was seen in the schoolyard

shackled to a ball and chain. The superintendent assured the
inspector that it must have been the children playing.

In 1970, the cause of training school reform was taken up by
Dr. Morton Shulman, the crusading Toronto coroner and inspiration for the television series "Wojeck." Shulman had entered
politics in 1967, after being fired from his coroner's post for
insubordination, and made it his mission in life to savage the
Tories. In one session of the legislature on June 1, 1970, he asked
Correctional Services Minister Allan Grossman to comment on
a magazine report that referred to St. Joseph's as a "hell-hole"
filled with sadists and homosexuals. "Will the minister look into
this matter and do an appropriate investigation?" asked Shulman.

Grossman was outraged that such an allegation would be thrust
upon him before he had even seen the article.

"Three million people know already," retorted Shulman.

In May 1971, the Christian Brothers at St. Joseph's fired a civilian employee for manhandling a child. Brother Maurice-Jacques
reported that the employee had been dismissed for assaulting a
boy for talking during the showing of a track-and-field movie.
He had allegedly seized the boy by the hair and dragged him to
the back of the hall where he struck him and slammed him into
a wall.

Were the brothers at St. Joseph's finally changing for the better?
The ministry scarcely had time to speculate about this before
another round of crises and investigations got under way at
St. John's.

In January 1971, fifteen-year-old Jerry Hills (not his real name)
had been sent to St. John's under section 8 of the Ontario Training

Schools Act. This section allowed for a child to be admitted to a training school if his parents were unable to control him or meet his social, educational, or emotional needs, providing that there was no other alternative. At the court hearing, Hills had told the judge he wanted to go. He was sure that if he stayed at home, his father would one day kill him.

His father often beat Hills' mother and on several occasions had attacked Hills. Once he chased the boy with a knife; another time he tried to smother him with a pillow. Hills did not know what saved him from the attempted smothering. When Hills regained consciousness, his father was crying and begging forgiveness. It got even scarier when Hills' mother left his father. In a rage, his father broke his brother's arm.

At St. John's, Hills quickly discovered brutality similar to that from which he had fled. A civilian supervisor named James Clarke taunted and beat him at every opportunity. When Hills reported the abuse to Brother Daniel, the superintendent hugged him and assured him that it would not happen again. As long as Hills stayed under his protection, he would be all right. Hills liked the easygoing Brother, who habitually shuffled around the institution, wearing his thick, steel-framed glasses.

Brother Daniel often dropped by Hills' dormitory in the evening and would sit on the edge of the bed, chain-smoking, while the two chatted. He seemed genuinely concerned about Hills' welfare and Hills was not overly concerned when the man gave him an affectionate kiss on his forehead before leaving one night. But soon the kissing became more sexual. Brother Daniel would lean over Hills as he lay in his bed and kiss him directly on the lips while pressing his hand down on the blanket over the boy's genitals.

On one occasion, he slid his hand under the covers and fondled the boy's penis. After that incident, Hills made sure his sheets were wrapped tightly around him and tucked under his body before the Brother entered the dorm. "He would almost look at you for acknowledgement that it was okay," Hills recalled later. "It was almost like when you fondle a girl on a date and you are trying to get to first base. As long as she isn't saying no, your hand is moving south."

Another time, Hills and another boy were returning from a trip to Hamilton with Brother Daniel when the monk tried to slip his hand down Hills' pants. And again, when the Brother took him and another boy to see a movie at a drive-in theatre, Hills noticed that the pair had their hands under their coats, which were spread over their laps, and were fondling one another's genitals.

"I just stayed glued to the movie screen. I have no recollection of the movie. I was absolutely frightened. But it never occurred to me once to run away. As far as I was concerned, they were in charge. I remember thinking: who ever will believe this?"

Hills didn't tell anyone about Brother Daniel during the seven months he was in St. John's. The story came out later.

Two months after Hills left the school, Brother Daniel had a new quarry, a twelve-year-old North Bay boy named Dwayne Dopp (not his real name). On October 15, 1971, the monk invited Dopp to accompany him on a trip to North Bay. It would give the boy a chance to visit his family while the Brother did a few errands. Soon after they set out, Dopp fell asleep in the front seat of Brother Daniel's car. They were not far out of North Bay when the boy was startled out of his sleep by the pressure of a hand sliding down the front of his pants. At first he rolled away, pretending he was still asleep, but when the hand pursued him, he raised himself up and shouted at the Brother to stop. For the remainder of the trip, he sat pressed against the passenger-side door, out of the range of the monk's roving hands. Brother Daniel drove on as though nothing had happened and dropped him off at his home.

The boy said nothing about the abuse until his second night home, when, sobbing, he spilled out the story to his sister. When Brother Daniel arrived to take him back to St. John's, Dopp's mother, backed up by the boy's uncle, was waiting for him.

Mrs. Dopp accused the monk of making "immoral advances" against her child and advised him that Dwayne would not be returning to St. John's with him as a result. When Brother Daniel pretended not to understand, she told him he "knew damn well" what she was talking about. "Oh, you know, Brother," she snapped. "Do you want me to say it in plain language?"

"No, that won't be necessary," he responded. Before he left, he offered Dwayne twenty dollars. "Don't say anything about this because it will leave a black mark against me," he begged.

Dwayne refused the money.

Back at St. John's, Brother Daniel began making hasty arrangements for the boy's release from the training school. His plans were dashed when Garraway, the administrator of training schools, called to advise that he was investigating an allegation against him. A few minutes later Brother Howard Jobin – who was filling in for the Brother Provincial, Brother Benedict – called, demanding to know what was going on. He had been summoned to the ministry's offices to provide an explanation. Armed with the scant information Brother Daniel gave him, Brother Howard then met with ministry officials. At the end of the meeting, he agreed to have Brother Daniel provide a statement within two days.

Nearly a week passed before Brother Daniel complied with the order. He handed over a four-page document denying the allegations, but apologizing for his "error in judgment" in attempting to arrange the boy's release. He stated that he made the error out of "confusion and embarrassment."

Garraway arranged to transfer Dopp to the Cecil Facer Centre, a new 120-bed, interdenominational, bilingual training school that had just been opened in Sudbury. Rather than call in police to probe the boy's allegation, the ministry, on the recommendation of its deputy minister, Leo Hackl, sent a nun — Sister Elise Rasch, Harry Garraway's assistant — to conduct the investigation.

Sister Elise interviewed the boy and his mother in their home. Although Dwayne was reluctant to talk about the incident, his mother explained that when she confronted Brother Daniel, he had not denied the allegation. But Sister Elise wasn't convinced.

In her five-page report, submitted October 26, 1971, she deduced that because the road was hilly and Brother Daniel had been travelling quickly, making what was usually a four-hour trip in three hours, it was unlikely that he would have been able to assault the boy. Furthermore, she noted, Dopp had been wearing tight-fitting trousers with a two-inch-wide belt at the time of the alleged assault. She also pointed out that Dopp never mentioned the incident to a friend he played with in North Bay.

The family pressed in vain to have Brother Daniel removed from the school. Dopp's uncle urged the ministry to take action. "Consider this matter carefully as I feel a man with this type of sickness should not be in a school for boys."

At the time of the incident, a child's allegation, without corroboration, was insufficient evidence to press charges. Nor were such allegations sufficient to lead to the dismissal of a man of presumed high moral standing. No effort was made to probe the matter further or to question other boys at St. Joseph's. The ministry was, however, concerned that Brother Daniel had shown poor judgement in dealing with the situation. Garraway wanted Brother Daniel out, but because he couldn't fire him, he attempted to negotiate with the Brother Provincial.

He did not get far. When Brother Benedict returned from a brief absence, he made it clear that Brother Daniel would be staying on as superintendent for a simple reason: no one else wanted the job. The congenial superintendent accordingly picked up where he had left off. He continued to visit the dormitory on an almost nightly basis to cuddle and kiss the boys. He visited boys in sick bay and held their hands in what they described as "a queer manner." He approached one boy in solitary confinement, lay down on the bed beside him, with his face just inches away, and began to rub the child's bare chest. When he inched forward to kiss the boy, he was rebuffed.

In January 1973, nearly two years after Jerry Hills had been molested by Brother Daniel, the ministry became aware that it had a problem. Hills' father had written to Attorney General Dalton Bales, with a copy to Premier Bill Davis, warning of a deviant homosexual at St. John's Training School. He was certain that others knew about this man as well, but had remained silent rather than disturb the status quo.

"This is a serious matter and I am fully aware of the possible ramifications of causing focus on it, but I feel duty bound to speak up." He said his boy's statements either made him "a dangerous liar or an unfortunate victim," but, if it was the latter, it meant that other boys could be victimized as well. "My revealing all this is to cause a thorough investigation into the allegations immediately and to cause steps to be taken to preclude the possibility of its continuance," he wrote.

He hoped that by copying the letter to the premier, there would be "sufficient motivation to cause appropriate and complete action." To disavow the allegations, he wrote, would be like "sweeping dirt under the rug and would allow continuation under the government's nose of an obnoxious and potentially scandalous situation. . . . I suggest that the safe cloak of the clergy can provide a shield such as to make persons involved untouchables."

Bales forwarded copies of the letter to John Yaremko, the Ontario solicitor general, who was responsible for the province's police, and to Syl Apps, the former National Hockey League star who had replaced Grossman as minister of Correctional Services in 1971. It wasn't until month's end that the assistant deputy minister, Glenn Thompson, assigned Stan Teggart, the director of his inspection and standards branch, to "conduct this delicate investigation personally."

Teggart first met with senior OPP officials, including Staff Supt. Stewart Loree of Toronto's Criminal Investigation Branch. Then, accompanied by another inspector, he interviewed Jerry Hills and thirty-five other former St. John's wards who had been in the institution over the previous three years. After the interviews, in mid-February 1973 Teggart advised Thompson that he believed he had uncovered sufficient evidence to warrant a police investigation and criminal charges. "There is no doubt that there is a requirement for an extensive investigation which may support criminal charges being laid of indecent assault."

Brother Daniel was summoned to the minister's office and confronted with the accusations. Although he denied having made sexual advances, suggesting the wards had misinterpreted a show of friendship, he tendered his resignation, saying his health was failing and that his effectiveness as a superintendent had been undermined by the investigation. He was transferred to Scarborough to run the order's retirement home for elderly Brothers and priests.

With Brother Daniel out of the picture, neither Teggart nor the OPP showed much interest in pursuing the investigation. Wrote

Teggart in a March 12, 1973, memo to Thompson, "I am satisfied that at this time there are not sufficient grounds to support criminal charges."

Teggart claimed that Jerry Hills was the only complainant and that he had refused to testify. The boy who Hills saw sexually abused at the drive-in had moved out of the province and was not interviewed. No wards in the school at the time were interviewed, nor were members of the school staff.

Thompson sent a four-page summary of Teggart's findings — stamped "confidential" on every page — to Loree on April 6. A sealed copy also went to Teggart for his files. The letter to the police, however, made no reference to the earlier allegations of sexual assault against Brother Daniel by Dwayne Dopp nor was there any explanation why interviews had not been conducted with boys or staff at St. John's at the time. "It would appear that there is very little supporting evidence of actual indecent acts or assaults, other than those alleged by the (Hills) boy," Thompson noted. "I am satisfied, after interviewing Brother Daniel LaBelle and after thoroughly discussing the matter with Mr. Teggart, that no further action is required by this ministry."

Brother Daniel was quietly replaced by Brother Adrian, who had previously headed the school and been a director of the order. Once again, public scandal was avoided and the names of St. John's and the Christian Brothers were untarnished in the public's estimation.

At St. Joseph's, it was neither the changing tide of public opinion, nor allegations of abuse, that ended the Brothers' reign of terror. Rather, it was a combination of factors relating to declining membership and inadequate funding from the province. Membership in the order dwindled as the influence of the Church in society eroded. Fewer children entered the religious life.

And the walls built up between different religions were coming down. It was becoming feasible to accommodate Catholics and Protestants in the same facilities.

St. Joseph's, tucked away in the eastern corner of the province, had been poorly situated to service the north. Once Cecil Facer Centre opened in Sudbury in August 1972, the writing was on the wall.

The Brothers did not fight hard to keep St. Joseph's open. Once the school had been operated by the three-hundred-member order based in Montreal, but when control was transferred to the eighty-member Ottawa district, it became more and more difficult to staff the facility.

Many of the Brothers who had toiled at St. Joseph's were poorly trained and educated. Some were suited for nothing more than maintenance jobs. Others, lacking teaching certificates, were nothing more than glorified babysitters. Few Brothers with ambition stayed long at Alfred and those who did found the time they spent there unpleasant. The order had missions in more than eighty countries around the world: St. Joseph's was considered a hardship post and a dead end.

St. John's, drawing Brothers from a larger population base and supported by a wealthier organization under the protection of the powerful Toronto archdiocese, would survive. The school hired lay professionals to deliver modern rehabilitation services to the boys who passed through its doors. But St. Joseph's had squandered its government grants on an indoor pool, bowling alley, and recreation complex, and had nothing left to attract top professional staff. The province kept pumping more and more money into the institution until it was carrying almost the entire operating cost of the facility.

On October 18, 1973, Correctional Services Minister Syl Apps made the announcement at Queen's Park. "The Brothers have experienced increasing difficulty in recent years in providing staff from their Order to work in the training school and feel it is appropriate at this time that the ministry assume full responsibility for the operation of the school," he said.

Unlike the school's grand opening in 1933, little fanfare marked the passing of what had become a Correctional Services dinosaur. In 1974, the province opened a new co-ed training school, called Champlain School, on the site and kept on many of the Christian Brothers and staff to work as civil servants. But the experiment was short-lived. In 1978, the last wards were shipped to the new Cecil Facer Centre in Sudbury.

Throughout the late 1970s, the debate over training schools continued to rage in Ontario. When, in April 1975, a probation officer was fired for telling a family court judge he couldn't recommend sending juvenile delinquents to any of the province's training schools because of their "organized brutality," Stephen Lewis, the vocal Scarborough West opposition MPP, demanded a public inquiry into the man's allegations. Hearings were subsequently held from which the media was formally banned. The ban did not, however, snuff out the controversy. Newspaper headlines bellowed: "SCRAP JUVENILE TRAINING SCHOOLS," "SCHOOL DAMAGE IRREPARABLE, PARENTS SAY," and "BOYS SCHOOL TURNED SON BAD."

A citizen's group, the Committee for the Abolition of Training Schools, was formed to focus attention on the province's eight remaining training schools and their twelve hundred wards. Dennis Conly, a twenty-five-year-old who had worked at Grandview Training School, was the driving force behind it.

In February 1975, the committee advised the government that the institutionalization of juvenile offenders was ineffective and inappropriate. It published a paper that claimed the training schools were having a damaging effect on children. "The alienation of children from their own communities and their placement in highly regimented institutional environments where strict routines, solitary confinement and locked doors must be used to maintain control all too frequently lead to homosexuality, self-mutilation and various manifestations of emotional disturbance."

In May 1975, the committee hosted a two-day conference at Ottawa's Carleton University. Its efforts garnered support from the Carleton University School of Social Work, juvenile court judges, criminologists, and editorial writers.

The committee charged that solitary confinement, routine brutality, sexual activity, and drug abuse were common in Ontario's training schools. "The kids always come out worse than when they went into these places," complained committee member Bob Crook, a thirty-year-old social worker who had spent six years working at the Ottawa Youth Services Bureau.

Citing statistics from a 1972 study by consultants Leah Lambert and Andrew Birkenmayer, Crook, Dennis Conly, and Sandra Ross claimed that 34 per cent of training school wards committed offences after leaving the institutions and 48 per cent were returned or sent to another institution within eighteen months of their release. They argued that the statistics proved that training schools were ineffective. They charged that they were also costly. It cost $42.85 a day to send kids to training schools while they could be accommodated in group homes or foster homes for between $7.00 and $20.00 a day. The province was estimated to be spending about $20 million annually locking up delinquents.

The Ministry of Correctional Services announced in June 1975 that the controversial section 8 of the Ontario Training Schools Act, which enabled the incarceration of children for non-criminal behaviour, would be dropped. The Committee for the Abolition of Training Schools had claimed that half the children sent to training schools were admitted under that clause. Although the measure was announced in 1977, it didn't take effect until January 1, 1979, because of a lack of alternative facilities. But the legislation marked the beginning of the end of the training school era.

Since 1969, the federal government had advocated moving control of juvenile delinquents out of provincial Corrections departments and into Welfare departments. The federal health minister had even offered to pay half the cost of keeping juveniles in institutions if the province went along with the plan. Ontario had resisted the move, however, because it believed the plan was ill-conceived, and was piqued that it had been formulated without consultation.

In 1977, the province did initiate a major overhaul of its child welfare services in an attempt to slice through the bureaucratic red tape that had bounced children back and forth between several ministries under seven separate acts. It was a big job. The province had twenty thousand children in its care, including those in training schools, group homes, mental health centres, and other institutions. George Thomson, a Kingston family court judge, who, at the age of thirty, was one of the youngest judges in Canadian history, was named to oversee an overhaul that encompassed four departments, thirty-two hundred staff members, and a $275-million budget. Thomson pushed forward the transfer of the responsibility for juvenile delinquents to the provincial Community and Social Services Department, which was what the federal Health Department had long recommended. The newly empowered provincial department wasted little time closing training schools and moving troubled children into group-home environments.

The province still owned the former St. Joseph's Training School and transformed it into a francophone food and agriculture college. With its shops, barns, and fields, it was ideally suited to the purpose. The dormitories were partitioned into classrooms and the Brothers' bedrooms over the shops became a student residence.

The Toronto Brothers continued to operate St. John's under contract to the province. A Brother still served as the institution's superintendent, but most of the Brothers on staff were eventually replaced by civilian professionals with experience and training in child social work.

Despite the reforms, the province continued to keep more than 10,000 children in its care, including 2,000 children who were held in custody. About 150 children were locked up in maximum-security, closed-custody detention centres for young offenders.

St. John's became one such institution. In 1995, in its hundredth year, 80 children were confined behind its locked doors and steel fences.

6

Fallen Angels

•

"The coverups of the past have sown the wind.
Now the Church reaps the whirlwind."
— Andrew M. Greeley, Roman Catholic priest
and author, March 20, 1993

A FTER THE closure of St. Joseph's, silence descended over the events of the previous decades. Former wards, Christian Brothers, government and Church officials all – albeit for different reasons – developed a sort of collective amnesia.

The shock waves that would eventually break down the walls of silence started not in Ontario, but thousands of kilometres away, in Louisiana, and to the east, on the windswept island of Newfoundland.

At the centre of the American storm was Father Gilbert Gauthe, a Roman Catholic priest with a Jekyll-and-Hyde personality, who had been accused of molesting more than one hundred boys in four Louisiana parishes, starting in 1972. It ended in October 1984 with his indictment on thirty-four counts of sexual assault.

Perhaps even more shocking than Father Gauthe's lengthy string of sex crimes was the revelation that the Catholic Church hierarchy had been told several times about his sexual deviancy. In every instance when his transgressions were reported, the Church had merely confronted him with his sins, sent him for counselling, and then turned him loose on another unsuspecting parish. When the outraged families of his victims finally figured out what the Church had been doing with Father Gauthe, they successfully sued it for $15 million.

Father Gauthe, however, was not the only deviant Catholic priest. After he found seven other priests in Lafayette parish who had been engaged in activities similar to Father Gauthe's, Jason Berry, a freelance journalist based in New Orleans, began to look at the problem across the country. He finally exposed what he called a massive cover-up by the Roman Catholic Church and related institutions in his book, *Lead Us Not Into Temptation: Catholic Priests and the Sexual Abuse of Children*. Berry claimed that four hundred priests in North America had been reported to authorities for sexually abusing children between 1984 and 1992 and that the Church had already paid out $400 million in legal fees and settlements. He estimated the tally would hit $1 billion by the year 2000.

Church officials accused Berry of sensationalism, but the noted Roman Catholic priest and author, Andrew M. Greeley, soon leapt to his defence. Greeley, too, claimed that sexual abuse by members of the clergy had reached alarming proportions. Using one diocese as a basis for his calculations, Greeley estimated that as many as four thousand of the fifty thousand priests in the United States were sexual abusers and that their youthful victims numbered more than one hundred thousand. Then a psychotherapist, A. W. Richard Sipe, entered the debate. Sipe, who had conducted interviews with twenty-seven thousand Catholic priests over a thirty-two-year span, estimated that 6 per cent of all American priests were at some point in their adult lives sexually preoccupied with minors.

Canada's 11.4 million Roman Catholics got the first whiff of a similar scandal in the fall of 1988 during the trial of the Newfoundland priest, Father James Hickey. Hickey, a graduate of St. Peter's Seminary in London, Ontario, had been host to royalty and had welcomed even the Pope himself when they visited the Rock. But Father Hickey was attracted to adolescent boys. He enjoyed fondling them, masturbating them, having oral and anal sex with them. When he pleaded guilty to twenty charges of sexual assault, indecent assault, and gross indecency, he was sentenced to serve five years in Dorchester Penitentiary. He died a little more than three years after his conviction.

After Father Hickey, a stream of Catholic priests was paraded before Newfoundland courts to face sexual assault charges. Soon children in schoolyards across the country were joking that daredevil stuntman Evel Knievel's next feat would be to cross Newfoundland in an altar boy's gown.

The worst, however, was still to come. On February 13, 1989, Newfoundland's Archbishop Alphonsus Penney worried in a television interview that there was "something loose somewhere" in the structure of the Church. Almost at the same moment, a Newfoundland politician informed a St. John's radio phone-in show that there had been a massive, fourteen-year cover-up of sexual and physical abuse at the Catholic-run Mount Cashel Orphanage for boys.

By March 1989, the Royal Newfoundland Constabulary had laid seventy-seven charges against eight members of the Irish Congregation of Christian Brothers who had been the subject of the earlier, muzzled investigation. Police also laid charges against a ninth Brother for offences after 1975 and seventeen charges against three civilians.

Three months later, a royal commission, headed by Samuel Hughes, a retired justice of the Ontario Supreme Court, began to hear testimony about the humiliation and brutality that children had endured or witnessed during their stay in the orphanage.

Over the course of nine months, three hundred people, including thirty-one former residents of Mount Cashel, together described a conspiracy between Church and government to stop a police investigation into the boys' complaints. Despite repeated denials and convenient memory lapses by government officials, the full story gradually, painfully emerged. Brother Provincial Gabriel McHugh, the head of the Roman Catholic lay order, revealed that he had made a deal in December 1975 with Newfoundland's justice minister to send two Christian Brothers out of the province for treatment rather than have police lay charges against them for sexually abusing boys at the orphanage. He also removed three other Brothers from the orphanage, including the superintendent, for mistreating boys.

"I sincerely was not aware of the terrible impact that this kind of abuse has on individuals, on the victims," Brother Gabriel said. "The best procedure was thought to be to try to rehabilitate the perpetrators."

At the height of the controversy, some Church officials continued to deny there had been a cover-up and instead blamed the victims. One bishop went so far as to intimate that the boys who were abused had consented to the sexual activity. "What I'm suggesting is that maybe some – a few of them, many of them, most of them, who knows? – had some kind of an inkling that this was wrong and could have said: 'No. Thank you very much,'" he said in a radio interview and a newspaper column.

The report of the Hughes Inquiry, more than a thousand pages long, and costing some $2 million, was released in April 1992, after having been withheld for eleven months while the trials of the Christian Brothers were completed. The report concluded that sexual abuse at the orphanage had indeed been covered up by officials who were terrified that the scandal, if made public, would rip the order apart. Hughes said the victims should be compensated. But he also declared that there was insufficient evidence to warrant charges against Church and government officials for obstructing justice – a conclusion that infuriated some of the former wards.

Michael Harris, publisher and editor-in-chief of the *Sunday Express*, the St. John's newspaper credited with forcing the establishment of the Hughes Commission, called the scandal a "conspiracy of indifference." In his book *Unholy Orders: Tragedy at Mount Cashel*, he offered this summation: "By the time the Hughes Inquiry had finished its sombre deliberations on Mount Cashel, it had laid bare a stunning, collective failure of the judicial, police, religious, media and social services establishments to protect the interests of hopelessly vulnerable and cruelly abused children. In the intervening fourteen years, at least eighty-seven people in positions of authority had learned about the dread happenings of 1975, but none took action to drag the scandal out of the shadows and into the healing light of day."

Eventually, nine Brothers brought to trial were convicted and received sentences ranging from one to thirteen years in prison. Mount Cashel's superintendent, Douglas Kenny, the last to be tried, received a five-year term.

In delivering the sentence, Mr. Justice Leo Barry of the Newfoundland Supreme Court chastised Kenny's "self-indulgent search for sexual gratification" which wrecked seven lives. Kenny "preyed in a calculated manner," said Barry, "with utter disregard for their psychological well-being, upon the bodies of young, often orphan boys who were completely within his control when he was supposed to be looking after their welfare."

Archbishop Alphonsus Penney of St. John's maintained a resolute silence for seventeen months while the controversy swirled around him. By the time he finally made a public statement in February 1990, his parishioners were clamouring for his head. They would get it. When, in July 1990, a Church commission he had appointed to investigate the scandal produced a scathing report condemning his leadership, Penney tendered his resignation.

The five-member commission, headed by former Newfoundland lieutenant-governor John Winter, revealed that Church leaders heard complaints of abuse at Mount Cashel and elsewhere as early as 1975, but had taken no steps to investigate the abuse, halt it, or inform parishioners of the risk to their children. The commission called the Church leadership weak, defensive, and unChristian.

Shaken by the Newfoundland disclosures and similar incidents involving priests all across the country, the Canadian Roman Catholic Church hierarchy began to search for a meaningful way to address the issues. In October 1989, the Canadian Conference of Catholic Bishops created an *ad hoc* committee on child sexual abuse by priests and male members of religious lay orders. The conference wanted the committee to develop guidelines to aid bishops in responding to allegations of abuse.

Three bishops – the Most Reverend Roger Ebacher, Archbishop of Gatineau; Adam Exner, Archbishop of Vancouver; and James MacDonald, the new Archbishop of St. John's – sat on the committee along with four priests and lay members. The committee advocated radical changes to prevent child abuse and offered stinging criticism of the secrecy that had prevented exposure of previous abuses.

Their report, *From Pain to Hope*, published in June 1992, offered fifty recommendations intended to break through the silence that had protected child abusers in the Church for years. "The ideal breeding ground for the development and repetition of child abuse is a general conspiracy of silence, motivated by the fear of scandal and of major repercussions of institutions. . . . [T]he

fear of scandal often conditions our instinctive reactions of inad-
vertently protecting the perpetrators and a certain image of the
Church or the institution we represent, rather than the children,
who are powerless to defend themselves."

The report recommended that Church dioceses pay the costs
of therapy for the victims and that abusers be required to contribute as well. It called both for better screening of men entering the priesthood and related institutions and for courses on
sexual abuse and sexuality in seminaries. While the committee
could find no link between sexual abuse and celibacy, it called
for further research of the issue.

"We want, more than ever, to shed light on this problem and,
more than ever, we will continue our efforts toward zero toler-
ance," explained Archbishop Exner. "As far as we are concerned,
the credibility of the Church itself is at stake."

It may have seemed that, before Mount Cashel, the Church preferred to counter any threat of sexual scandal with silence and
denial, followed, if necessary, by a cover-up involving strategic
transfers of personnel and discreet one-on-one settlements with
injured parties. In fact, the Church was not entirely dodging
the problems it faced. In both the United States and Canada,
the Church had established institutions and treatment centres
to assist priests, ministers, and members of lay orders to deal
with their problems. However, the existence of these centres –
the Institute of Living in Connecticut; Servants of the Paraclete
in New Mexico and Missouri; the St. Luke Institute in
Maryland; the House of Affirmation in Massachusetts – was
not much publicized.

In 1965, the Emmanuel Convalescent Foundation established
Southdown, a therapeutic residential centre in Aurora, Ontario,
forty kilometres north of Toronto. At first its primary concern

was to assist clergy in breaking the grip of alcoholism, but in 1974, it broadened its program to include other problems. Paedophilia did not become an area of treatment until well after St. Joseph's closed its doors.

In 1989, Southdown's executive director John Allan Loftus painted a pathetic picture of the men who sought treatment at the clinic. In a paper on child sexual abuse and the clergy, Loftus noted that abusers among the clergy are often immature sexually, "woefully out of touch with their own bodies, with sexual energy itself, and in general, with themselves."

Some didn't know if they were homosexual or heterosexual. Others still felt sexually like adolescents. Many, explained Loftus, were starved for affection and often felt they had no one to care for or who really cared about them.

While it was difficult for therapists to agree upon a standard of successful treatment, clergy who demonstrated gross sexual immaturity and profound sexual repression were generally good candidates for counselling, psychotherapy, and behaviour modification, Loftus wrote. Those whose deviant sexuality was already well established, however, were almost impossible to "cure." They could be treated with drugs to modify their sexual drive and they could be taught to avoid situations which might tempt them to reoffend, but, like alcoholics battling drink, they would always have to struggle to resist their deviant sexual urges.

Loftus noted that there was no evidence of a direct link between celibacy and the deviant sexual behaviour of priests, but he refused to rule it out as a factor. While many of their victims have blamed clerical celibacy for their suffering, the issue is a confusing one. In the early years of the Church, most priests were married, and a long line of popes descended one from the other, much like the monarchy. It was only when the Church began to view chastity as a blessed condition that the notion of celibacy gained currency. By the twelfth century, the Church had rid itself of married priests, and in succeeding centuries, seminaries were established in which novitiates were required to be, among other things, celibate. Today the Roman Catholic Church strictly enforces celibacy among the clergy. In this respect, it stands alone among the nineteen Catholic rites. All others, including the Ukrainian Catholic and Maronite rites, permit their priests to marry.

Some argue, of course, that celibacy has nothing to do with paedophilia, that most paedophiles outside the Church are, in fact, married. For psychotherapist A. W. Richard Sipe, the problem is that the Church "demands celibacy, but does not train for it."

Some psychologists believe that men who abuse boys may not even be attracted to them sexually. They use them for sexual gratification because they are available and vulnerable. Similarly, incest offenders often feel no particular sexual attraction to children, but exploit them sexually when factors such as alcohol, depression, and low self-esteem enter the picture.

Unquestionably, some of the Brothers at St. Joseph's and St. John's, like their counterparts at Mount Cashel, led tormented lives, haunted by the demons of alcoholism, depression, low self-esteem, and confused sexuality. Some had been abused as children. But this only explains, it does not excuse, the suffering they inflicted on their helpless charges. The day of reckoning would come.

When the angels fell in Newfoundland, memories began to stir in Ontario. Ancient wounds became fresh again and the ghosts of the past returned to haunt the boys of St. Joseph's and St. John's.

7

Breaking the Silence

•

"I never thought this story would ever come out. We kept quiet about it because no one believed us when we tried to talk about it."
– Claude Larocque, former St. Joseph's ward, April 2, 1990

FOR SEVERAL months in 1989, David Richard McCann was unaware of the Mount Cashel scandal raging in Newfoundland. The forty-three-year-old bachelor was fully absorbed in his life as a gentleman farmer, raising rare Irish-bred Kerry cattle, as well as pigs and sheep, and pampering three dogs on a 160-acre farm near Kingston, Ontario.

He had packed a lot of living into the years that followed his departure from St. Joseph's. When he was sixteen, he dropped out of high school and moved into a tiny cabin on the shore of Lake Ontario rather than live with his parents. He soon drifted back into his criminal ways. When police picked up his accomplice in a series of burglaries, McCann hopped a bus for the United States, knowing it would not be long before a warrant was issued for his arrest.

Eventually, he made his way to California, where after working for a time, he enrolled in a bachelor of science program at San Diego State College. It was a great place for a young man in the 1960s. He spent his free time surfing, jogging, and going to rock concerts.

After he graduated in 1971, McCann launched a small business cleaning up housing subdivision construction sites. But he missed Canada and his family. He contacted a lawyer about the outstanding charges against him and turned himself in to the police. He was sentenced to eighteen months at the Rideau Correctional Centre, a minimum-security jail south of Ottawa. He was released on parole after six months, received a pardon for his offences, and in the fall of 1977, entered McMaster University in Hamilton, Ontario, with the idea of studying medicine. It was an ill-fated plan.

His father became terminally ill and McCann's grades started to slip. In September 1978, he was asked to withdraw from medical school. McCann went on to Toronto and began working in the home renovation business. In the summer of 1982, he became addicted to cocaine and began peddling it to support a $300- to $1,000-a-week habit. In July 1983, he was arrested for bringing a half-kilogram of cocaine into Canada from the United States.

For the next six years, McCann – having kicked his drug habit following his arrest – worked as a freelance agent for practically every law enforcement agency in North America, as well as some intelligence agencies, setting up drug smugglers, arms dealers, and spies. Under the direction of an RCMP sergeant in Kingston, he worked for the Metro Toronto Police, the Quebec provincial police, the U.S. Customs Office, the U.S. Drug Enforcement Administration, the FBI, and various NATO-member intelligence agencies. Sometimes all that was asked of him was an introduction. He would develop his underworld connections and introduce undercover officers to "targets" or "marks." Sometimes an undercover officer would introduce him as a person wanting to buy a chemical, like methylbensokytone (P2P), a legal substance used in the illegal manufacture of amphetamine ("speed").

Once he penetrated a Texas bike gang for several months so he could pass on information about its activities to authorities. Since he was never called on to testify against any bike gang members, he assumed this had been a reconnaissance mission. He was told only what he needed to know. He was given a cover story and he expanded upon it as needed.

As a civilian, he had more latitude than an undercover police officer, who, for instance, cannot break the law. But it was his ability to deceive bad guys that was most valued by his employers. He was an accomplished confidence man, better at what he did than most police officers, for it was a talent that could not be taught. McCann had come a long way from breaking into parked cars – and now he was working for the good guys. He liked the excitement, and he could handle the long hours of boredom and loneliness involved in setting up a sting operation. There was no one waiting for him at home.

Between assignments, he puttered around his farm. Sometimes he had difficulty keeping his two lives separate. He told one of his neighbours that he had been a doctor in a California hospital, but had left the intense world of the emergency room for a quiet life in the country. Eventually, around the county, he gained a reputation for telling tall tales.

When he wasn't on assignment, McCann enjoyed kibitzing with his neighbours and spoiling their children with pastries he bought in town. He was happiest, however, when he was alone in his fields. He could often be found on his tractor, wearing a work shirt and patched overalls, and with a battered Tilley hat crumpled over his brow. He didn't own a television and spent his quiet hours reading, indulging the passion for books that he had formed in his youth.

He was sitting in a Toronto hotel room one night in the fall of 1989, waiting for instructions concerning a new assignment, when he turned on the television set and caught a news report about the Hughes Inquiry. The more he saw and heard, the more he was struck by the similarities between his own experience at St. Joseph's and the revelations about the scandal at Mount Cashel. Could these Christian Brothers in Newfoundland, he wondered, be from the same order that operated St. Joseph's? Had some of them served in both institutions?

McCann purchased a television set so he could keep up with the developments in Newfoundland. When government and religious officials began to testify before the Hughes Inquiry, some of them denying all memory of the initial police investigation at Mount Cashel in 1975, McCann felt his gorge rise. As the inquiry continued, he began to be plagued by nightmares. He dreamed of Brother Léo in his black robe, of children with bleeding noses and heaving chests, of men going from bed to bed in the darkness.

McCann was not alone with his nightmares. Across Canada, hundreds of men were sitting in front of television sets, crying bitter tears, realizing for the first time that others had been through the same kind of hell as them. The Hughes Inquiry gave them a measure of comfort.

Gerry Sirois, a Timmins cabinetmaker and contractor, became infuriated while he watched the drama unfolding in Newfoundland. His children looked up in astonishment when he suddenly cursed the Christian Brothers, threw down his newspaper, and stormed out of the room. In North Bay, Gerry Belecque, a forty-three-year-old social worker, had often recounted his experiences at St. Joseph's to his psychologist, but he knew he was not believed. As he watched the Mount Cashel victims testify before the Hughes Commission, Belecque wondered why people could believe their stories but not his.

On his farm several hundred kilometres away, David McCann was wondering the same thing. He had complained at the time, but as far as he knew, no action had ever been taken. His story had either been rejected or ignored. Were people prepared to listen now? Had the world changed?

He knew that the training school at Alfred had been closed for a long time. But how many of the Brothers who ran it were still alive? Had there been an investigation at St. Joseph's like the aborted Mount Cashel investigation of 1975? Once, after he had escaped from the school, his mother had taken his complaints to a judge, the parish priest, and his probation officer. Had anyone looked into them?

On Saturday, November 4, 1989, McCann picked up the phone. It was almost midnight in St. John's, Newfoundland, but Hughes Inquiry counsel David Day was still in his office.

He answered the call on the third ring. The sorrowful voice on the line from Ontario asked if the Hughes Commission could probe incidents of abuse outside Newfoundland. Day took notes as McCann described life at St. Joseph's.

"He is deeply troubled this evening, although not for himself," Day wrote. "He repeatedly spoke, sometimes in tremulous voice, about other boys, his chums, that he claimed to have observed being mistreated at St. Joseph's."

Day told McCann that the Hughes Commission did not have a mandate to look into St. Joseph's, and urged him to take his allegations to the police or a lawyer to lay civil charges against the people who had abused him.

Later McCann called a reporter at the St. John's *Evening Telegram* and spoke to her at length. He was keen to discover the names of the principal accused Brothers at Mount Cashel and whether there had been any exchange of staff between the institutions.

It happened that I had interviewed McCann four months previously for a *Toronto Star* story about witness protection programs in Canada and the United States. I had asked Toronto criminal lawyer (now Judge) David Cole to put him in touch with me.

Now, in mid-November 1989, McCann wanted to talk about

St. Joseph's. I had never heard of the place. I'd never even heard of the village where it had been located.

"Halpurn?" I asked.

"No, Alfred, halfway between Ottawa and Hawkesbury," McCann explained. "It's now an agricultural college, but it used to be run by Christian Brothers."

McCann said he understood that charges of abuse had been levelled against the Brothers by parents and their children back in the 1960s, but that nothing had ever been done. He offered to call back in a few days if I required more information. When he called the second time, he stayed on the line for nearly half an hour, but it wasn't until near the end of the conversation that he said he had been a ward of St. Joseph's himself.

"They physically abused kids," he said. "They would kick the living shit out of them. In some instances, some of the kids went to hospital. I am not saying this happened on a daily basis, but it was quite regular."

He described several attacks on children without, at first, admitting that he had been the victim.

"I didn't start thinking about this until the whole thing on the East Coast started coming out," he explained. "I think they're trying to make this out to be an isolated case with these Christian Brothers, but my feeling is that it wasn't, that when there were problems, they transferred [the Brothers] around."

His detailed allegations had the ring of truth to them. The *Star*'s Ontario editor, Vivian Macdonald, authorized me to work on the story when I could find the time, between other assignments.

Tracking down the abused wards McCann had named proved to be difficult. I traced one to prison, but he had since been released and I was unable to pick up his trail. The provincial Ministry of

Corrections and provincial social services agencies had scarcely any information about the school, although several officials recalled that it had a bad reputation. Finally, a sympathetic official suggested I try the provincial archives.

It was at the Archives of Ontario that I found a catalogue listing the file headings of various documents relating to St. Joseph's. There were twenty boxes of general administration files, microfilm reels of ward case files, and a box of files on the use of force.

One notation jumped off the page. Filed under RG 20, H-I, BOX 11.2 was a document described as "St. Joseph's Training School, Alfred, Inquiry into, 1960." There was no information about the scope and mandate of the inquiry, but my curiosity was piqued. I filed a request to view the document under the province's recently proclaimed access to information legislation. The legislation provided that all such requests be filled in thirty days, but it was March 1990 before I was given the inch-thick bundle of Department of Reform Institution reports and correspondence. I read the documents with a trembling hand and a pounding heart. They corroborated everything McCann had suggested and more.

Although heavily censored, the documents, which covered the years 1958-60, outlined a series of internal investigations into both St. Joseph's and St. John's training schools. The letters, memos, and reports documented allegations of abuse at both schools and the feeble efforts of the department to bring it to a stop.

My excitement was dampened by senior editors at the Star who complained that the events described had "happened over thirty years ago" and had little significance today. McCann, however, was thrilled, and anxious to see the documents for himself. We met face-to-face for the first time in a Yorkville restaurant in early March. McCann, who was sitting at a window table reading a

newspaper when I arrived, had a slight build and a receding hair-
line, and wore aviator-style wire-rim glasses. He looked more like
an accountant than an undercover drug agent.

Of all the documents in the bundle, perhaps the most interesting was Donald Sinclair's March 15, 1960, report of his investigation into allegations of abuse at St. Joseph's. Listed on the
first page were many of the allegations McCann had raised earlier
with me. The report referred to allegations that staff were trying
to engage boys in sex, that boys were being strapped, forced to
wear handcuffs and carry weights, and that they were being cuffed,
kicked, and shoved by staff. There was also an allegation that a
boy had been beaten so badly that he was hospitalized.

I told McCann I wanted to track down as many of the officials
who were still alive as I could find. The key question, it seemed
to me, was why no one had ever called in the police to investigate these complaints?

Back at the Star, I learned from newspaper files that George
Wardrope, the colourful former minister of Reform Institutions
in the late 1960s, was dead. So were former deputy minister Archie
Graham and former training schools advisory board chairman
Martin Pinker. And so was Ralph Ross, the man who had been
instrumental in initiating the first 1960 investigation with a letter
to Wardrope.

A number of the senior probation officials at the time were
still around, but when I contacted them, few remembered the
problems at Alfred. I tracked down Maurice Egan, now living
in semi-retirement in Sechelt, B.C. Egan offered a frank assessment of the situation. "I had no hard evidence," he recalled.
"All I had was the word of the young boys themselves. Kids tell
you things which, if they tell you often enough and the stories
are similar enough, you kind of get a sense that something isn't
right."

Egan said he could not recall any specific complaints of abuse, but he remembered allegations of fondling and sexual activity. "I reported it and there was an investigation," he said matter-of-factly. "It was a very delicate subject in those days, much more than now."

Egan said he had been ostracized for his actions. "You have to keep in mind the conditions of the times, the attitudes of the times, the morals of the times," he explained. "The fact no charges were laid was not at all surprising. The mentality was to get them out, to get them away. That was the practice of the day. It went on all the time. It was not unusual."

The documents from the archives also led me to the mother of one of the former wards. When I telephoned Ruth Jenkins in Ottawa and began to explain the reason for my call, she said, "You're a little late. It's thirty years after the fact."

Ruth Jenkins was still angry that nothing had been done at the time. "I guess they figured that sending a new Brother Director in there and moving a few Brothers out would solve the whole thing."

Jenkins, aged sixty-one, disabled, and legally blind, lamented that her son's life had been ruined by his experience at Alfred. "It really blew his whole life up into nothing," she said. "He didn't know if he was coming or going. He never got over it."

Bobbie Jenkins had joined the Navy after he was released from Alfred. He had gone around the world, spending considerable time in Japan and San Francisco. He could not bear to stay in one place, his mother explained.

"It was as if something was chasing him. He was acting as if he had a monkey on his back. Ten or fifteen years ago, he came home and the person who stood at my door was not the boy who had left. He was sick as a dog. We took him in and got him back on his feet and off of drugs and back to work. He still needs help yet."

Despite her anger, Jenkins was doubtful that anything was to be gained by raising the issue now. "The boys didn't do anything to be ashamed of, but on the other hand, you don't want to hang it out on the wash line for all the neighbours to see. If it does nothing else, I hope it will get Bob some help. He needs to go to a psychiatrist."

As for the Christian Brothers, she had definite ideas.

"They should castrate them," she said. "Fix them so they can't have sex no more. I can't see any other way."

Later, when I called the Jenkins household again, hoping to talk to Bobbie, I was greeted with stony silence, then the line was disconnected.

It was discouraging to say the least. When I spoke to McCann the next day, it was clear to both of us that we had reached a crossroads. Despite the considerable documentary evidence now in our hands showing that boys had been badly mistreated at the training schools, McCann was the only survivor I knew of in a position to give personal testimony. But McCann, as an undercover agent, was obviously reluctant to have his identity made public. I was left with the prospect of writing a story in which serious allegations were made against the Catholic Church and the Brothers of the Christian Schools for which I could offer no named source.

Worried that the story might never be published, McCann said he would consider allowing himself to be quoted by name. Eventually, he did agree to be cited, but only by his middle and last names, hoping that the people he had helped put in jail would not make the connection. He began to grow a beard to mask his facial features.

Neither of us realized how big a story we had uncovered or how many lives would be affected by our actions. Later, our efforts to conceal McCann's identity would seem laughable.

In mid-March, the story suddenly acquired much greater urgency. In tracking down the operators of the detention home Gerry Champagne and his fellow runaways had visited in 1960, I learned that the man who had operated the home then had since suffered a stroke and could not come to the phone. "But it is strange that you should be inquiring about this," the man's wife (his second) remarked. "Yesterday there were two police detectives here asking about the very same thing."

A Corrections Ministry official confirmed what she had said. The OPP were, in fact, investigating the thirty-year-old allegations that I had found in the archives.

"After we had gone through the files that the archives made available to you, we thought it would be appropriate for us to advise the OPP of the situation," ministry spokesman Judi Richter-Jacobs told me. "When we reviewed the record, we found that although the training school and various committees took immediate action, there didn't seem to be any police involvement. It is at our request that they are looking into it."

Robert Macdonald, the deputy minister of Corrections, had sent the request to the OPP deputy commissioner of investigations, Murray McMaster, who in turn, on February 15, 1990, passed the request, with his okay, to the OPP headquarters in Toronto and to Tim Smith, a criminal investigation bureau detective inspector with the OPP in Kingston.

Smith, a twenty-three-year veteran on the force, started his police career as a constable in Barrie in 1967. After moving into detective work in 1975, he had risen quickly through the ranks, becoming a corporal in 1983, a sergeant in 1987, and an inspector in 1988.

When the St. Joseph's investigation was assigned to him in mid-February of 1990, he thought it would be relatively routine. He would try to track down the principals in Donald Sinclair's 1960 internal investigation and determine to what extent, if any, police had been involved and whether criminal charges were warranted. Although there was a six-month statute of limitations on common assault, there was none on serious assaults or sex crimes.

In March, Smith was joined by Det. Const. Ron Wilson, and together they set out across Ontario to interview as many of the people named in the archival documents they could locate. The pair talked to former police officers, government officials, Christian Brothers, and former St. Joseph's wards. They talked to Corrections and probation officials – even the former secretaries of long-dead government supervisors. And they came up with virtually nothing.

"Yup, there were physical assaults there," former wards would tell them. "They were pretty rough on us. Sure, I heard about the sexual assaults. But it never happened to me."

When the duo dropped into L'Orignal, the seat of the judicial district in which Alfred was located, to advise the Crown attorney of their investigation, Robert Pelletier, thirty, had been running the L'Orignal office for all of six months. Ronald Laliberté, a year his junior, had been prosecuting cases as the assistant Crown attorney for just four months. They had no idea that the investigation being mounted by Smith and Wilson would consume the next four years of their lives.

The next meeting was a formal one. Smith had arranged an interview with the Ottawa archdiocese officials responsible for the training school. A former altar boy himself, Smith had a working knowledge of Church hierarchy and procedure. He was comfortable around the clergy and counted priests among his friends. Wilson, however, a non-Roman Catholic, was ill at ease, particularly when Smith advised him to call the archbishop "Your Eminence" and to kiss his ring.

The meeting took place at the Ottawa archdiocese office on March 13, 1990. The police officers, dressed for the occasion in grey business suits, were escorted into a room with plush red carpets. Wilson took a few steps towards a low-slung couch, but was pulled up short by Smith, who gestured towards a pair of high-backed chairs. He did not want to be in a position where he would be looking up at the Church officials.

They waited several minutes before Ottawa Bishop Gilles Belisle walked in followed by his assistant, Father Gilles Lavergne, and the Brother Provincial, Brother Jean-Marc Cantin. Neither Archbishop Marcel Gervais, nor the Ottawa archdiocese auxiliary bishop, Brendan O'Brien, were in attendance, although Smith had expected them to be there. The Church officials assured the officers that both the archdiocese and the order would co-operate with the investigation. Brother Jean-Marc would be their principal contact.

The Brother Provincial was a likeable figure. He had joined the order in 1965, turning down a job offer from a radio station in his home town, Timmins. After earning his undergraduate and master's degree at the University of Ottawa, he taught at Académie de la Salle in the capital as a layman for two years before joining the order. By the age of twenty-four, he was the school's principal. In the years that followed, he served as a consultant to the Ottawa Board of Education, as president of the Ontario Teachers' Federation, and as deputy secretary general to the Canadian Teachers' Federation. In 1988, he had been appointed head of the Ottawa order for a three-year term.

Brother Jean-Marc explained to Smith and Wilson that the

Brothers of the Christian Schools were in no way affiliated with the Irish Congregation of Christian Brothers now being vilified in the Mount Cashel Orphanage scandal. They were separate and independent Roman Catholic lay orders. He promised to provide police with the proper names of the current and former Brothers, and, where possible, the present whereabouts of those being sought in the investigation.

Smith left the meeting with an uneasy feeling. He had never been involved in an investigation involving any church, let alone the Roman Catholic Church. As he drove back to Kingston with Wilson, he decided it was imperative that he meet with police investigators in Newfoundland to learn what pitfalls might be looming ahead. He also purchased a Latin-English edition of Canon Law. He wanted to know what rules governed the people he was dealing with and who would be calling the shots.

By late March, Smith and Wilson had made little progress. Then, on March 28, while driving in northern Ontario, they heard a CBC Radio news report about a story, published in the *Toronto Star*, claiming that a police investigation was underway into thirty-year-old complaints of abuse at St. Joseph's.

"Holy mackerel!" exclaimed Smith, pounding the dash. "The cat is out of the bag!"

The *Star* article, headlined "POLICE PROBE 1960 ALLEGATIONS OF ABUSE," quoted Richard McCann saying he was still haunted by the brutal beatings he had witnessed during his years at the school. "I saw kids literally have the crap kicked out of them. I don't mean hit. I mean, down on the ground, being kicked. I still see a guy with a cross around his neck and robes billowing as he's thumping some kid with his boot."

The story was printed on page 14 of the *Star*, but it got top billing in other newspapers. A wire-service version was splashed across the front page of the Kingston *Whig-Standard*, and Ottawa newspapers scrambled to follow the scoop.

The news coverage served to break the silence that had enshrouded the training school. Callers flooded police switchboards with stories of their mistreatment at St. Joseph's. Over the next two weeks, more than a hundred former wards called the police. Another twenty took their stories to the media.

"I never thought this story would ever come out," said a distraught Claude Larocque, an Ottawa man who had spent six years at St. Joseph's. "We kept quiet about it because no one believed us when we tried to talk about it."

"It was like Dachau with games," said Gerry Sirois. Although he hardened himself to the task of emptying his soul of the pain and anguish he had carried since his days in St. Joseph's, Sirois wasn't optimistic it would help in the long run. "There will be no winners over this situation – only losers," he predicted. "But it has to be brought to light. People must see this place for what it was."

As one sobbing former ward after another told his story on camera, provincial Corrections officials rushed to defend the administration of the schools. Retired or former Brothers attempted to minimize the extent of the abuse or depict it as rare. They provoked more angry responses from still more former wards who might otherwise have kept silent.

Lucien Dupras, who ran St. Joseph's for thirteen years under his religious name, Brother George, conceded that the Brothers were sometimes violent with the boys. "At the time I thought it was okay. But I would not say that today," he told a reporter. "I would be against it." He added that an inquiry might be in order.

A former civilian supervisor at St. Joseph's acknowledged the abuse had gone on for years, but said that people had chosen not to believe it. "All the kids were liars, even if there were twenty-five of them with the same story," the Alfred-area man explained. "People said staff couldn't be like that. But it was like that."

I contacted Donald Sinclair, now in his seventies, while he was on holiday in Arizona. After his stint with Reform Institutions, during which he rose to deputy minister, he had moved through the ranks of various provincial ministries, retiring in 1984 as deputy justice minister. Sinclair could not remember there having been a discussion about calling in the police. It was not even contemplated, he said. The department cleaned up its own messes. Sinclair believed he had solved the problem when the Christian Brothers agreed to remove offending Brothers from the school. "Things were done differently in those days," he explained. "It was not the practice of the minister of Correctional Services to charge people. They were discharged from the services."

Sinclair believed his actions had been appropriate for the time. He confessed, however, that he was dumbfounded by allegations that the abuse had continued at St. Joseph's until it closed fourteen years after his investigation. "I look back and think: how could I have been so stupid, so callous, so naïve? But in an attempt to be fair to myself I have to look back into the times and see the decisions I made in the context of those times. A lot of people had suspicions about things happening, but getting proof of them was a very different cup of tea. I couldn't stand up in court and say I knew and had hard evidence of abuse, but I knew damn well from what the kids said that there was a great deal of brutality at St. Joseph's."

The *Toronto Star* followed developments with almost daily articles and local television stations beamed the horrendous stories of the victims into living rooms across Ontario nightly. Premier David Peterson quickly pledged to support the former wards, whose stories, he admitted, touched his heart. "I see some of these men on television and it just makes me weep," he said, adding that he and his wife, Shelley, could only imagine what it would be like if one of their three children had been sent to a place like

St. Joseph's. "I mean think about it, think about it in terms of your own kids," he said. "It's just awful."

Many of the former wards were in a sleepless daze, alternating between tears and fury. Their families were frightened and bewildered. David McCann warned the government that it was sitting on a powder keg. These were shattered men who were barely hanging on to their sanity, he explained. The walls behind which they had hidden throughout their lives had just come crashing down. They were exposed and vulnerable. "I'm scared to death that some people may not be able to deal with what happened to them at St. Joseph's," he said. "The provincial government must make social and psychological counselling available to the victims. Without it, there's no telling what will happen."

Within a few weeks, Peterson's government announced that counselling would be made available to the former wards. The province also doubled the size of the police squad investigating the complaints.

McCann had asked reporters to pass on his phone number to other former wards and he listened to many of their stories firsthand. The more he heard, the angrier he became. It was becoming clear that the abuse had occurred for decades before and after his own time in the school, and there were literally hundreds of victims.

How could this have been allowed to happen? Gradually, he became convinced that only a public inquiry like the one aimed at Mount Cashel could find the truth. He wanted people to know who did what and why. "I am interested in making sure this doesn't happen again," he told the *Star* on March 30, 1990. "I am angry enough that I will stand up and be counted. The reason the abuse went on as long as it did was not a failure of the justice system. It was a failure of government officials to act when they were duty bound to do so." Over the weeks and months that followed, the first former wards to follow McCann's example by making their memories of the training schools public would be joined by scores and, ultimately, hundreds of others. Under McCann's leadership, they came to share something of his determination to make the government, the Church, and the Christian Brothers answer for the suffering they had caused or condoned.

8

Stirring the Pot

•

"They ripped the kid out of me. It was nothing but absolute
terror. That's the only way I can describe it."
— Gary Sullivan, former St. Joseph's ward, April 22, 1990

O N APRIL 5, 1990, barely a week after the scandal exploded in
the *Toronto Star*, David McCann brought together some of
the former wards who had so far come forward. About twenty-
five men from across Ontario gathered in a room at Ottawa's
Westin Hotel for a school reunion like no other.

McCann called the meeting to order and was asked to chair
the proceedings. He reviewed the events that had brought them
together, not omitting his own involvement, and summarized the
present situation as he understood it. Then he turned the floor
over to the victims. One by one, they stood at the front of the
room to relate their own experiences. On a table beside the speak-
ers were two mementoes of their experience at St. Joseph's: a worn
hymn book and a wooden paddle fashioned from a sawed-off
goalie's hockey stick. The emotion-charged meeting soon took
on the air of a group therapy session.

Among the first to speak was Normand Mallette, a slender
thirty-seven-year-old St. Catharines man, who pleaded with his
peers to help end the cycle of abuse. In a plaintive voice, he

described the effect of four years of abuse at St. Joseph's between 1965 and 1969. Pleading, sobbing, even shouting, he urged the others to find the strength and the courage to come forward with their stories.

"I am not crying for the boys here now," he said. "I'm crying about the boys still out there, and for the boys that did not make it." Mallette said it was difficult to fathom how he had largely blocked the experiences from his mind all these years, but the hurt had always lingered, smothered under shame and embarrassment.

"I know how a woman feels to be raped now," he said. "I know how a woman feels to hide it, hold it, keep it a secret. This has to stop. There are other institutions out there now and if we don't put a stop to any and all of those institutions or at least have them well looked after, we will come back here in another thirty years and maybe we'll have more atrocities to talk about. Will we really be able to stomach it then?"

Grant Hartley, a bearded fifty-year-old with tattoos on both forearms, described what happened when he was recaptured after each of his seven escapes.

"Every time they caught me, I would tell the provincial police – if it wasn't my so-called compadres who caught me – what I was subjected to and instead of them marking it down and putting it in their daily report, they would bring me in and tell Brother George what I had told them," he said.

Telling the police only made things worse.

"Now I am getting twice the beating. Handcuffed to the knees, handcuffed to the ankles, with a Brother with his hand on your back to steady you so you don't fall, with the strap in the pail soaking between strokes, they worked their way down from the small of the back to the back of my knees. My legs and my ass were so bloody sore and blistered and raw, but as soon as it was healed, I was gone again. Every chance I got. Stupid? Maybe.

"I remember one time I went on the run before Police Day. Remember Police Day? What a wonderful fucking day. I had just gotten back and I was just out of cells, but because I was a continuous runner, the handcuffs stayed on me for thirty days.

"I am standing in the middle of the field, hands cuffed behind my back, with two ten-pound ball shackles on each foot. An Ottawa detective came up to me. He says to me, 'What's a little guy like you doing all shackled up like that?' I said, 'I will show you.' And I spit in his face.

"Brother Joseph [the Hook] saw it and came running over, looked at the detective, looked at me, and suckered me. I went down. He jumped on me and started pummelling me with his fists. The detective reached over and grabbed him and said, "Hey, hey, hey, ease off. He's just a kid.'

"Brother Joseph says, 'He deserves to be punished for what he did to you.' 'Not like that, he doesn't,' says the cop. 'Now go away, I want to talk to the kid.'

"You know, I apologized to that cop. I was crying, no two ways about it. I was hurt. I was hurt more for spitting on him because he was good enough to pull this idiot off of me. I told him this happens frequently. I turned around and lifted my pants leg. This is almost three weeks after being strapped for being a Go-Boy. I showed him the back of my legs."

Hartley, now a taxi driver and former head of the Ottawa taxi drivers' union, said the years at St. Joseph's had never left him. They were buried in his subconscious and came back in nightmares even after twenty-six years. It was time to deal with it, he said. "I want to demand, not request, that they have a judicial inquiry."

On and on it went, late into the evening. One man described the beating a friend had received. He said he would be sent to jail for twenty years if he ever touched his own children like that.

When approached by a CBC reporter after the meeting, he was asked if he had ever complained to anyone. "Who would I tell? Who? My father was an alcoholic. My mother was dead. She died in 1959. Who would I tell?"

When the news of the St. Joseph's investigation had first broken in the local media, the memories stirred up such a fire in Eddie Graveline that he marched down to the Brothers' residence in Ottawa and demanded the former superintendent of St. Joseph's, Brother George, pay him what he was owed for the years he was contracted out to local farmers.

"I was angry," Graveline said at the meeting. "I wanted to see his face, to tell him I wasn't a kid anymore and that what he did to me was wrong. Thirty years ago, he was big and strong, and we were just little kids, but now he's an old man. It was something to see him like that. He was so afraid I thought he was going to cry.

"To me, this is all about revenge. Pay them back for what they did to us. If it was up to me, they would all be dead today."

Then Gerry Belecque, a slight, bespectacled, soft-spoken man stood up. He had travelled from North Bay to Ottawa for the meeting, not to rage against the Brothers, but to find some sort of peace for himself.

"I'm not here to cast stones at the Brothers," he said. "I don't like what they did, but what I want is some help for me. I don't need some ninety-year-old man with one foot in the grave being brought to court."

Some former wards made it clear they could not co-operate with the police investigation because they no longer had any trust in the authorities. They did not trust the police, they did not trust the Catholic Church, and they did not trust the government. "You are asking us to put our trust in an authoritative regime that put us in Alfred in the first place," complained one man. "You are asking us to go back to them now and believe these guys are okay. They didn't listen to us then and they won't listen to us now. For thirty years they shut it up and they are going to try to shut it up again."

There wasn't a man in the room who didn't realize what they were up against in taking on the Church and the Brothers. It was clear by meeting's end that they were profoundly worried that their cries would be ignored once again. Some worried about reprisals.

"They are big, they are strong, and if they can eliminate one head, one shit-disturber, one troublemaker through an accident, through violence, through kidnapping, they are going to do it," Hartley warned. He suggested that all archival documents linking the Christian Brothers to abuse be kept in safe hands in case anything should befall David McCann.

McCann chuckled at the notion. "This is called paranoia,' and this paranoia was instilled in us by St. Joseph's Training School for Boys," he told the meeting. "My prime concern is that the Church will hire the most expensive and best legal talent this country has and destroy me legally. They have done it at Mount Cashel, and they have done it in many other investigations. They can afford it, and they will do it again.

"Only by disseminating the information that we gained will we get a royal commission to finally bring this whole dirty stinking mess to the public. By everybody having it, nobody has to worry about it because the heads are too many to cut off – either legally, through character assassination, or whatever."

McCann recognized that individually they were lost. Only by working together would they not be ignored. Their numbers gave them credibility. But he also realized that the former wards were up against formidable opponents.

The meeting wrapped up near midnight after electing an executive committee made up of half a dozen former wards. Their job would be to deal with the media, contact prison organizations, liaise between the French- and English-speaking former wards, and help sift and sort through the blizzard of information that was coming in from the victims.

Over a late dinner of lobster and wine, McCann mused over the night's events. A stress headache with which he had opened the meeting had subsided. And, aside from a long and pointless argument over the best way to approach wards who were in prison, the meeting had gone well. He had stepped boldly forward, hoping others would follow, and they had not let him down.

The group formed in Ottawa would quickly become the voice of the abused survivors of St. Joseph's and, later, St. John's training schools. Through the group, the former wards addressed those who once had been responsible for their welfare – and manifestly failed them. They demanded redress, but it wasn't altogether clear, when they began, how best their demands could be met. Over the spring and summer of 1990, they explored a number of options including a civil lawsuit, political action (a public inquiry), and some form of acknowledgement from the Church.

As time went on, David McCann and Grant Hartley heard that large settlements had resulted from civil actions carried though the courts in the Gauthe episode in Louisiana and in some other U.S cases. Was a similar class-action suit possible in Canada?

The two men approached Roger Tucker, an Ottawa lawyer Hartley knew as the legal adviser of a fellow taxi driver. Tucker, a forty-two-year-old Collège militaire royale graduate, had served four years as a naval officer aboard Canadian Forces submarines and destroyers and often drew upon his military background in shaping courtroom strategy. Hartley and McCann were looking for a scrappy lawyer with a fresh approach and they liked what they saw in Tucker. He was equally impressed by them.

Tucker advised them that there were good reasons why the civil litigation route was not the way to go. In 1990, the liability in assault cases lasted only four years after the assaults occurred. Before 1963, it had been impossible to sue the government, and the majority of the St. Joseph's cases predated that. Similarly, the former wards could not apply for compensation from the province's Criminal Injuries Compensation Board because the board was not established until 1968 and had no jurisdiction to assess damages for crimes that occurred prior to that.

Tucker also recognized that many of the former wards lived marginal lives and were unlikely to find the resources, either emotional or financial, to support a lengthy civil litigation process. "I had visions of filing a statement of claim knowing guys would kill themselves because of it. Every time these guys were examined in the witness box, they would relive the experience. It was obvious that the conventional legal practice wasn't going to work. They had no money, no psychological strength. They couldn't stay the course."

Tucker proceeded to have McCann's rudimentary organization formally recognized as St. Joseph's and St. John's Training Schools for Boys Helpline. And, after talking to a lawyer involved in the Mount Cashel investigations, he made one positive, and as it turned out, deeply significant recommendation. He suggested that they seek a negotiated, rather than a judicial, resolution to their differences with the Church, the Christian Brothers, and the government.

By the time of their second meeting, about sixty former wards had come forward. Following Tucker's suggestion, they began to draft a list of what they expected out of the negotiations.

Tucker was struck by the expressions on the faces of the men in the room. "What used to stick out in my mind was their eyes.

They had eyes like sick puppies. You could feel the pain. Every time I was tempted to quit, I would remember that."

While Tucker dealt with the legal matters behind the scenes, McCann, as the group's chairman, kept a high public profile. Between April and July 1990, McCann recruited victims to take calls from other former wards on a network of regional telephone helplines set up in homes in Kingston, Ottawa, Timmins, and North Bay. The volunteers publicized the phone numbers in the local media in order to provide former wards with information about the organization, contact numbers for police, and help in getting counselling. Often they were simply a shoulder for fellow wards to cry on.

McCann formed the opinion at an early stage that he, backed up by other former wards, would have to find ways to keep the pressure on the government if a public inquiry was ever to be established. The political campaign preoccupied him over much of the summer.

It was soon obvious that they would meet with resistance from the government. A Corrections official characterized McCann's request for a public inquiry as "premature." And the province's attorney general, Ian Scott, interpreted a Supreme Court of Canada decision that had recently stopped a provincial inquiry into an Ontario political fund-raising scandal as an impediment to any inquiry in which criminal charges might arise. Scott maintained the province would have to grant immunity to witnesses to get them to testify at a public inquiry, and he refused, he said, to grant immunity to people who might have raped and beaten boys.

McCann argued that Scott was comparing apples and oranges. The type of inquiry envisaged by the court was different from that which would probe the government's dealings with St. Joseph's. He had a great deal of support for this opinion.

In the April 11, 1990, issue of the *Toronto Star*, an editorial wondered if Scott and his boss, Premier David Peterson, had read the forty-six-page Supreme Court judgment carefully. "That ruling makes it plain that the court killed the Houlden inquiry because the government had misused the inquiry process in an unprecedented way to get evidence of criminal misconduct against targeted individuals," it stated. "Moreover, the court points out that inquiries set up to explore broad public policy objectives can function legally even when there is some overlap between the subject matter of the inquiry and criminal activity."

The editorial suggested the provincial government wanted to defer the inquiry because an election was coming and it wasn't anxious to expose itself to the kind of embarrassing revelations that public inquiries can generate.

The newspaper's Queen's Park columnist, Thomas Walkom, followed up on the same theme the next day, noting that the allegations from St. Joseph's made revelations from Newfoundland's well-publicized Mount Cashel inquiry sound tame by comparison. "The premier says he is horrified by the stories and he probably is," wrote Walkom. "However, weeping is not enough."

McCann wasn't about to let Scott's announcement go unanswered. On April 12, he took his campaign to Queen's Park.

Still using his middle name, Richard, and sporting the newly-grown beard in an attempt to conceal his identity from his underworld connections, McCann presented the case for an inquiry to Queen's Park reporters. "I am very angry," he said. "Justice has been denied me for twenty-nine years. I will not let the issue die."

Opposition Leader Bob Rae wandered into the legislature's media studio just as McCann's press conference was coming to a conclusion. Rae greeted McCann, together with NDP justice

critic Peter Kormos, who had appeared with McCann to signal
his support, and the three men discussed the issues that had been
raised. The NDP, and Kormos in particular, had endorsed
McCann's call for a public inquiry shortly after the scandal broke.

Earlier, in an effort to expedite the police probe, the government announced it would double the size of the OPP investigation team from six members to twelve. The gesture was appreciated,
but it wasn't enough, McCann told Rae. "I just find this whole
thing extremely frustrating that we have this type of documentation and the province won't call an inquiry. The government
knew about this back then and they moved the offenders and to
hell with the victims. I just get angrier and angrier the more I
find out they knew."

Later, as he stood in a Queen's Park corridor waiting to be
called in to talk to the premier, McCann seemed overwhelmed
by the events that had overtaken him. He felt as though he were
in the eye of a hurricane. "I was abused and I saw other children
abused during my stay there, but never in my wildest dreams did
I think it [the scale of the abuse] was this big," he said.

When introduced to the premier, McCann seized Peterson's
hand and kept a firm grip on it until he had said all he wanted
to say. He knew the minute he let go, the premier's aides would
whisk Peterson into the legislature for question period, which had
already begun. Peterson assured McCann that he would look at
the issue of a public inquiry "in the long term. I certainly don't
rule it out," he said. "There's nothing to hide. Our objective must
be to make sure this kind of thing never happens again."

While the Ontario government continued to hedge on committing itself to a full public inquiry, it did take one modest step
towards reform. On April 30, 1990, it announced that it would
review existing safeguards against abuse within its institutions.

Joanne Campbell, a former Toronto city councillor who headed the provincial social assistance review board, was given six months in which to complete her inquiry and submit a report.

Campbell's six-month investigation into the treatment of the ten thousand children in the province's care resulted in sixty-seven recommendations for improving safeguards in the system to ensure children were not abused. While noting that a wide range of safeguards did exist, she expressed concern that they "were not as effective as they were meant to be."

Her January 1991 report, which McCann termed "far-reaching," called for better screening of staff, better training for investigators, new standards for investigating abuse, and better programs to teach children to report abuse. Campbell complained that there were dramatic differences between the way children aged twelve to fifteen were treated by the Ministry of Community and Social Services and the way sixteen- and seventeen-year-olds were treated by the Ministry of Corrections. She recommended that responsibility for all children in the system be placed under one ministry. Over the next four years, the province would implement most of Campbell's recommendations, but care for children remained split between the two ministries.

Although she met with McCann and Helpline, Campbell chose not to endorse or reject the group's call for a public inquiry. "I think the call for a public inquiry is very important to the victims and I absolutely respect that, but I am not going to advise the province on it," she said.

McCann and Helpline next took their campaign to the village of Alfred. What they wanted was a formal endorsement of their call for a public inquiry from Alfred's political leaders. "The resolution would be a symbolic gesture," McCann told the *Ottawa Citizen*. "I want the council to publicly state its opinion. They had to be deaf, dumb, and blind not to have known what was going on."

On May 1, 1990, McCann presented the village council with the findings of the 1960 Sinclair investigation and reminded them that "there were boys beaten, there were bones broken, there were boys sexually assaulted in the school that sits less than a city block away from here."

But the campaign did not receive a favourable response. One councillor, Lorenzo Seguin, had worked at St. Joseph's as a monitor from 1965 to 1977. He maintained that the years he spent at the institution were good years. "As far as I am concerned, nothing happened at the school." Other Alfred residents accused the former wards of "gold-digging." Henri Charlebois, who had worked at the training school as a recreational supervisor from 1970 to 1981, publicly denounced them outside the council chambers. "You guys think the Brothers of the Christian Schools have enough money that you can get a couple of bucks out of it," he said.

McCann was not surprised. He had not expected his appeal to Alfred residents to succeed. He felt, however, that it was important for the victims to have the villagers, who had condoned the abuse by their silence, publicly upbraided.

One week later, McCann was on the offensive again, this time suggesting that the Ontario Liberals knew more about the abuse scandal than they were letting on. He told reporters that Ontario Treasurer Robert Nixon had once called for an investigation into "organized brutality" in the province's training school system. "The Ontario government today says it has nothing to hide, that it knew nothing," he said, "but the second most powerful elected official in Ontario, Robert Nixon, knew about it when he came into government. And he did nothing about it."

While in opposition, Nixon had once asked the attorney general if he was aware that a suspended probation officer had complained about the abuse of boys in the training school system. When McCann raised the issue, Nixon said he couldn't remember asking the question. "I'm sure you understand that, over a decade as leader of the Opposition, questions were asked on every conceivable subject," he told a reporter. McCann retorted that it was "mighty convenient" for Nixon to forget. Opposition Leader Bob Rae seized the opportunity to renew his party's call for an inquiry, saying it was even more valid in light of the new allegations.

If they achieved nothing else, McCann's attacks on the government helped to secure police the resources they needed to conduct a thorough investigation into the scandal. Many former wards remained sceptical that it would result in the laying of any charges. The police had never been their friends. What could the victims expect from the same authorities who had ignored them when they were children?

The third part of the Helpline strategy, besides exploring their legal options and pressing the government for a public inquiry, was to bring pressure to bear on the Roman Catholic Church for some kind of acknowledgement of the abuse that had occurred within institutions over which it possessed at least nominal authority.

Nearly a month after the scandal broke, the Church had yet to offer a comment on the issue. Its silence did not go unnoticed by parishioners in Toronto. Joanna Manning, a member of the Coalition of Concerned Canadian Catholics, called on senior Church officials to address the needs of the victims. The coalition, formed in response to the sexual abuse scandal at Mount Cashel, suggested a freeze on Church construction in order to channel building funds into counselling for victims. She said many Catholics were appalled at the reluctance of the Church to speak out against the abuse.

"There's a deafening silence on the part of the Church leadership in all this," said Manning, a former nun. "People are just incensed, but nobody in the leadership seems willing to address the depth of feeling. Everything is being done for the priests and the Brothers – and the victims have been totally shut out."

Manning accused the mighty and powerful in the Church of closing ranks against the powerless and voiceless. "The course the hierarchy of the Church took in responding to the abuse was a cynical betrayal of the weakest members of the Church in favour of saving its own face," she later complained in an opinion piece published in the *Toronto Star*.

McCann kept stirring the pot. In August 1990, nine former wards, each wearing a white T-shirt with an illustration of a Brother pulling a child from his bed, picketed a meeting of the Canadian Conference of Catholic Bishops in Ottawa. Grant Hartley carried a placard which read: "Christ cared for the children; Why don't you?"

About an hour into the demonstration, two bishops emerged from the building to talk to the former wards and declare that they understood their concerns. Their meeting, in fact, had been called to draft new guidelines to help victims, treat offenders, and research the "whole question of sexuality."

"I know the Church is beginning to face up to the issue," McCann said. "But we won't be happy until we see the guidelines."

Later in the day, he was invited to address the conference.

Winnipeg Archbishop Adam Exner, one of seven members of the conference's sexual abuse committee, said the bishops believed the victims of St. Joseph's and St. John's should be treated seriously. "We believe they deserve an apology, and we believe they deserve assistance," he said.

Hartley was elated by the bishop's response. "I think we

achieved a lot today. I expected things were going to go in a neg-
ative way. Instead we've got a positive reaction. It's a big step."
But former St. Joseph's ward David Hollinger was not as easily
impressed. "You can't live on promises," he told reporters. "When
it happens, then I'll believe it."

Ten days later, McCann took a group of former wards to
Toronto to deliver a message to Archbishop Aloysius Ambrozic.
McCann told reporters he had tried without success to reach
Archbishop Ambrozic forty times by phone and had written
three letters, each of which had gone unanswered. "He refuses
to acknowledge that there's a problem," McCann complained.

On August 12, a Sunday, twelve protestors demonstrated
outside St. Michael's Cathedral in downtown Toronto, much to
the chagrin of parishioners attending mass. Some parishioners
called the former wards a disgrace to the Church. There was a
confrontation between protesters and Church ushers before Father
Michael Facey emerged to calm the brewing storm. A few days
later, in another small victory for Helpline, Archbishop Ambrozic
agreed to a meeting.

Two weeks later, on August 25, fifteen former wards, includ-
ing McCann and Hartley and members of the Coalition of
Concerned Catholics, paraded in front of the Apostolic
Nunciature, Canada's Vatican Embassy, upriver from Parliament
Hill. On this occasion, McCann presented a letter intended for
Pope John Paul II to his Canadian representative, Father Dante
Pasquinelli. Dated August 25, 1990, the letter called on the Church
to take responsibility for the abuse of children at St. Joseph's
Training School for Boys. "The failure of the individuals, who
were the abusers, to live up to their responsibilities and their vows
is tragic," it said. "However, the failure of their superiors and the
Church hierarchy to act and protect these children is an even
greater tragedy. Many lives have been ruined. Many people have
lost their faith, and many more will continue to leave the Church

unless a strong, continuous, and powerful message is given that the Church will no longer tolerate such abuse and that the Church will move quickly to assist those whom it failed to protect in the past. Help us find the light that was lost in our youth."

The letter went on to ask the Pope to prepare a homily to respond to the needs of the victims and to acknowledge the Church's responsibility to them. When Father Pasquinelli met with McCann and Hartley, he first admonished them for making the letter to the pontiff public, but eventually agreed to forward it to Rome. The Pope never responded to the letter.

Throughout the summer of 1990, Helpline, headed by McCann, had confronted the Ontario government and the Catholic Church. It had publicly begun to detail the abuse its members had suffered. Now its work would begin in earnest on two fronts: it would attempt to get the institutions to address the needs of the victims and force the criminal justice system to investigate their allegations.

9

Looking for the Truth

•

*"To investigate is to determine the truth, and
this is what we are determined to do."*
– OPP Det. Insp. Tim Smith, April 2, 1990

THE SWIRL of media attention that began in spring 1990 with
the first story in the *Toronto Star* led to a flood of allegations
from former wards of the two training schools. Each new report
prompted more phone calls, letters, and faxes. It was soon obvious
that the investigation was going to take on mammoth proportions. Every day new names were added to the list of suspected
abusers while the list of the abused grew at ten times that rate.

At first, OPP Det. Insp. Tim Smith spent most of his efforts
setting up the administrative structure to run the investigation.
Based in an office in Long Sault, near Cornwall, he went about
the business of finding investigators, secretaries, vehicles, office
space, phone lines, and a computer system to cross-reference all
the allegations, alleged victims, suspects, and witnesses. He set
up a telephone hotline for former wards of both schools to register their complaints, but there had been such a deluge of calls
already that it would be weeks, and in some cases months, before
he could assign investigators to follow up each one.

It soon became obvious he would have to move his investigation team out of the tiny Long Sault detachment. The office was too small. On April 15, 1990, the team moved into a plain two-storey office building in southwest Ottawa, and a new hotline phone number was released. The team of investigators, which swelled to twenty-two at the investigation's peak, included several bilingual officers to interview both francophone Christian Brothers and victims. Vehicles were seconded from detachments all over the province.

One of Smith's first decisions was to send a researcher to the Ontario archives to hunt for additional documents. He wanted to determine whether the police had investigated any of the allegations at any time. The researcher sent Smith reports on every inspection conducted into St. Joseph's and St. John's by the ministry, as well as correspondence between the training schools and the ministry. He also pulled the ward files containing the background, progress, and medical history of wards who had filed criminal complaints against the Christian Brothers. Although there were literally reams of material, much of the information was sketchy and often in such poor condition that it was barely legible.

Smith's prize catch was a computer program called ASK SAM, which had been used by U.S. federal attorneys in the Iran Contra hearings. Once all the victim statements were entered, the program allowed investigators to match witnesses to crimes and victims to offenders merely by typing in a few key words. If a former ward told police he saw a boy being sexually molested by a Brother in a barn, investigators could match the witness to the possible victim simply by typing in the word "barn." The system was invaluable in organizing the statements of hundreds of victims. By the time Smith's investigation into St. Joseph's was ended, more than ten thousand allegations would be keyed into the computer's memory banks.

The lanky, chain-smoking detective ran the investigation out of a windowless second-floor room. The walls were covered with yellow construction paper. On some sheets the police had written the names of the suspects, their dates of birth, and their period of service at Alfred. On one they had inscribed the names of the Brothers who had died. Photographs of the Brothers, as they appeared in the 1950s and 1960s in their crewcuts, black horn-rimmed glasses, and bib-collars, stared from another wall. Yet another wall was taken up by floor-to-ceiling aluminum shelving stacked with bound, gold-embossed, blue-covered case files on each accused.

Two tables, bare except for telephones, were pressed against a large map of Ontario on one wall. The locations of complainants were marked. Rather than sending officers back and forth across the province to interview victims as complaints came in, investigators were sent on trips that allowed them to conduct five or six interviews.

Smith developed a list of specific questions to be asked in sequence by his investigators. Later, as expenses rose, Smith simply mailed the questions to out-of-province complainants because he couldn't afford to fly anyone out to take their statements.

Not surprisingly, the interview sessions were traumatic for many of the victims. Most didn't trust police or authorities and expected the worst. When Armand Jobin, Jr., went to give his statement to an OPP investigator at an Ottawa hotel, he concealed a kitchen knife in his sock for protection.

The stories the investigators heard were so horrific that many – who thought by this point in their careers they had heard everything – were taken aback. One former ward said he witnessed a sexual assault in which a Brother attempted to shove a tree branch up a child's anus. Another man told of how a long-running feud with a Brother had resulted in a brutal rape. He tearfully described being beaten unconscious in the school's maple sugar shack and awakening as the Brother cut open his jeans to sodomize him.

"None of us had heard any stories like this before – even hard-ened, long-time cops," Smith explained. "You had to see the pho-tographs of these kids, the way they were – not the way they are now – and listen to their stories. It was gut wrenching. It was hard for me to go home and play with my son and think about what could have happened to him if he was in the hands of those Brothers."

Some of the statements of the men were so moving that the secretaries wept as they keyed them into the police computer. One officer could not cope with the anguished tales he was hearing almost daily and had to be sent home. Investigators were surprised at the candour of the victims. The pain in their faces left little doubt about their sincerity. Many broke down repeatedly as they tried to tell their stories. "The emotion was genuine and obvious," said Det. Sgt. Bob Carpenter. "These are strong, tough men breaking down in front of you."

In June 1990, Smith and Crown attorney Robert Pelletier went to St. John's, Newfoundland, to consult with detectives and attor-neys about the investigation into the Irish Christian Brothers there. For five days, they heard about the many pitfalls that had threatened to derail the Mount Cashel investigation and tried to predict the response they could expect from the hierarchy of the Catholic Church in Ontario.

During a tour of St. John's, the pair were taken by the dark and empty Mount Cashel Orphanage. Someone joked about mooning the building. But the laughter was strained. It seemed so strange to Smith and Pelletier, both Roman Catholics, that their Church was now their adversary.

In the fall of 1990, as Bob Rae's New Democrats were in the process of sweeping David Peterson's Liberals from office, police were busy planning simultaneous raids on the offices of the Christian Brothers in Toronto, Ottawa, Uxbridge, and in Laval, Quebec, where the order's archives were located.

The search warrants, which formed a stack of paper five centimetres thick, had been delivered to justices of the peace two weeks prior to the planned mid-September raid date to give them ample time to review their contents. The court officials would need all that time to pore over the three hundred pages of allegations against forty Christian Brothers and other employees of the training schools. By comparison, the search warrants issued in the Mount Cashel investigation numbered only four pages.

Since the investigators didn't know precisely where the material they sought would be found, they planned to search all four locations simultaneously to ensure documentation could not be shunted from one to another between raids.

They struck on September, 13, 1990, two days after Peter Kormos reaffirmed his intention to push for a public inquiry now that he was a member of the new governing party. Smith accompanied investigators to the order's Ottawa headquarters. Other teams hit the Toronto headquarters and the administration offices of St. John's in Uxbridge. And a fourth team, led by Det. Sgt. Bob Carpenter, visited the archives in Laval.

Ottawa district Brother Provincial Jean-Marc Cantin was remarkably calm when police arrived unannounced at his door. The police waited politely until the order's lawyer arrived. "My reaction was to co-operate to the fullest measure possible," Brother Jean-Marc said after the raid. "I think the whole purpose of this exercise is to get to the truth."

The investigators noticed immediately that there was little dust on the thirty-year-old boxes, stamped "St. Joseph's," but that was hardly a surprise. The Brothers had had ample time to comb the files in anticipation of charges. Indeed, much of the material was in boxes strewn around the Brother Provincial's office when police arrived. Some files contained precious little information. One, about a Brother who had been in the order for decades, contained only a holy card marking his twenty-fifth anniversary in the order. At one location raided that day, police found a paper shredder still set up in the filing room. The Brothers had had plenty of time to pull incriminating material from the files, but what police were really looking for was what they called "identifier" information, including the Brothers' chosen religious names, the years they had worked in the training schools, the responsibilities they held, and their current names and addresses.

Carpenter's team in Laval was greeted by an elderly archivist who led them to the St. Joseph's files. He was adamant that all the information was there until Carpenter pointed out that there were reference numbers on the files he had seized indicating that there were additional files. Using the reference numbers, Carpenter found several other files the archivist had neglected to mention. But each time a new file was found, the archivist assured him that it was the last. Finally, Carpenter sat the archivist down in a corner and took the room apart methodically, first photographing each area and then going through the shelves file by file. When he was finished he could trace each document in his possession to its precise location in the room.

Under the terms of the search warrants, the investigators had a month to sift through the material and file returns with the court to indicate what they had taken with them. While police found file cards listing the religious and secular names of the Brothers, as well as where they had been stationed and when, they found no records of any internal complaints against any of the Brothers. The only material relating to a Brother's conduct was recorded in the scant minutes of a meeting of a council called the Chapter of Vows. The chapter, which consisted of the heads of, or senior Brothers in, a number of the order's key institutions, reviewed the applications of fellow brethren seeking to have their vows renewed.

Investigators found it ironic that three suspects on their list had sat on the council that passed judgement on Brother Sylvio, who had been dismissed following Sinclair's 1960 investigation. The hypocrisy of their decision astounded the officers.

It was obvious that the investigation into St. Joseph's and St. John's was going to dwarf the Mount Cashel investigation. Smith, at this point, had more than forty-five suspects and two hundred alleged victims. In Newfoundland, nine Brothers and three civilians had been charged with abusing just forty-one victims. After the raids, Smith told the media he expected that a number of charges would be laid. This was welcome news for the former wards, some of whom were experiencing considerable anxiety as they waited for a tangible sign that they were believed. Even McCann was excited. "I can feel a chill running up my spine," he remarked. "Somebody, after all these years, is finally doing something."

In December, three months after the raids, Smith gathered up his case files and carted them to L'Orignal to Crown attorney Robert Pelletier and assistant Crown attorney Ronald Laliberté. The two spent the holiday season reading the horrific statements of the abused. They had to toss out hundreds of allegations because of the six-month statute of limitations on common assault. Only if there was visible injury could the Crown proceed with charges.

The prosecution was further hampered by changes in the Criminal Code of Canada since some of the offences were committed. Charges would have to be laid, in some cases, under the statutes that existed at the time. That meant that rather than being charged with sexual assault, many of the Brothers would face such now-obsolete charges as buggery and gross indecency. And that could mean problems down the road if the defence challenged the fairness of the outdated charges. The charges had been replaced with the offence of sexual assault in the revised Criminal Code because they pertained only to acts committed by men. There were no corresponding charges for similar acts committed by women. While the defence could not challenge the charges under the Canadian Charter of Rights and Freedoms, since it had not been in effect at the time of the alleged offences, they could challenge them under the Bill of Rights.

The complexity of the legal issues, combined with the many other difficulties entailed in an investigation into crimes that had been committed, in some cases, thirty years earlier, made progress towards the laying of charges slow. From the perspective of the former wards, the process sometimes seemed interminable, but it had finally begun to yield results.

IO

Confronting the Past

•

"I forgave the Brothers a long time ago. They have got their own demons they have to deal with. I am really searching for inner peace and that won't come without forgiveness."
— David McCann, February 14, 1991

MORNING. February 14, 1991. Outside the community centre at Kanata, twenty kilometres west of Ottawa, where the press conference was about to begin, several bleary-eyed detectives from the OPP stood in the newly fallen snow, smoking cigarettes and telling jokes. Past them streamed a parade of journalists anxious to learn of the latest developments in the OPP's year-long investigation into the Brothers of the Christian Schools. Most of the television crews had already arrived, their brightly marked vehicles covered with a light dusting of snow in the crowded parking lot.

The detectives were enjoying the crisp air. The night before they had been boisterously celebrating the culmination of an investigation that had concluded in one hundred and forty-nine charges being laid against nineteen former employees. The list included sixty-nine charges of assault causing bodily harm, fifty-nine charges of indecent assault, fourteen charges of buggery, five of gross indecency, and two of attempted buggery, some dating back to 1941 and all perpetuated on boys between the ages of seven and seventeen.

Of the nineteen charged, only seven were still in the order. The eldest, eighty-one-year-old Léo "Puss Eyes" Monette, faced twenty-seven charges, including buggery, gross indecency, indecent assault, and a staggering twenty-one counts of assault causing bodily harm. Six others were in their seventies. The youngest, Réjean Nadeau, aged forty-five, a provincial bureaucrat from Toronto, faced single counts of indecent assault and buggery. They had been spared the ordeal of being arrested. Police had quietly arranged for them all to be issued summons in Ottawa the day before. They would have to appear in court in L'Orignal in five weeks.

Their arrests had been timed to coincide with what were expected to be the arrests of another thirteen Christian Brothers and two civilians who had worked at St. John's, but at the last moment, senior Crown officials demanded more time to review the files. While this action stunned police, it created near panic among some of the former wards of St. John's, who wondered why not a single Brother from their school had been charged. "There is no possible way they should get away with the severe beatings they laid on us," lamented former St. John's ward Nick Sapusak. "I took a baseball bat over the head. Who does that to a fifteen-year-old?"

At the press conference in Kanata, OPP Supt. Wib Craig noted that another sixteen Brothers who had worked at St. Joseph's would have been charged if they had still been alive. Craig said 177 former wards of St. Joseph's were identified by the investigation as victims. There were probably more, he said, but they did not come forward "for one reason or another." (Within three weeks of Craig's comments, another 25 wards offered their stories to police.)

If convicted, the Brothers faced an array of penalties. The

Criminal Code of Canada set the maximum for buggery at life, indecent assault and assault causing bodily harm at ten years, and gross indecency at five years.

Not surprisingly, reporters demanded to know whether there had been a cover-up by the province and the Church akin to what had happened at Mount Cashel in 1975. Craig didn't think so, although he conceded he didn't know what went on behind the scenes. All he could say was that there was no evidence to indicate such a deal.

"Let's keep in mind it was thirty years ago and the social climate has changed," he said. "I think they investigated it and made the decisions that they felt were appropriate at that time. They decided as a group that was the best approach."

And why the delay in laying charges against the Brothers at St. John's? The veteran OPP officer provided little insight. "There have been no charges laid against anyone at St. John's and I am not at liberty to talk about why no charges have been laid," he said. "It is now in the hands of the Crown attorney and I think it would be very unfair for me to make a comment."

Both David McCann and Roger Tucker attended the press conference. It was a day of vindication for McCann, a milestone on what he termed his "journey towards inner peace." But if McCann was thrilled by the developments, he concealed his feelings well. He looked and sounded rather like a lawyer, which is how the *Globe and Mail* described him in the next day's newspaper. He was polite, calm, and generous in his praise for the police investigators, whom he described as being extremely sensitive to the victims. When he spoke it was not of retribution, but of healing. "This is a significant step to finding that inner peace that I think is important to all victims of abuse," he said. "The court proceedings will close maybe a chapter on this story for the government, but my search will be an ongoing process."

He told reporters he had become most concerned with helping

former wards find the financial, medical, and psychological help they required. Interestingly, McCann did not use his appearance at Kanata as a platform to hammer the province on the need for an inquiry. When pressed on the issue by reporters, he simply said the premier was aware of their concerns. "We've had our opinion made known to him."

The door on a royal commission inquiry was slowly closing. McCann was well aware that by the time the trials and appeals were out of the way, the chances an inquiry would be called were slim. Premier Bob Rae would later say that, as a result of the charges, there could be no inquiry until the courts had dealt with the matter. McCann also realized that the criminal trial process would not delve into the government's role in allowing the abuse to continue. Although he considered the trials important, McCann was coming to the conclusion that the real needs of the former wards could be best met through negotiations with the province and the Church, away from the media spotlight and the frenzy of criminal litigation.

Still, if McCann did not want to ruffle the feathers of the parties he hoped to bring to the negotiation table, other Helpline members did not feel similarly constrained. "I don't want revenge, but the law has to take its course," said former ward Sylvio Goulet. "The politicians that were there at the time knew what was going on. They should be charged, too. Even the judges who sentenced us kids. Why shouldn't they be charged? There were a lot of people hiding behind the Brothers' robes."

The Christian Brothers responded to the onslaught of media queries with a single-page press release. It read, in part, "Our thoughts go out to those, at Alfred and elsewhere, who may have been victims of abuse. We do not condone such acts; this is why we have co-operated with the police throughout their investigations. We offer our apologies for any abuse that may have occurred and will provide counselling and assistance at an appropriate time. It is now for the courts to decide the innocence or guilt of these men in the eyes of the law." The order maintained it would work with secular agencies and the Church to try to prevent "the potential for such occurrences in the future."

In Alfred, the news of the charges being laid seemed to cause barely a ripple. On the first Sunday after Craig's press conference, Catholics turned out at St. Victor's Church as if nothing had happened. Rather than using the occasion to address the issue, Father Lucien Charbonneau gave a homily on the war then raging in the Persian Gulf. Confronted by an *Ottawa Sun* reporter after the mass, the priest flew into a rage and ordered the journalist "to get the hell out" of his church.

The Ottawa Brothers indicated shortly after the charges were laid that they would consider compensating the victims if members were convicted, but by and large the Brothers were still reeling from the shock of the charges. The order had brought in a priest psychologist to ease the trauma of its forty-four members.

Brother Provincial Jean-Marc Cantin said he refused to make any distinction in how he dealt with the Brothers who had been charged and the other Brothers. In his eyes, they were all his brethren. If anything, the charges would bring them closer.

The public and the former wards had their first glimpse of the accused when they were summoned to the 166-year-old courthouse in L'Orignal for their first appearance on a blustery March 20, 1991.

The nineteen elderly men who gathered in the second-floor main courtroom with its ornate ceiling and cathedral windows seemed to be throwbacks to another era. Wearing ill-fitting plaid sports jackets, polyester suits, and wide ties, they looked dazed and horribly out of place.

While the victims had been asked by police to refrain from attending, a dozen former wards, including one drunken man who waved a placard at passing cars on the highway, showed up anyway. "I waited nearly thirty years for this," explained forty-one-year-old Paul Gagnon, who said he had been sexually abused by one of the accused Brothers. "I have come to see justice done."

Former ward Wilfrid Marion took a day off work to be there. "My mom said I should come and hold my head up high," the burly thirty-four-year-old Ottawa man said as he stood outside the courthouse. "A lot of people think we're here for vengeance, but we're here to say, 'Let's get the show on the road.'"

The accused, some walking with canes or leaning on the arms of colleagues, filled the first three rows on one side of the court-room, sitting shoulder to shoulder on dark-stained oak benches that rose up the back wall like bleachers.

The twenty-minute proceeding was conducted entirely in French before justice of the peace Fernand Tittley. Some of the accused nervously chewed gum as they were asked to stand and hear the charges against them. One by one, they rose unsteadily to their feet while dates were set for pre-trial conferences – bracketed around the upcoming Easter holiday – on March 28 or April 2.

Once the brief court appearance was over, several Brothers shook hands and wished each other good luck before departing again through the throng of media. One Brother, seventy-five-year-old Camille Huot of Montreal, couldn't resist thumbing his nose at the photographers as he exited the building.

Afterwards, lawyer Robert Doyle told reporters that his client, seventy-four-year-old Aimé Bergeron of Ottawa, previously known as Brother Gabriel, had to be hospitalized when he learned he was facing sexual abuse charges. "He is anxious to be finished with all of this," Doyle said. "He denies the allegations and he is very disturbed by them."

Lawyer Denis Pommainville, who represented two former Brothers, Jean-Louis Jeaurond and Réjean Nadeau, echoed Doyle when he noted both his clients were having a difficult time dealing with the trauma of being charged. "Both are really affected – nervousness, sleepless nights, an inability to perform a regular workload." Each man, he said, would deny the allegations.

On the day the accused were making their appearance in court, McCann's Helpline was co-hosting a conference on male child abuse at the downtown Toronto YMCA. Hailed as "a national hero" when he was introduced by the head of a Toronto-area sexual abuse treatment program, McCann apologized for naming the conference "Betrayal of Trust." He said he still had a lot of anger and hate burning inside when he began organizing it, but that had passed.

On April 18, 1991, about a month after the charges were laid at St. Joseph's, police finally laid charges against former employees of St. John's. Six men faced seventeen charges, including twelve counts of assault causing bodily harm, four counts of indecent assault, and one of attempted buggery. Only one of those who was charged was still a member of the lay order. Another fourteen employees of St. John's could have faced charges if they had been alive.

Police used the occasion to announce that they were laying additional charges against several already accused Brothers from St. Joseph's. So far, according to the OPP, the investigation had cost taxpayers more than $1 million and had elicited allegations by three hundred former wards against a total of seventy-eight employees from St. John's and St. Joseph's.

David McCann called the numbers "mind-boggling," and this time he did not hesitate to revive his call for a public inquiry. "A public inquiry will show that for almost fifty years they failed to protect children from abuse," he said. "I think the premier has to say at the appropriate time that there will be a public inquiry."

Later that afternoon, in the Bay Street law offices of O'Donohue & O'Donohue, the Toronto Brothers apologized to both the public and any individual for "any abuse that may have occurred." Brother George Morgan, a member of the order's governing council, said the Brothers condemned the unacceptable behaviour alleged by former wards of St. John's. He pledged on behalf of the order to work with society and the Church to try to prevent future abuse. He also pledged to provide counselling and psychological assistance for the abused and accused "at an appropriate time."

Later, however, under questioning from reporters, he said the order would not enter into any mediation process with the victims while the court cases were in process. "My feelings go out to those who may have been victims of any of these allegations," he said. "Secondly, it is a difficult time for those who are accused. The needs they have for their own psychological well-being and healing are foremost in my thoughts and my prayers."

Brother George assured reporters that none of the Brothers who had been charged had worked at St. John's in more than two decades. Indeed, the only Brother still on staff at the institution was the superintendent of the past eleven years, Brother Norman Hofley. Morgan said Brothers who historically had staffed the facility had been replaced over the years by professional social workers, counsellors, and custodial staff.

One month later, the six accused from St. John's made their first appearance in Ontario Court, provincial division, in Whitby,

east of Toronto. Each was remanded to appear for separate preliminary hearings between August and October.

They were an interesting mix. Robert Morrissey, aged fifty,
who was known as Brother Frederick at St. John's, was now a
priest in an Alberta parish; Bernard Recker, also aged fifty, who
was known as Brother Mark, ran a market garden in the nearby Peterborough area. Fifty-one-year-old Bernard McGrath,
who was known as Brother Hugh, worked for the province's
Corrections Department, counselling adult inmates in Brampton.
Fifty-seven-year-old Timothy O'Donnell, who was known as
Brother Sean, was a Scarborough school teacher. Joseph Dugas,
aged sixty, known as Brother Basil, lived in retirement with his
wife and two children in Welland, Ontario, and Robert Radford,
also aged sixty, who was known as Brother Michael, had settled
near Dorval, Quebec.

Crown attorneys in charge of prosecutions at both St. Joseph's
and St. John's were facing a number of legal challenges over the
inordinate length of time that had passed since the alleged
offences occurred and the laying of the charges. Lawyers for the
Christian Brothers also planned to argue that the indecent assault
charges that had been laid violated the Bill of Rights because there
was no similar charge relating to indecent assault by a female
against a male. If the Crown lost this argument, about two-thirds
of the charges would be thrown out of court.

L'Orignal assistant Crown attorney Ronald Laliberté convinced Madam Justice Louise Charron in Ontario Court, general
division, that people being prosecuted for offences in the 1940s,
1950s, and 1960s had to be prosecuted under the standards of the
day. In that era, long before the advent of the Canadian Charter
of Rights and its guarantees of equal treatment before the courts,
the standard was considered fair. Charron agreed and her decision would later be upheld by the Supreme Court of Canada.

But verdicts in several other cases would have a direct bearing

on the Christian Brothers' cases. In October 1990, Ontario lower
courts interpreted a decision by the Supreme Court of Canada
to mean that trials must begin within eight months of charges
being laid. In what subsequently became known as the Askov
ruling, the court had dismissed charges of extortion against Elijah
Askov and three others because it had taken thirty-four months
for their case to get to trial. The startling judgment, in which
the high court ruled that waiting six to eight months between
trial and committal might be deemed to be the outside limit of
what is acceptable, prompted the withdrawal or dismissal of more
than fifty-two thousand cases that had been waiting to get into
Ontario courts.

   Although Pelletier wanted to get all the St. Joseph's cases
through the court by April 1992, he knew he would have to be
extremely lucky. Fortunately for the Crown, the rules changed
again. A later decision by the Supreme Court clarified its earlier
position and resulted in the reinstatement of serious cases that
had been dismissed amid a great public outcry. New rules would
permit cases to run longer in extenuating circumstances.

   The defence benefited tremendously from a November 7, 1991,
Supreme Court decision. In what became known as the
Stinchcombe decision, the court ruled that the Crown had to
make full disclosure of all information in the case to the defence,
with the exception of the identities of informants and information which could harm an ongoing investigation.

   A lawyer for Étienne Fortin, who was known as Brother Étienne
when he served at St. Joseph's, used the Stinchcombe decision to
win a stay of proceedings on the charges against his client.
According to Mr. Justice Jean A. Forget's decision, the stay was
granted because the Crown had failed to produce documents
pertaining to a potential witness for the defence. In his ruling,
Forget said that while it appeared a lack of resources, either in
personnel or finances, was the root cause of the Crown's failure

to produce the documents to the defence, that wasn't sufficient reason to deny the application for a stay. Fortin, who won the stay on a technicality, subsequently launched civil action against the police for false arrest.

Preliminary hearings for the accused Brothers of St. Joseph's began in August 1991 at Ottawa's Elgin Street courthouse, just a few blocks from Parliament Hill. It proved to be an emotional time for the victims, who had to face their abusers in the stillness of a near-empty courtroom while a judge decided if there was sufficient evidence to send each case on to trial. By this time, many victims were relying heavily on a victim services team established and funded by the provincial government to guide them through the process.

They depended on co-ordinator Cosette Chafe, who had been seconded from the attorney general's victim-witness program, and Jeanette Desjardins, to arrange for their food, lodging, and transportation. But, even more importantly, the two women, and the counsellors they brought in to assist them, also provided the witnesses with emotional support.

To sail on the turbulent waters of justice was perilous, of course, and some victims never made it beyond the preliminary hearing stage. They were simply too fragile, too frustrated, or too contradictory in their recollections to survive cross-examination by the defence team. Others begged off with letters from psychiatrists warning that they might commit suicide if put through the stress of testifying.

Among the first Christian Brothers to face his accusers was "the Horse," André Charbonneau – Brother André. A balding, broad-shouldered man with a beard and glasses, Charbonneau looked younger than his sixty years. He walked with an awkward gait, the result of several knee operations. He faced a total of thirty-one charges, ranging from assault causing bodily harm to buggery. As his alleged victims filed into court one by one, he sat unflinching in the back of the room, arms crossed, appearing almost indifferent to the proceedings.

Charbonneau had arrived at St. Joseph's in 1963, already a seventeen-year veteran of the Christian Brothers. Almost immediately he began to abuse boys. Some wards attributed his nickname to his legendary strength and athletic prowess. Others, however, recalled that he liked to punish boys by driving a knee into their thigh muscles, giving them a cramp or charley horse.

At the preliminary hearing, Charbonneau was portrayed as a sadistic paedophile who liked to hurt and humiliate his victims. For instance, after he sexually abused one boy, he urinated over him, then wrapped him up in the soaking sheets and made him stand that way for several hours. Another boy, allergic to dairy products, was beaten and had a tooth knocked out when Brother André tried to force him to drink a glass of milk.

But this was another Brother André the former wards were seeing now. Twenty-five years after the fact, some could not recognize him as the once notorious Horse as he sat in the back of the courtroom. One witness, serving a six-year term for robbery with violence, was asked to point out his abuser. As he walked towards Charbonneau, the chains of his shackles clinked together in the still courtroom. An alarmed police officer rose to intercept him, but the witness stopped just short of where Charbonneau was seated with two other elderly gentlemen. The witness studied their faces, then pointed to a thin man in a brown suit. It was not Charbonneau. "Well," he shrugged, "they don't look like the person I remember." He then turned and shuffled back to the witness box.

The court was told that Brother André had had a knack for

ingratiating himself with the Indian wards. At least at first. He
was always smiling and willing to play cards with them. He always
had reassuring words for them, or a candy bar. One former ward
told how, at age thirteen, he had confided to Brother André that
he had been sexually abused by another Brother shortly after he
had arrived two years earlier. Brother André responded by raping
him, too, while the youth was in solitary confinement.

"On the second night, this guy I thought was my friend, opened
the door. I was so happy to see him. I thought he was going to
help me get away from that place. He came into the cell. He pulled
down my pyjama bottoms. He was laughing all the time. He
rolled me over on the bed. I remember him spitting on his hand
and rubbing it against my bum and I remember the pain as he
forced himself into me.

"I don't care what they do to you, man," he sobbed as he
pointed at the expressionless Charbonneau.

Another man, sent to St. Joseph's in 1969, said Brother André
also raped him in a solitary confinement cell. "He put his hand
around me and started to kiss me on the cheek, and I started to
resist. He grabbed my arm and twisted it behind my back. He
pushed my head into the bed, and then he forced me to start
taking my underwear, my pants, down. I was under the impression I was going to get a spanking. But that's not what happened."

Another victim described how, after a series of sexual assaults
by Brother André, culminating in anal intercourse, he was sent
to the school's infirmary. He tried to tell the school's priest about
what was going on. "I told the priest that I didn't like what the
Brothers were doing to me in the school. He sat down beside me.
He started rubbing my back and I knew exactly what he was up
to. But what was I supposed to do?"

Charbonneau, along with his eighteen colleagues from
St. Joseph's, was remanded for trial. In January 1992, more charges
were laid by the OPP against the former employees of St. John's

– two former Christian Brothers and a former civilian employee
– as well as one from St. Joseph's. The charges against Laurence
Lessard (Brother Albert) and Stanley Clark (Brother Andrew) of
St. John's, and James Clarke and André Desjardins (Brother
André) of St. Joseph's, brought to twenty-nine the total number
of men charged, and pushed the total offences near the two
hundred mark. All the while, still more former wards were coming
forward with their stories.

It pained the Christian Brothers to hear the allegations and see
their brethren marched off to court. Once he knew he was being
transferred to Rome, Ottawa district Brother Provincial Jean-
Marc Cantin shook OPP Det. Const. Ron Wilson's hand and conceded he was glad to be leaving the scandal behind him.

"I know you are probably a nice man," he told Wilson, "but
every time I see you my heart stops."

As the police investigation chugged along one track, McCann
headed down another, intent on forcing the Catholic Church, the
Christian Brothers, and the Ontario government to accept moral
responsibility for the tragedy and to do something about it.

II

At the Table

•

*"Let us approach our task humbly, moving forward in a manner
which truly reflects Christ's healing mission, and recalls that what
we do for these victims, our brothers and sisters, we do for God."*
— bishops' adviser Paul McAuliffe
to Douglas Roche, January 1991

A S EARLY as summer 1990, Roger Tucker had suggested that
a negotiated settlement among the victims, the government,
the Church, and the Christian Brothers might be the most desir-
able outcome as far as the Helpline victims were concerned. Such
a deal would constitute an acknowledgement of fault by the
transgressors — Helpline wanted formal apologies from them —
and would also include provisions for counselling and some form
of compensation. During the summer, David McCann made a
visit to Newfoundland that left him thinking that Tucker's suggestion was a good one.

The Mount Cashel scandal continued to interest McCann for
obvious reasons. But he found it hard to judge, based on reports
in the media, just what, if anything, the Church in Newfoundland
was doing in the aftermath of the revelations. He was also curious
to know what the effect of the Hughes Inquiry had been from

the point of view of the victims. What had it done to the men
who had bared their souls?

McCann had also wanted to meet Newfoundland's archbishop,
the Most Reverend Alphonsus Penney. When they did met, in
July 1990, Penney had just tendered his resignation because of the
scandal, and was awaiting a response from the Pope. It was a somewhat unsatisfactory and inconclusive meeting.

As McCann took his seat, he saw before him a tiny, frail,
almost childlike man seated on a small couch. "He struck me as
someone who was totally lost," McCann said later of the sixty-
six-year-old archbishop. "He was out of his depth. He didn't have
a clue about what was going on despite the fact that he had made
a number of public statements and had resigned."

McCann gained little insight from the encounter, but he took
away with him a stack of copies of the independent report the
archbishop had ordered into the tragedy. The Winter Report,
which found that the alleged sexual activities of at least five priests
were personally known to Archbishop Penney, urged the Church
to end the denial and cover-ups and work harder to help the
victims of abuse. However, McCann had the feeling that Church
officials were far from ready to deal with the issue. They seemed
to be still in shock.

McCann met with the Crown attorney who handled the Mount
Cashel trials and came away with the belief that some form of
victim assistance program was going to be necessary to help the
former wards through the trauma of testifying. He talked to
several Mount Cashel victims, to inquiry counsel, and to anyone
else who would see him or who would spare a comment, including police, taxi drivers, reporters, and his hosts at the bed-and-
breakfast where he stayed. He wanted to know how the scandal
was perceived from every standpoint and, to that end, he would
return twice more to Newfoundland to monitor developments.

By the fall of 1990, McCann and Helpline's seven-member

executive were coming to the conclusion that a public inquiry was, at worst, unlikely and, at best, a distant prospect. Having seen firsthand the results of the Newfoundland inquiry, they were no longer sure that it was worth campaigning for. Did they really want to submit themselves to such an exhausting, painful process? Was it worth the time, money, and terrible personal anguish to continue to pursue it as a strategy?

Either a negotiated settlement or mediated reconciliation, in contrast, looked increasingly attractive. Clearly, however, it would be no easy matter to persuade the other parties to participate in it. Already they had contacted the archdioceses, the government, and the Christian Brothers in Ottawa and Toronto. Their reception had been polite but non-committal. No one, it seemed, wanted to make the first move.

On paper, the notion of negotiation rather than litigation was interesting, but it had never been done before in similar circumstances. Clearly for the strategy to work, the victims would need someone with clout to bring the disparate groups together. Someone who could walk into Queen's Park and command immediate respect. Someone with an intimate knowledge of the workings of the hierarchy of the Roman Catholic Church. Someone the bishops and the Christian Brothers could not ignore.

Such a man, as it turned out, was available. Douglas Roche, former Canadian ambassador for nuclear disarmament, had rubbed shoulders with the leaders of the world's superpowers. He had been outspoken about American escalation of the arms race in the 1970s and 1980s. And when he felt the Canadian government was kowtowing to American interests during arms talks, he had quit on principle.

He had been raised a staunch Roman Catholic and was the founding editor of the *Western Catholic Reporter* newspaper. His political and negotiating skills had been honed over twelve years as the Conservative MP for Edmonton–Strathcona. The sixty-one-year-old Roche was now disarmament adviser to the Vatican delegation at the United Nations, and among his eleven books, he had co-authored one advocating reform in the Church. All things considered, he appeared to be suited to the job of intermediary.

When McCann contacted him in mid-December 1990, Roche was working part time as a visiting professor at the University of Alberta in Edmonton. Roche, as it turned out, was already aware of the plight of the victims of St. Joseph's and St. John's. Roger Tucker was his son-in-law. Although Roche's daughter, Evita, and Tucker were in the process of obtaining a divorce, the estranged couple remained friends and colleagues at the legal firm of Perly-Robertson, Panet, Hill & McDougall.

Roche immediately agreed to find out if the different parties could be convinced to negotiate with Helpline as "legitimate representatives" of the former wards of the Ontario Catholic training schools for boys. He would also have to persuade the other parties to pay his travel expenses and $800-per-day fee.

The series of meetings that Douglas Roche embarked upon started a process that was to last most of the following two years. Progress was often painfully slow. Some parties to the negotia-tions were undoubtedly wary and distrustful of the people they faced across the negotiating table. Others, however, showed remarkable goodwill and a determination to arrive at a reason-able resolution. Money problems, especially the obvious poverty of Helpline and its membership, were to be a recurrent theme. And the largest single impediment to progress was the obdurate refusal by the Toronto Christian Brothers to acknowledge the responsibility of their branch of the order.

Roche met first with Ontario government officials because, as he saw it, their endorsement as the most powerful of the parties would assist him in approaching the others. The key man for the province was Ron Cavalucci, executive assistant to the solicitor general. Cavalucci had been assigned to meet with lawyers from the Attorney General, Solicitor General, and Correctional Services ministries with respect to the issue, and to recommend a solution to cabinet.

Roche explained that the victims were seeking counselling, formal apologies, and financial compensation. Cavalucci agreed to include a letter from Roche with his submission to cabinet. Roche left Queen's Park optimistic that Bob Rae's government would participate in the mediation process.

Next, Roche visited the archdiocese of Ottawa, where he met Archbishop Marcel Gervais and Auxiliary Bishop Brendan O'Brien. Gervais told Roche he wanted to do what was proper, but was deeply concerned that participating in the process Roche outlined would be seen as an admission of guilt by the Church, and thus leave it open to legal action. The Ottawa archdiocese wanted to wait, he said, to see what the Christian Brothers and government planned to do. And before it agreed to sit down, it wanted to know what portion of the cost it might be expected to pay.

"The negotiation to bring Ottawa in will have to be finely tuned," Roche reported to McCann. "In the end, a process of mediation actually starting – to which Ottawa refuses to enter – could put Ottawa in a bad light. Thus for that reason, Ottawa may assent. The carrot – not the stick – is the only way for Helpline to proceed. My estimate of success: low to medium."

Roche went on to meet an official with the Canadian Conference of Catholic Bishops. Bernard Daly was secretary to the bishops' *ad hoc* committee on sexual abuse, which had been established in 1989 to develop policies for victims and their families. Daly told Roche the archdioceses would be wary of entering the mediation process because it could set a precedent. The

Church feared an onslaught of similar allegations from Indians who had been sent to Catholic Indian residential schools. He said the bishops doubted that mediation would, in the long run, be any cheaper for the Church than a class-action suit by the victims.

Reporting back to McCann, Roche said the bishops "not only want to do the right thing, but be seen to be doing the right thing. Helpline mediation could be perceived by the bishops as doing the right thing, but they are not there yet. And they are not likely to believe that Helpline is fundamentally interested in reconciliation if Helpline employs any more confrontation tactics."

The Ottawa Brothers had legal counsel when they met Roche on January 23, 1991. Brother Provincial Jean-Marc Cantin, joined by lawyer Ronald Caza and Cantin's eventual successor, Brother Maurice Lapointe, informed Roche that he wanted to meet his moral obligations to the victims, but he did not want to jeopardize his legal responsibilities in the process. He was anxious that the Brothers received a fair trial.

Brother Maurice was dismayed at the image of the order in the media and worried about a "cash grab" by the victims. "I have a hard time seeing Helpline as truly reaching out to improve the atmosphere," he said.

Caza warned that the victims better not get greedy. "The order is not the Bank of Canada, and if Helpline takes a pie-in-the-sky approach to financial compensation, the process will go nowhere."

Roche later told McCann that the Brothers were still in shock. He said the scandal threatened the order's survival and "Brother Cantin is a deeply worried man who will be affected by the advice he gets from his legal representative and the orders he gets from Rome." Still, Roche felt there was a good chance the Ottawa Brothers would join in mediation.

Roche went on to Montreal where, on January 24, he met representatives of the archdiocese. Brother Jean-Marc had explained

OPP Det. Insp. Tim Smith
was flooded with calls
when the scandal broke
in the *Toronto Star.*

DARCY HENTON

DARCY HENTON

OPP Det. Sgt. Bob Carpenter (right) and OPP Det. Cst. Mike Fagan
(left) flank assistant Crown attorney Ronald Laliberté outside the
Ottawa courthouse.

Michael Watters (left) and Helpline lawyer Roger Tucker (seated) work on the St. John's lawsuit with Brian Flaherty (centre) and Tom Bell.

Douglas Roche, a former member of Parliament, mediated the settlement between victims, the Catholic Church, and the provincial government.

Brother Joseph, the Hook, (left) poses in front of St. Joseph's workshops with Brother Irenée in 1960.

More than thirty years later, the sixty-seven-year-old former monk, Lucien Dagenais, appears at his trial to face charges of physical and sexual abuse.

Aimé Bergeron was known as Brother Gabriel when he worked as a maintenance man at St. Joseph's.

A frail-looking Bergeron arrives at the L'Original courthouse to face his accusers.

DARCY HENTON

Léopold Monette, known as Brother Léo when he worked at St. Joseph's, was among the most cruel of the Christian Brothers.

DARCY HENTON

The eighty-four-year-old Monette, escorted to court by Brother Étienne Fortin, was convicted on fifteen charges and sentenced to five years in prison.

Charges against Pierre Durocher, known as Brother Peter when he worked at St. Joseph's, were stayed when the defence argued successfully that he was mentally incapable of defending himself.

Maurice Perrault, known to St. Joseph's wards as Brother Gérald, was convicted on two counts of assault, fined, and placed on probation.

Aimé Bergeron, the first Christian Brother to be convicted of abuse at St. Joseph's, was sentenced to two years less a day.

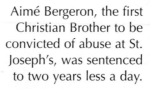

Brother Camille Huot was convicted of buggery and two counts of indecent assault and sentenced to two years less a day.

DARCY HENTON

Sent from an
orphanage to St.
John's, Trudel spent
four years at
the training school.

Nelson Trudel, haunted by the abuse he
suffered at St. John's, killed himself in 1993.
More than a dozen former wards have
committed suicide since the scandal broke.

In despair because of foul-ups in the
compensation process, former St.
John's ward Bernie Bafaro killed
himself with a drug overdose.

David McCann lobbied long and hard on behalf of the former wards of the training schools.

to him that prior to 1958, the provincial or governing body for the order operated out of Montreal. However, Montreal Auxiliary Bishop Leonard Crowley said he didn't believe the archdiocese had any jurisdictional responsibility for the training school. Roche suggested that Helpline write to Montreal Archbishop Monsignor Jean-Claude Turcotte to clarify the issue and inquire whether, prior to 1958, the archdiocese received complaints of abuse at St. Joseph's. "If the answers show no involvement and no complaints, I suggest Montreal be dropped." Subsequently, Helpline ascertained this was true and the Montreal archdiocese was no longer considered as a possible participant.

Roche completed his tour with a trip to Toronto to meet a delegation from the archdiocese of Toronto. Father Edward Boehler had been assigned by Archbishop Aloysius Ambrozic to represent the archdiocese. He was accompanied by the associate judicial vicar, Father Brian Clough, and Peter Lauwers, a lawyer with Holden, Day, Wilson.

Father Boehler wanted to know if the archdiocese was being approached to enter mediation on legal or moral grounds. If it was on legal grounds, he wanted to know what evidence there was that the archbishop had any knowledge of sexual abuse at St. John's. He believed the archdiocese had been more than fair to Helpline, but was dismayed by the air of intimidation and implied threats coming from the victims. He said the archbishop would not enter mediation in such an atmosphere.

Roche recognized that Archbishop Ambrozic's approval would be the key to the success of his mission. The archbishop would require delicate handling. "The archdiocese of Toronto is big, powerful, and run by an archbishop who will not be coerced, let alone intimidated," Roche told McCann. "It is well stocked with resources to fight that which it chooses to fight."

It was the Toronto Brothers who were going to be Helpline's most obstinate adversary. Tellingly, the head of the order, Brother

Provincial Francis McCrea, received Roche at the offices of his chief counsel, Melville O'Donohue of O'Donohue & O'Donohue. There were two other lawyers present – Angelo Callegari, O'Donohue's right-hand man on the file, and Peter Shoniker of Fedorson, Shoniker, who was overseeing the legal defence of the accused St. John's Brothers. The Brother Provincial hardly spoke during the ninety-minute meeting and then only to defend St. John's.

O'Donohue, who chaired the meeting, told Roche that he was concerned about the confidentiality of any mediation talks. "We're not going to bare our souls on the front page of the *Toronto Star*," he said. "It will be difficult for us to come forward without some protection."

Shoniker expressed fears that Mary Lou Dickie, the Crown attorney handling the St. John's prosecutions, would subpoena the mediation records to bolster her case. Shoniker also wondered whether a judge would permit a mediation process to proceed at the same time as the criminal process. However, Shoniker warmed to the notion that a Crown prosecutor might recommend leniency on the grounds that mediation was in the public interest. If the court would take the mediation process into account in sentencing and mediation records were protected from seizure, then the Brothers might be interested in pursuing the process, he said.

Roche recognized immediately that it would be the lawyers who would make the decision whether the Toronto Brothers joined the process. After the meeting, he told McCann that he remained hopeful. "If they can be convinced that the Crown will not use the mediation records to buttress the evidence, they would likely join, if for no other reason than that it might keep old men out of prison."

Meeting with McCann later, Roche frankly assessed his chances of bringing everyone together at no better than 50 per cent. It would take methodical work to build up a climate of trust. Roche recommended that, rather than wasting time arguing about liability, Helpline should immediately make it clear that it was appealing to the archdioceses solely on moral grounds. This would give the other side an opportunity to be seen voluntarily doing the right thing.

Roche wanted a session with McCann and Roger Tucker to draft strategy, and he insisted that once the strategy was set, McCann would remove himself from public view. He wanted McCann to let him implement the strategy, and he was concerned that an ill-considered public comment by McCann would sabotage the process. "As an injured party, you clearly have strong feelings which are understandable and which I respect," explained Roche. "But as a neutral convenor, I can rend[er] better service if all the parties come to repose a certain confidence in my judgment and actions."

McCann rejected the recommendation. As Helpline's chairman, he would not be muzzled. He had to be a visible spokesman. Roche warned McCann that his aggressiveness could lead to confrontation and failure. McCann compromised. He undertook to tone down his remarks but refused to give up his role as the voice of the aggrieved.

Roche had hoped to remove a source of tension from the process. In conceding McCann's leadership role, he resigned himself to mediating in a volatile atmosphere. He just hoped it didn't blow up in his face.

Roche asked Helpline to prepare a document that would outline the rationale for reconciliation while responding to the concerns raised by the parties so far. In the resulting proposal, Helpline called for a process similar to that used by Ontario's

Criminal Injuries Compensation Board. Victims would apply to an independent panel that would assess and validate their application and determine the appropriate level of financial compensation for suffering and lost wages, counselling, and educational upgrading.

In mid-February 1991, Roche drafted a letter inviting all parties to an exploratory meeting in Ottawa on March 21. He said he had sensed a desire for reconciliation. The dance was about to begin, but the tickets were going to be expensive: Roche asked that the Toronto and Ottawa archdioceses each put up $25,000 to defray Helpline's travel costs, its sponsorship of a male child abuse conference, and expenses for the mediation process. Roche also asked the province to pay $50,000 towards Helpline's legal costs in setting up the mediation process.

The meeting, held in a small Ottawa hotel, was attended by representatives of most of the relevant parties. The Toronto Brothers, however, were conspicuous by their absence. To ensure the victims would not be blamed for revealing the location of the meeting to the media, Roche did not even tell David McCann and Grant Hartley where it would be held. He simply sent a taxi to pick them up forty-five minutes before the meeting's start.

With Roche at the meeting was Ben Hoffman, president of Concorde Inc., a firm that specialized in dispute resolution. Hoffman had been behind the scenes all along, advising Helpline's lawyer Roger Tucker on the possibilities for a mediated settlement and briefing Roche on the process. Roche now brought him officially on board as his consultant.

McCann set out the proposed Helpline mediation model in a short presentation that he prefaced by setting out some ground rules. "We feel that all of us here today have a moral responsibility to work together for creative solutions to this crisis and

this moral responsibility supersedes all other questions of cul-
pability or liability."

McCann explained that Helpline would encourage its members
to co-operate with the authorities and tell the truth, to not publicly discuss allegations against specific individuals, to not interfere with the right of any individual to a fair trial, and to take a
leading role in the search for solutions. He emphasized that the
process was not a money grab. The victims would insist, he said,
that the standard of proof required to assess their allegations for
the purpose of mediation should be the civil standard – the
balance of probabilities – rather than the criminal standard of
proof beyond a reasonable doubt. Helpline would also insist that
the victims receive an apology from representatives of the various
other parties at the appropriate time.

McCann said that if the Helpline model for reconciliation was
accepted, the victims would want the right to appear before an
assessment panel that would determine the merits of their application for compensation. He called the process a window of
opportunity. "It is open now and Helpline will not close it," he
said. "But it is a tough road ahead and there is a great deal of
pain to be shared. Our work can be a model for others to show
there is a kinder, gentler way."

The meeting went on for three hours. At its end, Roche felt
sufficiently buoyed by developments to suggest another meeting
in the following month. But he had one nagging worry: How
could he bring the Toronto Brothers to the table?

The second meeting was held on April 19, 1991, at the Archdiocese
Pastoral Centre in Toronto. Again the Toronto Brothers did not
show. Representatives from the Toronto archdiocese had held an
hour-long meeting with Brother Provincial Francis McCrea and
the order's lawyer, Melville O'Donohue, but the Toronto Brothers

continued to assert that there had been no rampant sexual or physical abuse at St. John's. In addition, lawyer Peter Shoniker had discovered that Tucker was Roche's son-in-law and was furious that Roche had not disclosed the connection at the first meeting. Shoniker had also checked into McCann's background and was convinced the man was a fraud. This was to have consequences later in the course of the trials.

Money problems were to plague Helpline throughout the mediation process. Their legal costs were already well over $100,000 by the time of the first meetings, and Roger Tucker's firm was impatient to have them paid. The Ottawa Brothers came through with some financial assistance, but not enough.

Helpline's day-to-day operating costs were spiralling out of control as well. The organization was being carried on the backs of its executive members, notably McCann, who had shelled out $25,000 of his own money through personal lines of credit and mortgages. Monthly expenses were now running close to $4,500 and climbing fast as membership expanded. Roger Tucker made it clear to the other parties that if Helpline was not funded, the process would die. Fair mediation, he said, required some semblance of a level playing field.

The other parties proposed a solution. Roche called the plan a breakthrough. A few Helpline members would later call it a sellout. It was the Ottawa Brothers lawyer, Ronald Caza, who suggested that the Church and government officials might be willing to devote funding to the process and, eventually, to a negotiated reconciliation model, if they didn't have to worry about a public inquiry. If Helpline would suspend its calls for a public inquiry, well, they were willing to help finance the process.

Roche called a recess to give the Helpline executive an opportunity to consider the offer. He told the executive that it was time "to fish or cut bait." Since they had no way of knowing whether an inquiry would ever be called, all they would be giving up by accepting Caza's offer was the right to continue to lobby for one. After the recess, McCann gave the speech the other parties wanted to hear. "Helpline recognizes that resources are limited," he said. "Its aim is healing and reconciliation. The time and money would be better spent towards that end than on a public inquiry. If the process culminates in a funded dispute resolution model, I will recommend that Helpline not seek a public inquiry."

Caza was satisfied. "If we can work on that understanding, the parties will take care of the financial considerations," he assured McCann.

Caza set out a mechanism to fund the mediation and cover Helpline's ongoing operating expenses, but the issue of who paid the ongoing and past legal expenses remained unresolved. Tucker was not pleased, especially since David Hill, a senior partner in the firm, had made it clear that Perly-Robertson would not continue to represent Helpline if its arrears were not dealt with.

After the meeting, McCann pondered the difficulties that lay ahead. He wanted the mediation proposal to be approved by not less than 80 per cent of Helpline's membership. Without such support, he feared the deal would ultimately fail. "Fifty per cent plus one will not be sufficient to achieve what we are working towards," he told Helpline's lawyers Hugh Blakeney and Evita Roche. "We must be able to reduce dissension to a very small minority. If the dissenters are too large in number, they will organize and undermine the trade-offs agreed to at the negotiating table."

To win that kind of support, the Helpline executive concluded they had first to receive a commitment on apologies. They wanted a resolution in the Ontario legislature offering an apology, and they wanted Helpline members in the public gallery to hear it. They wanted apologies from the leaders of the Church, the archbishops, and from the orders of the Brothers of the Christian Schools. And they wanted to ensure that new policies and procedures to deal with child abuse in the Church were adopted, along with a commitment that the Church would adopt a code of ethics for priests, religious, and lay staff.

The executive was also clear about the compensation it was seeking. The financial settlements would have to range up to $100,000, which was the current ceiling on civil awards for sexual and physical abuse in Canada. It was also important that the awards, if granted, not cut into any other pension or benefit received by the victim. It would hardly benefit the victim if his social assistance was cut off when he received his compensation cheque.

The executive wanted the panel chosen to hear their applications for compensation to be mobile, so that victims would not have to travel long distances. And they wanted the applications to be processed within ninety days.

McCann further insisted upon benefits for widows of victims. And he wanted allowance made for victims to transfer benefits, such as educational opportunities, to their children or spouse if they were either too elderly or infirm to take advantage of them. "This process will have to be simple, non-confrontational, easily understood, and a process over which the victim feels somewhat in control," McCann said. Moreover, it had to be open. "If the other participants feel that this is a deal to be done behind closed doors and left that way, then this effort will fail. There must be a very strong commitment to support public awareness of this type of approach."

By late June 1991, the parties were engaged in a line-by-line examination of a draft agreement that called for education upgrading, counselling by recognized counsellors, and medical and dental services. Helpline members who had been forced to work for the Brothers without pay would be compensated for lost wages. And a fact-finder would write a public report to set out the victim's stories of abuse and the histories of the institutions. No one yet knew how much money they were talking about, but Ben Hoffman had been assigned to research the issue.

Roche, meanwhile, had considered ways to resolve Helpline's financial woes. At the May meeting in Ottawa, a plan was drafted to get the dogs off Helpline's heels. Tucker's law firm agreed to accept 75 per cent of what it was owed if it received an immediate payment of 25 per cent, followed by the remaining 50 per cent once the reconciliation model was established. The Ottawa Brothers agreed to advance the initial 25 per cent. Ronald Caza, however, still needed a formula to apportion Helpline's $60,000 operating costs among the parties and a deal to split future expenses.

The Ontario government, meanwhile, seemed to be stalling on its commitments. Promised funding had not been provided to renew counselling contracts that had lapsed four months earlier and, with no indication that anyone was going to pay their bills, some therapists stopped seeing former wards and their families. The province, which had also undertaken to pay a share of Helpline's bills, including Roche's wages, had yet to pay a cent.

Tucker sent an angry letter to Bob Rae in August 1991: "It is my duty to inform you respectfully that the reconciliation process, which will have the likely effect of saving the government of Ontario millions of dollars by avoiding litigation, is in extreme jeopardy at this moment and will be aborted on August 28, 1991, if the government does not make a serious commitment to the process."

On August 27, Rae assured Tucker that the province was committed to the process and that he remained hopeful a resolution could be achieved. Soon afterwards, the deputy attorney general,

Mary Hogan, advised Tucker that the province would, indeed, honour its commitment to provide funding for counselling and Helpline. The funds were subsequently made available.

Still, the Toronto Brothers held out. In an August 26, 1991, letter to Douglas Roche, Melville O'Donohue laid partial blame for their reluctance to participate on the Brothers' insurance companies. He implied that the companies might not honour liability clauses in their coverage if the Brothers went to the negotiating table. In the letter, he claimed some insurance companies had yet to locate the thirty-year-old policies, and the Brothers were reluctant to proceed when the status of those policies was ambiguous.

Privately, other parties at the table doubted that the training school would have had coverage to protect staff and the institution from liability in abuse cases. Even if they had such coverage, the sums offered in thirty-year-old policies would undoubtedly have been inconsequential by modern standards.

An angry McCann said the Brothers were listening to their lawyers when they should have been listening to God or their conscience. Was the order a religious or a corporate entity? As far as he was concerned, the letter from O'Donohue suggested that the latter was the case.

The Toronto Brothers were especially eager not to be associated in any way with the Ottawa order. They clung to the belief that there had been no rampant abuse at St. John's. The Ontario government, however, did not see it that way and told them so. It advised the other parties in the mediation process that it made no distinction between the two schools and insisted the Toronto Brothers take part. A Helpline survey of 150 of its (then) 300 members confirmed the province's contention. Although only 30 per cent of the 150 respondents were from St. John's, almost all claimed to have been assaulted, and 59 per cent claimed to have been sexually assaulted. Nearly half described the assaults as severe and 60 per cent said they had been permanently scarred. Comparing St. John's to Mount Cashel, the mediation parties noted that St. John's had four times as many alleged victims and substantially more serious allegations of abuse.

Roche arranged a meeting with the Toronto Brothers on September 26, 1991, at the Toronto Pastoral Centre's main boardroom. Representatives of the government and the archdiocese joined Roche in urging the Brothers to participate in the mediation. Again the order demurred.

In December 1991, Roche tried again. This time he called on the board of directors that operated St. John's to participate in the negotiations with the victims. Roche thought the board seemed to support the concept, but once again O'Donohue held them back, warning the board that its insurance policies could be made void if it agreed.

The Toronto Brothers still refused to budge in January 1992, when the negotiators indicated that they hoped to have an agreement ready for signing by the end of June. It seemed to some observers that the Toronto Brothers, by continually dwelling on the insurance issue, were reducing the parties to the status of claims adjusters. McCann told Roche at the January meeting that the victims had heard quite enough about insurance and would not listen to any further discussion about it. Roche quickly dispatched the issue to a subcommittee, and, in effect, decreed that it would never again be discussed in the presence of the victims. Later, when representatives of the ten major insurers involved met with the parties in a meeting, none had any serious objections to the mediation process.

As the June 30, 1992, deadline for an agreement approached, the stress induced by the mediation process began to take its toll on everyone involved. McCann, in particular, was under severe strain. It wasn't altogether certain that he would be able to carry on. He was suffering from severe migraines, insomnia, ulcers, and was haunted by nightmares. For the first time, he began to have doubts about his ability to pull off the deal. The most difficult days, he knew, were still ahead.

12

The Deal

———————————— • ————————————

*"They are not going to quit doing it because it is the morally sensible
thing to do. They will quit doing it because they got caught and it
cost them a lot of money."*
— David McCann, December 29, 1992

THROUGHOUT the early months of 1992, David McCann was
on the road almost constantly, attending victims' meetings,
conducting mediation talks, meeting with lawyers. The neighbours kept an eye on his farm and made sure his dogs were fed.

When he returned home one day in November 1991, he noticed
the latch on his screen door was broken. A quick search assured
him that nothing major had been stolen. His computer, television, and CD player were still there. However, a number of files
were missing from his filing cabinet, including a draft copy of
the tentative agreement, his own ward file from St. Joseph's, his
year-end statements dating back to 1984, and his curriculum vitae.
Sensitive documents relating to contract work he had performed
for police agencies in the United States had also been taken.

McCann contacted Helpline's lawyer Roger Tucker and the
provincial attorney general's office to report the theft of the draft
agreement. Who needed the headaches that its premature release
might cause?

Somewhere, some private detective was likely at work, checking out his background, visiting his old schools and business
partners, stirring up the past. McCann had heard from Helpline
members across the country that private detectives were interviewing their employers and relatives. Two had also questioned
former deputy minister of Reform Institutions Donald Sinclair
at his home.

McCann mentioned the theft at a mediation meeting the next
day. He told the parties he would not be discussing the matter
at the table, but he urged them to contact the police directly if
they had any information about the break-in. The negotiators
immediately set to work to develop a strategy in the event that
the document was made public.

The break-in just added to McCann's stress. Besides participating in the mediation talks, he was also drafting a schedule for
a series of Helpline information meetings across the country and
preparing for a preliminary hearing in which he expected to be
called to testify against Pierre Durocher. Migraine headaches
were now a constant companion. But there was no time to rest.

When the meetings got under way, McCann found the Helpline
membership despairing, angry, and only occasionally hopeful
that something positive would result from the mediation.
Lamented one North Bay man, "I am sorry I came forward
because people now call me a faggot. What good is an apology
now?"

Some were made anxious by the sums of money they saw
gobbled up by the process. Would there be anything in the trough
after the lawyers had finished wallowing? "When do our needs
get addressed?" asked one. Others announced that they could not
afford to keep attending endless meetings. And many were furious

that the Helpline executive would no longer be pushing for a public inquiry.

Douglas Roche attended some of the Helpline meetings and came back from them concerned that the negotiating parties had overestimated the time they had to put a reconciliation model in place. "A new cycle of trauma has occurred in which fear has been replaced by anger," he said. He told the other parties at the negotiating table that the men he had seen were sceptical, bitter, poor, marginalized, and lacking in self-esteem. "They are united in the bonding of their common experience. Volatility lies just beneath a veneer of patience."

A probing survey of former wards, commissioned by the mediation parties, confirmed Roche's worries. "The coping mechanisms which enabled the boys to survive their abuse have been dislodged as the men courageously attempt to face the horrors they have repressed," wrote two social workers who analysed the survey. "It is imperative that adequate educational, vocational, health and counselling programs be put in place to enable them to discover constructive ways to rebuild their broken lives. To abandon them now would be to re-victimize them. In our opinion, the repercussions would be devastating and unpredictable."

By late January, McCann, too, was beginning to show the effects of the strain. His hair-trigger temper was surfacing more often now at Helpline executive meetings and at meetings with Roger Tucker. Once, he lashed out at Tucker particularly harshly, then felt miserable about it. "The level of anger I have bewilders me at times," he said when he apologized for the outburst. "There seems to be no rhyme or reason to its appearance, and I have not yet developed a good strategy for dealing with it."

Tucker was more than Helpline's lawyer. He had become McCann's friend. McCann had come to realize that Tucker's discipline was a perfect match for his broad, freewheeling approach.

Tucker urged McCann to vent his frustration with him, rather than unleash it at the negotiating table, giving McCann the psychological support to stay at the table.

McCann was under a psychiatrist's care, but therapy could do only so much in the face of the unrelenting daily grind. At one point, McCann's furious attention was focused on allegations by former St. John's wards against an individual still on the staff there. When McCann announced plans to hold a press conference to express his concerns about the man, he ran into an angry Tom Marshall, the chief civil lawyer in the attorney general's office who was now the province's representative in the talks. Do that, said Marshall, and watch for a slander and defamation suit. In an emotional face-to-face clash over the issue, a livid McCann shouted "Cover-up" and stormed out of Marshall's office, smashing his knuckles on the elevator door as he left.

Later, when he had calmed down, McCann decided to call off the press conference. Within a few days, he learned that the Brothers, informed by police that the man was under investigation, had removed him from his position on staff.

No sooner was that issue resolved than McCann began to hear about problems in funding therapy for the victims. The inconsistent funding had put a strain on Ottawa–Carleton Family Services Centre. The therapists and several victims demanded a meeting with Helpline. "This is a tough enough file without the therapists becoming political activists," lamented McCann before the meeting. He and Tucker assured the therapists that they would be paid and pledged to iron out the wrinkles in the funding arrangement. Prodding the Church and government to honour its funding commitments on time was becoming a full-time job.

It was not only money for counselling that was required. As the mediation process dragged on, and previous funding arrangements expired, Helpline was locked in a continuous struggle for financing for its day-to-day servicing of its members needs, for mediation expenses, and for its legal representation. Sadly, since there was no charitable foundation established to empower victims of sexual abuse, the organization had to rely on the generosity of its adversaries in negotiation – an awkward situation and a continuing source of aggravation for everyone involved.

Helpline's expenses for the first six months of 1992 were just over $250,000. By the end of the mediation process, Tucker estimated his law firm would be owed a whopping $379,000.

Both the Toronto and Ottawa archdiocese were claiming "donor fatigue" and said they would not pay another cent towards Helpline's legal fees. Tucker replied that an inquiry had been launched into the compensation awarded to Donald Marshall, a wrongly imprisoned Micmac, when it became apparent the lawyer representing him had been "negotiated into the ground" by the province. "We don't want to see that happen here," he cautioned. "Let's keep the playing field as even as possible."

Negotiations, in the meantime, were still proceeding at a snail's pace – despite Helpline's insistence that it had to have a signed deal by June 30, 1992, to take to its members.

Although the Toronto Brothers continued to resist full participation in the negotiations, there were some small indications that they might yet come around. On the invitation of Jim George, the new chairman of the St. John's School Corporation, Douglas Roche attended a meeting of the board in January. He later met privately with George, who told him it was on the advice of the board's lawyer that the board – a separate entity from the Toronto Brothers – was not participating. Such participation, according to the lawyer, was premature. George himself seemed impressed by the process. "All in all, we want this to happen," he said.

The Toronto Brothers had stopped attending meetings, however, and continued to sit on their hands, even after Toronto

Archbishop Aloysius Ambrozic made a personal appeal to Brother Provincial Francis McCrea to join the full process. The archbishop responded to every objection the Brother Provincial raised and expressed his conviction that the process was a useful enterprise. But the Brothers claimed Helpline couldn't be trusted. They did suggest that any of the alleged victims of abuse who approached them on an individual basis would be welcome. Not surprisingly, there were no takers.

McCann didn't know if he had any energy left to continue. Setbacks in the criminal proceedings, including the staying of charges in a case in which he had expected to testify, had been a disappointment. So, too, were accusations by some Helpline members and others that McCann was feathering his own nest and engaging in "empire building." It was true that McCann had received a $42,500 annual salary from the Ontario government for his Helpline work – but this was a far cry from what McCann received through his contract work with police agencies. McCann, in fact, was now living largely on credit cards and whatever assets he could liquidate.

On June 7, he attended a meeting of the Helpline membership in Toronto, but he told Tucker he was far too exhausted to make the reconciliation meeting set for the next day. He was, he said, going to see a doctor for admission into hospital.

McCann's absence from the mediation session did not go over well. Was it a negotiating tactic? some wondered. And if McCann was gone, could the other members of the Helpline executive proceed without him? Tom Marshall complained that the timing couldn't be worse, as he wanted to put a proposal before cabinet before the end of June. Only Brother Provincial Jean-Marc Cantin voiced concern about McCann. He told Roger Tucker he would pray for McCann's recovery.

In McCann's absence, there was some discussion about whether the deal they were making could survive if the Toronto Brothers refused to ratify it. Marshall pointed out that even if the Toronto Brothers refused to join, the victims would still be entitled to counselling and, under the terms of the deal they envisioned, a portion of any award for pain and suffering. Peter Lauwers, the lawyer for the archdiocese of Toronto, noted that the deal, when final, would protect all the parties from civil litigation. The Toronto Brothers, however, would be left exposed if they chose not to participate. Lauwers pointed out, however, that the Catholic Church and other parties could wind up funding a lawsuit by the victims against the Toronto Brothers. "We are creating a situation which is attractive to Helpline members and unattractive to the Brothers of the Christian Schools of Ontario – that Helpline members are given money which could be used to sue the Brothers of the Christian Schools of Ontario." Under the circumstances, he hoped the Toronto Brothers, or at least their insurers, would find the deal irresistible.

Negotiations later bogged down over the question of apologies. Some of the parties wanted the issue to be left informal, while others insisted that it be included in the agreement. Marshall said he wasn't in a position to have a decision on the government's participation in apologies by the June 30 deadline. While he agreed to a proposal that asked all members of the legislature to endorse a resolution containing an apology to the victims of the abuse at St. Joseph's and St. John's, he couldn't guarantee their agreement.

Tucker was at a loss to understand the fudging on apologies. The issue, after all, had been part of the negotiation since its inception. If the process was to be one of healing, an apology was essential.

The issue became even more critical when the negotiators,

including McCann, met in late June at Tucker's office in Ottawa to hammer out what they hoped would be the deal's final details. Roche advised the gathering to tackle the hard issues – the money issues – first, get them out of the way, then they could easily dispense with what he termed the "soft" moral issues.

McCann disagreed. He wasn't interested in talking money until the apology issue was settled.

Roche was livid. "You don't know what you're doing," he told McCann. He accused the Helpline chairman of attempting to hijack the process.

"Hey, Doug," retorted McCann, his voice rising. "I don't think *you* get it. If they are not willing to apologize, we're not going anywhere with this process."

McCann, Tucker, and the Helpline executive moved into a side room. Then they summoned, one by one, the representatives of the other negotiating bodies to determine where they stood on the issue of formal apologies. The Ottawa Brothers had no problem, but the archdiocese of Toronto was not so obliging. Peter Lauwers told the Helpline executive that since Archbishop Ambrozic had nothing to do with the operation of St. John's, and had not been the archbishop when the abuse occurred, he was not about to apologize. He said he had received specific instructions to that effect from his client.

The archdiocese of Ottawa was a little more receptive. While the archdiocese hadn't had any direct control over St. Joseph's, archival documents had shown the involvement of Archbishop M. Joseph Lemieux in the dialogue between the Ottawa Brothers and the government. So, yes, the archdiocese would offer an apology.

Tom Marshall said he realized the importance of the apologies to the victims, but was vague on committing the government. Still, he said, he would put the matter to the Rae government.

Lauwers left the meeting at 7.30 P.M. to catch a flight back to

Toronto, but called from the airport to see where the matter
stood. A Helpline representative told him that the negotiations
were probably over and that they had wasted two years. Without
an apology from the archdiocese, "the last hold out," the deal
was as good as dead.

Perhaps envisioning the headlines and their effect on the
publicity-conscious Ambrozic, Lauwers called back again at 11 P.M.
to confer with Helpline counsel Hugh Blakeney. When he called
again at 2 A.M., it was to dictate to Blakeney the protocol for the
archdiocese's apology.

In advance of the meeting scheduled for the next day, the
Helpline executive, along with the lawyers, held their own breakfast session. It was then that they decided they had to get something "more substantive" from Marshall.

When they summoned him to their caucus, he told them that
it was ridiculous to expect the premier to apologize. Bob Rae had
not been the premier when the story broke in the press, let
alone when the abuse had occurred. If Helpline didn't move on
to other, more important matters on the agenda, he'd leave the
meeting. At this, McCann went to a phone and called the premier's
executive assistant, Fraser Green. He told Green he had just
instructed Hugh Blakeney to write a media statement for immediate release. The statement would begin: "Government of
Ontario Torpedoes Mediation Talks; Refuses to Apologize to
Victims."

Ten minutes later, George Thompson, the province's deputy
attorney general, was on the phone asking what was going on.
He had been yanked out of a meeting to deal with an emergency
he knew nothing about. After McCann filled him in, he said he
would see what he could do. A short while later, Marshall told
McCann that the government had acceded to Helpline's demand.
But he was furious that McCann had gone over his head to his
political superiors.

Still McCann held back, insisting that he receive a commitment in writing. The government was saying "may apologize"
and Helpline was insisting the wording be "will apologize." It
was not a small difference.

"I'm fucking sorry, but if you are not willing to give an apology,
we're not going anywhere," McCann shouted at Marshall. "I don't
trust you guys."

Just after noon on June 24, Helpline felt it had an agreement on
the issue of apologies that its members could accept. Over the
next thirteen hours, the negotiators worked on all the outstanding financial issues. At 1 A.M., they had a deal. It called for the
Ottawa and Toronto Brothers to advance $6.2 million and
$3.6 million, respectively, into a reconciliation fund. The province
would provide $4 million. Although the Toronto Brothers had
not committed themselves, the other parties hoped that they
would see the sense of the arrangement.

Under the terms of the deal, the victims would apply to a panel
of independent assessors picked from the province's Criminal
Injuries Compensation Board, which would determine the valid-
ity of each claim and, if it was probable that the abuse had
occurred, would award compensation for pain and suffering.

The deal anticipated there would be four hundred victims, and
that the individual compensation awards would total nearly
$30,000. That figure was reached by assuming the average award
from the compensation board assessors would be $10,000, which
would be paid by the province. The Christian Brothers would
issue another cheque to the victim for 1.6 times the assessed
amount. In addition, the victims would all be eligible to apply
for an opportunity grant, provided by the two archdioceses, for
a maximum of $3,000 to use to further their education, pay
medical or dental expenses, or upgrade their job skills. A clause

in the agreement allowed the victims to apply for the grant on behalf of their children or grandchildren if they so chose. Another provided for widows to receive partial benefits.

There was also a provision to bolster the compensation to severely abused wards. An amount equal to one quarter of each award was set by the assessors, to be placed in a fund to be divided at the panel's discretion once all claims had been heard.

The province would pick up the cost of counselling Ontario victims while the Christian Brothers and the archdioceses agreed to provide $250,000 each for counselling services for victims living outside Ontario.

The Christian Brothers and archdioceses would also pay the estimated $1-million cost of ratifying and implementing the package and for funding a recorder, who would document victim accounts of the abuse at St. Joseph's and St. John's in a public report. The Reconciliation Process Implementation Committee, composed of representatives of the Church, Christian Brothers, government, and victims, would be assigned the task of implementing the deal and processing the opportunity grant claims. The committee would also award a token payment for lost wages to former wards who were never paid for the work they did – for farms, businesses, and the Brothers – while they were in the training schools.

The negotiators were tired, but happy to have finally reached an accord. Unfortunately, for the next six days, Douglas Roche received a raft of amendments from the lawyers of the various organizations. On the eve of the June 30 deadline, Roche concluded that more work remained to be done. The press conference planned for July 30 was rescheduled for August 13, and less than forty-eight hours before that date, the province and Helpline were still making amendments.

The press conference, held simultaneously via satellite hook-up in Ottawa and Toronto, with representatives from almost all affected parties in attendance in each city, was a well-scripted affair. Roche had even provided all the participants with a list of previously agreed-upon answers to anticipated questions.

The mere fact they were holding a press conference triggered a minor controversy. Police and prosecutors handling the criminal cases were furious that they had not been consulted and worried about the effect the announcement could have upon their efforts to gain convictions. Although compensation negotiations were known to have been under way, the announcement of an actual dollar figure made the prosecutors cringe. Now, they feared, victims could be seen to have "a motive" to lie.

In Toronto, Roche opened the press conference by introducing the agreement, which he described as "unprecedented in North America." He credited Roger Tucker and Helpline for its genesis. While the elements of the agreement were no panacea for the problem of child abuse, he said, they did provide strategies for dealing with the needs of the people involved. He hoped it would serve as a model for other groups seeking reconciliation and healing.

McCann, in turn, thanked Roche for his tireless efforts in bringing the parties together to create what he called an historic agreement. "We disclosed our pain and we told our stories so that others might be spared a similar fate," he said. "Children are our most precious resource. They are our most prized treasures. They are our memories and our future. If this process helps us spare only one child from abuse, then it will have been successful."

Grant Hartley boldly predicted that 97 to 98 per cent of the Helpline membership would find the agreement acceptable. McCann, however, said he had no idea if the membership would accept or reject the package. He would be going on the road to explain it and collect their votes.

The deal would be worth $16,135,250, which, if equally divided
among the approximately four hundred victims, would have given
each about $40,000. But Roche stressed that the figure was an esti-
mate, and since each victim had to apply individually and be
assessed on the basis of his own experience, the awards could
range from nothing to more than $40,000.

Reporters were told that victims who accepted the agreement
would be giving up their right to sue. However, should they
choose not to sign the agreement, the litigation route would still
be open to them. When the issue of a public inquiry was raised,
Roche answered without pause. "The participants do not want
to have a public inquiry."

Father Edward Boehler, of the Toronto archdiocese, was left
to explain where the Toronto Brothers stood, but he could not
confirm whether they would participate. "It's to be hoped that
at some point in the future, they will see fit to get involved in
this. We are hopeful of that."

No one asked what would happen to the agreement if the
Toronto Brothers did not participate. McCann, himself, did not
know what the outcome would be in that eventuality. As the
September 30 deadline for all parties to ratify the agreement
approached, he became fearful that the deal would collapse like
a house of cards.

The deal had its critics. Michael MacEachern, publisher of the
Ottawa Catholic newsletter *The Orator*, complained, "It is today's
taxpayer and today's Roman Catholic who is going to pay for these
things." He also was worried that the closed-door compensation
hearings might result in some of the guilty going unpunished by
the courts.

Reaction from former wards to the deal was mixed, too. In
North Bay, Gerry Belecque called it a fair deal, but he wanted to

see a clearer, stronger message sent to clergy that the Church would no longer tolerate such behaviour. As well, he was unhappy with the condition that he would have to relinquish his right to sue, then rely on the generosity of the authorities for compensation.

There was some dismay at the low amount of the financial awards that could be expected. Gerry Sirois said the Church and the government were getting away dirt cheap. McCann put it into perspective for reporters by telling them the average award would be about half a reporter's annual salary. It was, admittedly, not the millions some Helpline members felt they deserved, particularly those who knew of settlements in similar cases in the United States. Moreover, it was far less than the highest sexual abuse judgment awarded by a Canadian court, $100,000. At the same time, the Helpline executive reminded its members not to underestimate the value of the other benefits of the deal: the counselling, the educational upgrading, the medical and dental benefits, and the apologies. It was to be a much friendlier process than litigation.

After the deal was announced, an Ottawa lawyer, Stephen Appotive, put out feelers to see if there were enough victims unhappy with the deal to launch a class-action suit. In a letter dated September 4 and circulated to some Helpline members, Appotive advised those interested in exploring civil litigation to contact his office before the deal was ratified.

"I feel some individuals could get higher monetary compensation through the court system, but they have to decide whether it is worth the emotional upheaval and time delay," he explained. "In my view, the case would be successful, but it would be a long road to get to that point."

Ontario still had no legislation permitting class-action lawsuits, but such legislation was expected to be in place soon. Appotive's plan was to launch a suit in one victim's name, then add others once the legislation passed. The biggest hurdle would be funding such a suit. Appotive had heard the province might establish a fund to help launch some class-action suits, but he didn't know what conditions would be attached. Certainly, none of the former wards could afford it. In all likelihood it would be his own law firm that would have to fund the case, a very expensive proposition.

McCann was not happy about Appotive's proposal, but he need not have worried. Most members accepted Roger Tucker's opinion that their deal was the best deal available. When the ballots were counted after a series of meetings across the country, only seven members had voted against the agreement. The over-whelming majority agreed with McCann, who said he was "not interested in spending the next ten years of my life fighting in court. That won't address any of the issues that prompted me to come forward."

He continued, "We spent tens of thousands of dollars researching this thing. Lawyers across Canada looked at all the possibilities – good and bad. We felt the potential for re-abuse was great and [civil litigation] would not address any of the issues. No court is going to issue an apology. No court is going to go into the issue of public education and prevention and re-search into child abuse or provide benefits to the families and widows of these guys. We concluded that it wouldn't heal us or reconcile us."

At a press conference called by McCann on the eve of the September 30 ratification deadline, McCann tried to prod the Toronto Brothers into participating. "If they are Christian Brothers, they had better examine what Christian means," he told reporters. "It means Christ-like. If Jesus Christ was the head of the order today, what would his answer be?"

McCann said he had been all around the country, travelling almost non-stop, attending twenty Helpline meetings, talking to the victims, hearing their stories. More than 160 members were now in counselling, and the demand for the service was growing. Helpline now had 570 former wards signed up as members. Just over a third had joined since the agreement was announced.

"As they have talked about the effects of the abuse, I've watched grown men and their wives crying their hearts out," he said. "I hear their cries for healing and counselling and I hear the Christian Brothers say, 'We will do whatever we can to help these people.' The questions is – when? The victims are saying 'now' is the time."

But the deadline passed without action, or reaction, from Brother Provincial Francis McCrea or Melville O'Donohue of the Toronto Brothers. O'Donohue simply told the *Toronto Star* it would be improper for him to discuss the issue while criminal charges were pending against members of the Toronto order.

Tom Marshall couldn't comprehend the Brothers' reluctance. "Their view is the membership of Helpline is largely composed of people who don't have claims capable of being substantiated," he noted. "Well, I believe the process set out in the agreement is sufficiently tight to weed out spurious claims. I think the Toronto Brothers are torn between trying to recognize a community responsibility and recognizing that they have a duty and obligation to stand four-square behind their members."

Other members of Helpline were just as dismayed. Gerry Sirois said he likely would never have come forward with his story had he realized the amount of anguish he and the other wards would experience after the fact. The major fault with the reconciliation package, as he saw it, was that it forced him to put his faith back in a system that had already failed him.

In November, Helpline decided to launch a three-day phone campaign urging the Toronto Brothers to participate in the deal. The Brothers had said publicly that they wanted to talk to the victims so McCann sent the members the phone numbers of McCrea, O'Donohue, and Brother George Morgan, a member of the governing council. "Do not call if you are going to get mad at them," McCann advised. "It will not help. Let them know that you want them to deal with your needs and concerns through the reconciliation agreement and Helpline. They would like to deal with us one by one to divide and conquer us. Do not give them the opportunity."

The telephone campaign didn't work, however, and Roche finally recommended that the parties proceed with the agreement without the Toronto Brothers and without their proposed contribution to the compensation fund. "It's much better to proceed with five-sixths of the parties than none at all," he said.

Ronald Caza, the lawyer for the Ottawa Brothers, agreed. "With all the work that has been done, it would be insane to let that go down the drain."

McCann was concerned that to proceed without the Toronto Brothers would effectively split the Helpline membership into two groups, one group receiving 40 per cent less in compensation than the other. He and Tucker devised a plan to split the $6-million contribution from the Ottawa Brothers between the former wards of St. John's and St. Joseph's – a plan overwhelmingly approved by the wards of St. Joseph's in a separate vote. It would mean they would receive an award 20 per cent smaller themselves, but since the St. John's wards were not bound in an agreement with the Toronto Brothers, it freed them to launch a civil class-action suit against the order. If successful, all the former wards who were eligible for compensation would share in that settlement.

On December 11, McCann announced the signing of the historic $13-million compensation deal by the former wards, the Catholic Church, the Ontario government, and the Ottawa Brothers. At the press conference, it was revealed that the average cash settlement would now be roughly $23,000. However, the counselling and benefits package, worth an estimated $10,000 to each ward, would remain in place. Now, instead of receiving from the Ottawa Brothers an additional award 1.6 times the compensation board amount, victims would receive an additional amount that was almost equal to the compensation board figure.

Helpline made it clear that the membership would continue to press the Toronto Brothers, and threatened to launch a $300-million lawsuit against them. "I want to warn the Toronto Brothers that they will be facing a different kind of opponent in the courtroom," said McCann.

Melville O'Donohue called the threat absurd. "Why don't they make it an even $500 million and I will see them in court? Mr. McCann apparently thinks he can scare the Christian Brothers of Toronto into paying $3 million out of court."

O'Donohue claimed there was no comparison in the way the two schools were run and certainly nothing to justify forking out $3 million. "Our position is that the St. John's Training School for Boys is a well-run school and it has been for a hundred years."

13

Judgement Day

•

"Ye shall not afflict any widow, or fatherless child. If thou afflict them in any wise, and they cry at all unto me, I will surely hear their cry."
— Exodus 22, 22-23

Aimé Joseph Bergeron stood in the prisoner's dock of the Ottawa courtroom with arms folded across his chest as the court clerk read aloud in French the charges against him.

Buggery. Indecent assault. It seemed inconceivable that the frail, white-haired seventy-seven-year-old Christian Brother before Madam Justice Louise Charron could possibly have committed the horrific crimes against children of which he was being accused.

He stood, nervously fingering the crucifix around his neck, as his lawyer begged the court's indulgence to allow him to sit in a comfortable chair at the table behind him, rather than on the hard wooden bench of the glassed-in prisoner's dock. Thus began two years of trials of current and former Christian Brothers from St. Joseph's Training School in Alfred.

Bergeron was known as Brother Gabriel over the sixteen years he toiled at St. Joseph's. The tenth of thirteen children, he had joined the Christian Brothers on January 7, 1929, at the age of thirteen.

When his lack of academic prowess was discovered, he was

shunted into janitorial duties, first working alongside a plumber until he acquired sufficient skill and experience to work for seventeen years as a maintenance man at a grade school the Christian Brothers ran in Laval. He arrived at St. Joseph's in August 1949 and stayed there as plumber and handyman until 1964. Although now retired, he still did maintenance work around the Brothers' residence where he lived in Ottawa. Several elderly Brothers from the residence had accompanied him to court for moral support.

The Crown's first witness was Gerry Belecque. A slightly built man, with receding dark hair and dark eyes, Belecque was wearing a dapper navy-blue suit, white shirt, and maroon tie.

Thumbing through a personal photo album that he had brought with him, Belecque described for the court the events that led him to Alfred and the problems he suffered since. At times he would illustrate his narrative with drawings or with references to the photographs he had taken with a small Kodak camera at St. Joseph's.

Belecque had been fourteen when he was sent to St. Joseph's in February 1959 for breaching a probation order for an earlier theft. While on probation – for stealing chocolate bars from a transport truck – he and several friends had hitchhiked to Toronto. The short holiday cost him eighteen months at St. Joseph's.

He described walking into the workshop unannounced one day to find Brother Gabriel standing in front of a small boy, who was on his knees fellating the Brother. Not long after, Brother Gabriel approached Belecque from behind in the workshop and began to kiss his neck, rub his buttocks, then gently squeeze his genitals.

"I was exasperated," Belecque said. "I didn't know what to do. I pinched his penis a couple of times and he kept wanting me to do more. I turned around and looked at him in the face and I guess it was a confrontation. He knew I was mad and I wasn't going to let him continue."

Belecque said he had never spoken to anyone about the incident, out of fear and shame. "In my opinion, what happened with me was. . . ." He stopped, gave out a strained laugh, and sat silent in the witness box for a moment. "It was more of a sinful act as opposed to a criminal act that he committed upon me and, in my opinion, that act also made me a sinner. We didn't talk about that kind of thing. I was told that a sexual thing is taboo. I had no thoughts of telling anybody. It was too embarrassing for me. If I went to tell anyone else about it, they would call me a queer or something."

Belecque said he had complained thirty years after the fact to the OPP on the advice of a therapist who told him that if he did not confront his past, it would poison the remainder of his life. He told Charron he was still "damn mad" about what happened and he hoped the trial would help resolve his anger.

"I said at the beginning I was not interested in seeing an old man going to jail," he said, glaring at Bergeron, who was immersed in a worn black prayer book. "But if that person cannot stand and admit what he has done and apologize for what he has done, then I am going ahead with this and it's going to be a fight."

Belecque was followed to the witness box by a balding, bespectacled high-school janitor, Denis Oiseau (not his real name). Oiseau allegedly had been raped by Bergeron in 1957, and talking about it in open court was the most difficult thing he had ever been asked to do. A reluctant witness, he had initially refused, but the Crown attorney had stressed the importance of the first trial and had made it clear he could be subpoenaed if he didn't show up on his own volition. He finally agreed to testify, but on the condition that he would not have to testify against two other Brothers whom he also had accused of abusing him.

With downcast eyes, laboured breath, and a breaking voice, Oiseau told, in French, how he had been just twelve when he was

sent to St. Joseph's for theft in 1957. While there, he was raped
by another student and then gang-raped by Brother Gabriel and
Brother Joseph, the Hook.

In the latter episode, he said that Brother Gabriel pinned his
shoulder to the bed in Brother Joseph's room while the Hook
buggered him. "It hurt. I raised my head and Brother Gabriel had
his penis close to my face. I figured he was trying to put it in my
mouth so I hid my head in the pillow. After Brother Joseph was
done there, Brother Gabriel got on top of me and done the same
thing."

Oiseau testified that both these Brothers tried to rape him on
another occasion, but he resisted so strenuously that Brother
Gabriel decided against it, complaining that "it was no fun" when
Oiseau struggled so much.

Bergeron, sitting behind his lawyer, reacted calmly to the testimony. He set his beaded rosary aside and started to clean his
ears with a Q-tip.

Oiseau testified he did not want to see Bergeron put in jail —
retribution was of no interest to him — but he did hope counselling would stop the elderly man from abusing children in the
future. "Brother Gabriel will have to answer to a higher court,"
he concluded.

Paul Gagnon, who appeared on the stand April 14, was a stark
contrast to Oiseau. The stocky forty-two-year-old house painter
from Orleans, an Ottawa suburb, wanted the world to know what
happened to him at the hands of Bergeron. He sat in the witness
box, his arms across his chest, glaring at the monk. He pulled a
tattered photograph from his wallet and showed it to the judge.
It was a photo, he said, that was taken the day he arrived at
Alfred. He wanted the judge to see him as he was then.

When assistant Crown attorney Ronald Laliberté asked him
to point out his abuser, Gagnon levelled a finger at Bergeron. "I
will always remember that pervert's face."

Sent to St. Joseph's at age eleven for the theft of a bicycle on September 12, 1960, Gagnon said Brother Gabriel visited his home once in 1965. He found the monk in the basement with his younger brothers. "I rushed downstairs and he had his arm around my little brother. I told my brothers to get the hell upstairs as fast as they could, and I told that pervert to get out and never come back."

"Have you seen him since?" asked Laliberté.

"Only in my nightmares," spat Gagnon, eyeing Bergeron, who sat with his head bowed and eyes closed.

Gagnon's appearance at the monk's trial was both interesting and embarrassing for the authorities. Interesting because he was there at the behest of Laliberté to provide what the Crown called "similar fact evidence," as a sort of a credibility booster to the other alleged victims. The embarrassment belonged to the OPP who, having interviewed Gagnon in 1990, had planned to lay a charge against Bergeron on his behalf but failed to do so. His statement had been lost in the blizzard of information that the investigation had generated. "I was told somebody had goofed it up," Gagnon told the court.

Det. Sgt. Bob Carpenter explained later, "The long and short of it is, we missed it. We have thousands of pages of statements and millions of bits of information and, like I say, there is no fancy excuse. We simply missed the charge."

Gagnon said he had agreed to come forward, despite the foul-up, in the interests of justice. Yes, he was angry about the screw-up, angry that Bergeron would not be punished for his alleged offence against him but, he said, no person should be permitted to do the things Bergeron had done to children.

His first sexual encounter with the monk occurred when he was working in St. Joseph's boiler room. Gagnon had been ordered by Brother Gabriel to climb inside the boiler tank wearing only a bathing suit to scrub its walls with a wire brush. When he came out, the Brother used a towel to wipe the perspiration off Gagnon's body.

"He told me I had to take off my bathing suit so he could dry me better," Gagnon continued. "I didn't want to. He sort of grabbed me and started to play with my penis. The next thing I knew, I was in his office, sitting in the chair, and he got down on his knees and started sucking me off."

At this, Bergeron, who had been studiously examining his prayer book, made the sign of the cross, clasped his gnarled hands together, and started to pray.

Under cross-examination by defence lawyer Robert Doyle, Gagnon further detailed Bergeron's abuse. The monk, he said, liked to fondle his penis and would masturbate as he played with the boy. "Sometimes he ejaculated on my clothes, on the chair, on the floor. He would get his rocks off, get dressed real fast, and kick me out of the furnace room. He would do this two or three times a week."

When asked what he wanted from the court proceedings, Gagnon said he hoped they would put the Christian Brothers out of the child-care business forever. And, he added, "I personally think they should all be castrated."

The fourth and final witness against Bergeron, Anthony St. Louis, a forty-nine-year-old Salvation Army truck driver and born-again Christian from St. Catharines, described being assaulted by Brother Gabriel in the spring of 1955 when he was about twelve years old.

He was in the washroom, urinating, when a man he identified as Brother Gabriel grabbed his penis. "I remember being pulled in to the washroom cubicle. My pants were brought down. I was on a seat, a toilet, and he played with my penis and tried to masturbate me. Then, somehow, he got on his knees and took my penis and put it in his mouth and sucked on it very hard. *Très vigoureuse.*"

In spite of the manner in which Brother Gabriel abused him, St. Louis said that at the time he had looked up to him as something of a friend. It was the first time anyone had ever showed him anything resembling affection. "When I came into the school, it was very scary. The Brothers were rough. I had no love from my parents so going to a training school and meeting a Brother was something I needed. I needed someone to love me. I think I felt his friendliness as love."

He had even offered to assist Brother Gabriel, who was the priest's assistant, in the maintenance of the chapel. Even there, however, there was no solace. Moments after the monk greeted him in the chapel, he pulled off St. Louis' trousers and began to sexually assault him.

St. Louis said that when he finally told another Brother about the incidents, the Brother in whom he confided flew into a rage and began screaming at him. "He came at me like a fly. He punched me in the face, the stomach. I fell on the floor and he kicked me in the stomach and in the back. It was just brutal."

As he was being beaten, St. Louis saw Brother Gabriel standing behind his attacker, saying and doing nothing.

Aimé Bergeron began to testify in French in his own defence on April 16, the Thursday before Easter, and was still being examined by his lawyer, Robert Doyle, when court adjourned for the weekend. When court resumed April 21, after the Easter break, Doyle took his client through all of the allegations and asked the Brother to respond to each one. Bergeron said he did not remember most of the boys. He denied having sex with them. Or at least with the three named in the charges against him.

Pausing, Doyle slid behind the prosecutor and tipped him off to what was coming by whispering into his ear, "Here is your Easter present." Over the Easter break, Bergeron had confided in his lawyer that he did recall one of the boys, Paul Gagnon.

Returning his attention to his client in the witness box, Doyle asked Bergeron if he had had sexual relations with Gagnon. "I performed fellatio on him five or six times," Bergeron responded, adding that the two "took turns" fellating each other. Laliberté looked up in astonishment. Charron wasn't quite sure she had heard the response correctly.

Bergeron went on to say he also had made an unsuccessful attempt at anal sex with Gagnon. "There were moments where I was very tired – moments of weakness," he explained.

Under cross-examination by Laliberté later in the day, Bergeron told the court that, yes, he was a paedophile. "It's a weakness," he admitted. "We're not perfect. God can accept a weakness. The good Lord will forgive us like anybody else."

Laliberté asked Bergeron what kind of boys he found attractive. "Do you find me attractive?"

"You are a good-looking boy," Bergeron replied, "but you are too old." (Laliberté had just turned thirty-one.)

"So what attracts you?" asked Laliberté. "Boys, ten and eleven?"

"Yes."

When asked if he was stimulated by his encounters with Gagnon, Bergeron sat silent for a moment.

"Yes," he said finally. "I'm guilty."

"Do you know you can't be convicted for the assaults on Gagnon?" Laliberté asked him.

"Yes, that's what they told me," he answered. Indeed, the monk still denied abusing any of the other children in the school. He told the court he believed Gagnon was exaggerating the extent of the abuse and that the other complainants had conspired against him and the other Brothers. Lying is easy for them, but not for him, he maintained. "You can ask me fifty times and I can't lie because I swore on the Bible."

Outside the courtroom, Doyle conceded his client's admission could be damaging to his case, but he did not consider it fatal. "It doesn't automatically shatter it or blow it to smithereens."

The following day, Charron delivered her verdict. She was not, she said, impressed by the Brother's admission of committing a crime for which he had not been charged. If anything, his testimony showed the man had a "clear, but selective memory." At the same time, Charron said that she would not have allowed Bergeron's confession to the attack on Gagnon to be entered as evidence if there had been a jury. However, she had not relied on that evidence in her decision to find Aimé Joseph Bergeron guilty on two counts of indecent assault and one of buggery.

As Charron read the verdict, the monk stared straight ahead, rocking gently back and forth. He remained in his seat for ten minutes after the courtroom had cleared, then made his way through a throng of reporters and photographers to a waiting car.

Outside the courtroom, Paul Gagnon was ecstatic.

"Got him!" he exclaimed, throwing his arms happily around another former ward who had been in the courtroom to hear the verdict. "It is about time! For years I thought there wasn't any justice for little boys from Alfred. God bless that judge. I am forty-two years old and I've never felt as good as I do today."

The other victims were more restrained. "For thirty-four years I waited for this," said Oiseau. "Now it is over with. I just want to get on with my life. The justice system worked. We finally got justice."

Anthony St. Louis said the months leading up to and during the trial were a severe strain. He was exhausted. "Going to court was like going to hell and back," he said. He hoped the conviction could heal his wounded soul. "The scriptures tell you to speak the truth and the truth will set you free. We're going to put it behind us now."

The conviction, which Bergeron would later appeal, had wide implications. For months, the victims, the Church, and the government had been holding meetings to negotiate some form of compensation for the victims, but all the groups had been holding back to see what the courts would do with the first case. Bergeron's conviction spurred the process on.

But neither Gerry Belecque nor David McCann saw the verdict as cause for celebration. Although the conviction was important to them, it brought them no cheer. Belecque said he would have been happier if Bergeron had admitted molesting the boys. Instead, the man continued the denial that he and the others had lived with their entire lives. "If the man had apologized, it would have meant a lot more to me," said Belecque. "It's just the arrogance of the man." McCann said he felt vindicated, but also very sad. "That school didn't operate in isolation. People knew about what was going on. They let it go on for decades."

The *Ottawa Sun* had no compunction against calling for the monk's head. In an April 27 editorial headlined "PENANCE," it demanded that Aimé Bergeron be sent to jail. "We do not care that he's old, and small, and frail," it stated. "We do not care that the charges for which he is now been convicted go back three decades. Did he care, more than 30 years ago, that the victims he so graphically assaulted were young, and small, and frail in their vulnerability? No, he did not. . . . Well, the court has found him guilty of all charges and so too will his God."

Brother Provincial Jean-Marc Cantin apologized to the four victims, hoping that it would, at the very least, help them close the door on a troubling past. "Although we can never erase the past, the Brothers of the Christian Schools will make every necessary effort to find the appropriate means of helping the victims and preventing those types of incidents again."

Christian Brothers' lawyer Ronald Caza added that the Ottawa order was considering a compensation package that would include a financial settlement for each former ward once the courts determined whether or not he was a bona fide victim.

Also amid the fallout of the trial was heard the lament of a police officer with a guilty conscience. John Williams, a retired Ottawa Police constable, told the *Ottawa Citizen* how he had often visited St. Joseph's as a volunteer on the annual sports day. During one of those visits, wards at the training school tried to complain about the abuse, but were ignored. He said he had found hidden inside his sports day program a typewritten note describing the physical abuse being inflicted upon the boys by the Christian Brothers. The note told of an eleven-year-old boy who, after defecating in his bed, had been left to stand outside in the winter cold with the excrement-covered sheets wrapped around his head until they froze to his face. It described how, as punishment, boys were forced to stand, clad only in their shorts, in front of open windows in midwinter, how they were forced to perch on their toes with tacks under their heels to make sure their feet didn't touch the ground.

Williams remembered seeing the blackened eye and badly swollen face of one fourteen-year-old boy. When he inquired about the injuries, the boy told him he had been punished for poor behaviour.

Williams said he discussed the allegations with a senior officer who also attended the same sports day, but was instructed to ignore it. They were bad bastards and probably deserved everything they got, the officer told him. That evening, Williams showed the note to his wife, and while it made them both very angry, he never took his concerns further.

Thirty years later, Bergeron's conviction confirmed Williams' worst fears. He had been one of the men in authority who had turned his back on the children of St. Joseph's.

"I feel very guilty," he said. "I apologize to the men now for not doing something about it then."

At Bergeron's sentencing hearing on September 11, 1992, a psychiatrist testified that the monk was a paedophile, with an attraction to both young boys and girls below age fourteen. Bergeron, he said, had scored very poorly on sexual "aptitude" testing and demonstrated low intelligence. In another report prepared for the court by the defence, an Ottawa criminologist revealed that Bergeron had been sexually molested as a young boy by a friend of the family. The monk also told him that a friend of one of his brothers had tried to sodomize him. The criminologist's report claimed there was a deviant subculture operating in the school, "which conferred an air of legitimacy to the victimization acts." He attributed Bergeron's participation in this deviant behaviour to the same factors that motivated members of a reserve police battalion in the Second World War to murder eighty-three thousand Jews: isolation, peer pressure, victim desensitization, and ambition. "I am of the opinion that the constant abuse in Alfred is in great part the result of a combination of systemic factors," he wrote.

Robert Doyle asked for leniency for his client, saying the old man's cataracts, weak heart, and arthritis made him a poor candidate for the rigours of prison.

Charron sentenced the Brother to imprisonment for two years less a day. She recommended Bergeron be considered for a temporary absence program that would allow him to live in a halfway house. Had he not been old and infirm, he would have gone to prison for four years, she said.

Most of the victims were satisfied. "I wished he would have got more than that, but I'm satisfied as long as he is paying for what he did to us," said Gagnon.

The next former Christian Brother to go to trial was seventy-four-year-old Pierre Durocher of Longueuil, Quebec. Less than two weeks after Bergeron's trial ended, Durocher limped into court on the arm of his wife, Marie, to face charges of assault, attempted sodomy, and three counts of indecent assault. At a preliminary hearing in 1991, David McCann had testified that Durocher, known as Brother Peter when he taught at St. Joseph's, had fondled him on two separate occasions in the late 1950s. He told the hearing that under the guise of checking for contraband, Brother Peter would stick his hands in McCann's pockets and fondle his genitals.

Another former ward, who was in Brother Peter's class from 1956 to 1959, testified at the same hearing that the Brother often would play with his penis in the classroom. Sometimes the Brother engaged in mutual masturbation with him at the quarry. He also alleged that once Brother Peter attempted to have anal sex with him, but stopped when he complained of the pain. At the same time, the former ward testified that he admired Brother Peter and enjoyed the sexual encounters with him. "When he molested me, I enjoyed it and I am telling you I enjoyed it," said the man, who was convicted of sexual assault in 1987 and who had been under psychiatric care. "It felt good."

When the legal arguments in the case opened May 4, 1992, Durocher's lawyer, Gabriel Lapointe, declared that his client and other Brothers were being unfairly singled out for prosecution since no civilians who worked at the school were charged. He pointed out to Mr. Justice Pierre Mercier that at least fifteen former wards had complained that they were abused by civilian staff at St. Joseph's, yet no civilians had been charged.

Police and Crown attorneys were quick to dismiss the claims, saying the Brothers and civilians were all assessed in similar fashion to determine if there was evidence to lay charges. "The same yardstick was used as to whether the Brothers were charged," explained Det. Sgt. Bob Carpenter.

One week later, Lapointe, a prominent Montreal lawyer who had been hired to represent eight Christian Brothers, tried to stay the proceedings again, this time by arguing that his client's poor health impaired his ability to defend himself.

Psychiatrist Jocelyn Aubut testified that a stroke Durocher had suffered in 1985 left him with short- and long-term memory lapses that caused him to get lost in shopping malls and made even simple tasks difficult. "He can be a bit like a child in that he can find himself at the information centres of the shopping mall paging his wife to come and get him," Aubut said.

Another doctor, a specialist in biological psychiatry, told the court he put Durocher through a series of tests in 1991, which, when analysed, pointed to serious memory problems. Durocher, for instance, could remember only two of the subjects he taught during the ten years he spent at the school. Nor could he remember the names of the principals of the school during his tenure. "Those are things that a teacher, if he taught in the same place for ten years, should remember," he said.

Marie Durocher testified that her husband relied upon her for his daily needs. He forgets birthdays, names of friends, and can't remember at suppertime what he had for lunch, she said.

Mrs. Durocher, who had married her husband after he left the Christian Brothers in 1975, said she had reviewed with him the statements made by former wards, but he couldn't remember the students.

On May 14, the judge stopped the trial from proceeding, saying it would be impossible for the former monk to have a fair and just trial. "I am convinced that Mr. Durocher could not give full answer in defence," Mercier ruled. "For reasons beyond his control, he could only have come here and said, 'I don't remember.'"

After the ruling, David McCann, surrounded by reporters outside the courtroom, bemoaned the fact that he was denied the opportunity to give his evidence to the court. "I waited over thirty years to stand up and make my allegations," he said. "Justice delayed is justice denied."

In June, lawyer Gilles Charlebois tried to derail the trial of his client, fifty-three-year-old Sylvio Valade of Sudbury. Appearing in Ottawa before Madam Justice Louise Charron, Charlebois argued that it was an abuse of the judicial process for officials to conduct an investigation in 1960 into allegations against Valade and then wait thirty years before laying a charge. His client had admitted to authorities that, in 1960, when he was known as Brother Sylvio, he had fondled Bobbie Jenkins, and he had been punished by being dismissed from the order.

"He thought it was all behind him," Charlebois told Charron. "The facts seem clear. The ministry not only had the choice to lay a charge [in 1960], but every reason to believe it happened." Why, he wanted to know, had his client not been charged then?

It appeared, Charlebois continued, that no one at the time of the incident was interested in having charges laid – not the Ministry of Reform Institutions, not Jenkins' mother, and not Jenkins' lawyer. So why lay the charges now?

Ronald Laliberté, however, countered that Valade had committed a serious breach of trust. It was in the public interest to pursue the prosecution of Valade even if it was thirty years after the fact.

On June 3, Charron dismissed Charlebois' motion, and Valade stood up to plead guilty to indecent assault. He had been astonished, he said, when police showed up at his door thirty years after his dismissal from the order. Now, he just wanted the anguish to end.

After leaving the Christian Brothers, Valade had led an exemplary life. He had returned to his home town of Sudbury, obtained a job as a lab technician, married, and raised three children, who were now between the ages of eighteen and twenty-eight. He worked with the Boy Scouts and other children through various volunteer groups. No complaints had ever been lodged about his participation in these activities.

Charron retired to consider whether Valade should receive a short jail term, an absolute discharge, or a suspended sentence. Bobbie Jenkins, for his part, was satisfied that justice had arrived for Brother Sylvio. The real punishment, he told reporters, was having to admit the crime publicly. "If he does an hour in jail, I would be happy," said Jenkins. "I feel sorry for his wife and children. I don't want to see them hurt."

Jenkins had spent the better part of his life trying to forget the incident. Valade was twenty at the time of the assault, Jenkins, twelve. Such a long, long time ago. It seemed another lifetime.

Charron gave Valade a suspended sentence, thirty days' probation, and ordered him to write a letter of apology to the victim.

Later that June, seventy-six-year-old Camille Huot of Montreal hobbled into Ottawa's Elgin Street courthouse, clutching a wooden cane in one hand. With his large glasses and grey side-burns, he seemed the very soul of a kindly senior citizen.

A member of the Christian Brothers for fifty-four years, Huot, too, was represented by Gabriel Lapointe, whose often brilliant legal manoeuvres in defence of clients had led some to call him "the Eddie Greenspan of Quebec." Lapointe, brother of Quebec comedy actor Jean Lapointe, planned to retire after his $2-million defence of the Christian Brothers.

Two witnesses carried the Crown's case against Huot, who had been the placement officer at St. Joseph's from 1962 to 1964. The first was Boyd St. Brieux (not his real name), a large, dark, mus-cular Sudbury man, who had been sent to St. Joseph's in 1963 at fifteen for being "unmanageable."

Brother Camille, he said, liked to give the impression that he was a caring, friendly man, but virtually every time he had St. Brieux alone somewhere, he would molest him. The assaults often occurred when he was in the car with the Brother en route to a work assignment in the community. Once, while working on a farm, he became sick during the night and asked to be returned to the training school. Brother Camille was sent to fetch him.

"As soon as he got into the car, he says, 'Why don't you sit closer to me? I will take care of you.'" St. Brieux said Brother Camille would either grab him by the genitals or try to coerce him to touch his genitals. "He was a sex maniac. I am angry, you know. Like shit, man, when I needed understanding and love, he would try to molest me."

He testified that once Brother Camille grabbed him by the head and pressed his face against his groin. "He was rubbing my face on him. I just felt scared. I remember him saying [in French], 'You're such a nice boy. You're such a fine boy.'"

St. Brieux said he had complained to the school superinten-dent, but to no avail. The abuse had stayed with him all his life.

He couldn't talk about it. It made him confused about his own sexual orientation.

"If Brother Camille is pleading not guilty, then he is calling me a liar, and I have had this all my life and I am here to prove that it is not a lie. I hope some day to come to terms with this and basically just be a part of society – a normal human being. I am just sick and tired of putting on a mask and not really knowing who the hell I am."

In his cross-examination, Lapointe vigorously pursued the issue of compensation. He wanted to show the court that the former ward had a motivation to lie to collect money through the compensation package.

But St. Brieux, who was living on a disability pension of $756 a month, said he hadn't testified in the hopes of receiving money. That was not what the negotiations were about. "We're hoping to get a chance to change the system of how young boys are being treated," he said. "I hope to regain some of the education I have lost and medical benefits. Some people need dental care. Those are the areas I am interested in."

The second witness for the prosecution had crossed the country for his day in court. A tall, forty-five-year-old widower from British Columbia, Lawrence Siple had been sent to St. Joseph's in 1962 at age fifteen. Like St. Brieux, he remembered Brother Camille as a friendly, outgoing man who seemed to care about his welfare. He said the Brother often invited him into his office for a beer and talk. Sometimes the Brother would make a pass at him, said Siple, but he was easily rebuffed.

After Siple left St. Joseph's, Brother Camille had visited him one day at his parent's cottage near Kapuskasing, in Northern Ontario. Siple had come in from a day's fishing to find the grinning monk waiting on the dock. It was his job as the training school's placement officer, he told Siple, to check on him. The monk stayed for dinner, and subsequently accepted the family's invitation to spend the night at the cottage, although Siple's mother and father had to return to Kapuskasing that evening.

After his parents left, Siple said Brother Camille gave the under-age youth a beer from the fridge, and they drank and chatted until nearly midnight. But when it came time to turn in for the night, Brother Camille showed a decidedly less amiable side.

"When we were in the bedroom," Siple explained, "he pulled me closer to him and started to grope around with his hands, started to kiss me on the lips, penetrating my mouth with his tongue. He kept on groping, and I kept on trying to get away. He pulled me down on the bed and kept saying, 'Relax. Take it easy.' He started to choke me with his forearm, and he kept insisting everything was going to be all right."

Siple said the Brother told him that if he didn't co-operate, he would drag him back to St. Joseph's, this time to stay. Then the Brother removed the boy's shirt and bathing suit, rolled him on his stomach, and proceeded to have anal intercourse.

"I was crying and I was angry and upset and I was ready to kill him, and I think at that point I could have quite easily killed him," Siple told the judge.

Afterwards, he said, he had told Brother Camille that if he ever attempted to abuse him again, or had him dragged back to St. Joseph's, he would kill him. He said he paced around the cottage all that night crying, wondering what to do. The next morning Brother Camille left as if nothing had happened, he said.

Lapointe apologized in advance as he began his cross-examination. "Buggery isn't my favourite subject," he told the court. He asked Siple if he had submitted to the sexual encounter.

"Willingly, no," responded Siple.

"You say you unwillingly submitted to buggery? What does that mean, exactly?"

"What part are you getting at?" asked Siple. "He used force. He was choking me. The emotion he used was fear."

"What I would like to know is did you relax yourself?"

"I didn't deliberately spread my legs for him."

"Did you relax your anus?" prodded Lapointe.

"Did I relax my anus? There must have been some relaxation because he penetrated."

"Did you relax?"

"I don't recall."

Time and time again over two days, Lapointe continued to goad Siple about the encounter. Was there any fellatio? Were you incontinent? Was an instrument used? Was a lubricant used? Was there bleeding? Was there co-operation? When did penetration occur?

"Did you at any time try to disengage?"

"By the time he had penetrated and was doing what he was doing, I was ridden with fear," Siple answered, "and I just wanted it over with as quickly as possible."

Lapointe retorted that it would have been impossible for his client to rape the boy without some kind of preparation.

"Are you familiar with the word 'metaphor'?" he asked Siple. "Are you trying to tell us it is possible to insert a marshmallow into a piggy bank?"

"I'm not talking about marshmallows and piggy banks," replied Siple, clearly frustrated.

Taking the stand in his own defence, Huot testified that he never invited Siple to his office, never drank beer with him, and never talked to him. The sexual assault at the cottage never occurred, although Huot did remember details of the visit, including what he ate and the precise timing of Siple's parents' departure. He also recalled that he had seen a reference on the boy's file about a weakness for alcohol.

In his testimony, Huot talked about his lengthy career. He had entered the order in the United States in 1937 and had spent fifteen years as an English professor at various Christian Brothers' schools in Quebec, followed by an assistant directorship at Montreal's St. Jean Baptiste de la Salle school, and a school principalship at Montreal's St. Paul College. Given this achievement, it seemed astonishing that in 1962 he was then sent to Alfred as a "lowly" placement officer. Two years after that, Huot was in a retreat.

How, Laliberté asked, could a man with such qualifications and positions have ended up in a reform school?

"How come? Certainly not for my nice hair," Huot joked.

The work at Alfred, he conceded, was not easy and he did not enjoy it. He had been happy to leave.

Laliberté wondered if Huot could shed some light on the psyche of a Christian Brother. How, for instance, did they deal with their own misconduct? "If you break a vow or promise that you make to God, is it God that will forgive you for that?"

"Certainly."

"Then in your mind, Mr. Huot, [if] God has forgiven you, I believe your conscience becomes clear?"

"Yes, once the sin is forgiven, the conscience is clear."

In his summation, Laliberté told the judge that he was intrigued by Huot's narrow yet specific recollections of his days at St. Joseph's. Why could Huot remember so clearly the two accused and not remember any of the hundreds of other young men he dealt with at the training school? It was, suggested Laliberté, because he remembers them as his victims. Lapointe countered that since Huot had had a year after being charged to focus his memory on his two accusers, this helped explain his clarity.

On June 22, 1992, Charron delivered her verdict: guilty of buggery and two counts of indecent assault. Huot stood motionless, his hands resting on his cane as the judge read her decision. But as she began discussing a date to sentence the man, he began to breathe deeply, his shoulders moving up and down.

"I feel vindicated," said Siple outside the court. "I'm glad I had

a chance to testify. It's almost like going to confession – except
that until a year ago, I thought I was the guilty one."

Huot and his two victims met again at the sentencing hearing in
October. In a victim impact statement presented to the court,
Siple said he had "lived an empty life. I was never able to commit
myself to any one thing or person because I felt dirty, ashamed,
and guilty." After St. Joseph's, he had joined the Armed Forces,
been dishonourably discharged, and later fired from a host of jobs.
One of his three sons was dead, a suicide. Another was in prison.
The other was addicted to drugs and alcohol. A stepdaughter was
a stripper.

When Huot entered the witness box to tell the court about
his troubles, including a heart condition and hypertension, he
took the occasion to deny again the charges against him. The two
former wards had lied to convict him, he told the judge, "but I
have forgiven them and I have asked the Lord to forgive them."
At this, St. Brieux dropped his face into his hands and groaned.

Charron sent Huot to jail for two years less a day, but recommended that he, too, be a candidate for the temporary absence
program. He was able to move to a halfway house within weeks.

His lawyer appealed on his behalf and eventually Huot was
released on bail. When the court of appeal upheld his conviction, he sought leave to appeal to the Supreme Court of Canada.

In August 1992, the Crown went up against the youngest and most
astute former Brother from St. Joseph's, forty-seven-year-old
Réjean Nadeau of Toronto. Known as Brother Rhéal in the late
1960s, Nadeau had a master's degree in criminology and was now
French-language co-ordinator for the Ontario Ministry of
Community and Social Services. Nadeau's older brother, Gilles

Nadeau, also from St. Joseph's, had also been charged with assault. Réjean himself was facing one count of indecent assault and one count of sodomy – charges levelled by a thirty-six-year-old Mohawk named Gerrard Hinds (not his real name).

Sent to St. Joseph's in 1967 at age twelve, Hinds had gone on to spend six years in a federal prison in British Columbia on sexual assault charges. Hinds, whom his police escorts nicknamed "Filthy Al," had a tendency towards exaggeration and an idiosyncratic sense of humour, qualities that did not serve him well in the witness box. He gave the Crown an indication of what it might expect at a preliminary hearing held the previous August when he was asked by defence counsel Denis Pommainville if he remembered whether Nadeau was circumcised. Hinds had replied, "I don't know. The thing was so small, I couldn't tell. I mean, we're talking about a person with a two-inch dink, max. I mean, what's there to say?"

Hinds described the sexual assaults in a casual way, using vernacular or profane expressions. Brother Rhéal, he testified, would give him cigarettes as a reward or enticement for sex. "I just went up to his room and he began to offer me cigarettes, which was great, and that's when he began to get close to me and started doing his thing."

"What do you mean, 'doing his thing'?" asked Crown attorney Murray MacDonald.

"Well, whatever, you know. Just taking my clothes off. He would get me to jerk him off, give me head, and stuff. I don't know what you call that – blowjobs or whatever – stick his finger in my arse, try to screw me."

Sometimes, Hinds testified, Brother Rhéal would molest him during walks or drives on the school's property. On one occasion, the Brother attempted to have anal sex with him, he said, but usually they engaged in oral sex and mutual masturbation.

The last sex Hinds said the Brother had had with him occurred on the boy's last day at St. Joseph's. Afterwards, Hinds said, Brother Rhéal gave him a going-away present, a wallet, which he promptly threw in a garbage can on the way out of Alfred.

He described the view from the window, and the furniture, in the monk's room. He said Brother Rhéal had "hair all over his body like a monkey." He remembered encountering a cleaning woman as he was coming out of the Brother's room one day. But more often than not he was short on specifics, and the ones he did provide got him into trouble.

Despite the apparent humour and the banter, Hinds said it had not been an easy decision to testify. He was also slated to be the sole Crown witness in the upcoming trial of Nadeau's brother, Gilles. Hinds said that, before the preliminary hearing, he had sat in a room with a loaded pistol and two cases of whisky and contemplated ending his life so that he would not have to testify. "I didn't want to come here. It's too embarrassing. It screwed my head up bad and my head is really screwed up right now."

At Nadeau's trial, Hinds said he realized that his lengthy criminal record damaged his credibility, but that he didn't really care. He said he wasn't seeking revenge. He had nothing to gain and did not wish to see Nadeau jailed. "I just wish I could forget it."

Nadeau's lawyer, Denis Pommainville, pointed out a number of contradictions in Hinds' testimony, including the fact that he had testified at his preliminary hearing that he had never told anyone about the abuse, but at his trial testified that he had told Nadeau's brother. Hinds also conceded that one assault he described at the trial he had neglected to mention to either the police or the Crown prosecutor, saying it had "popped" into his mind recently.

When it was his turn in the witness box, Nadeau meticulously refuted all of Hinds' allegations. He said he never assaulted the boy, not in the gully behind the school, not in the field, not in the car, and not in his bedroom.

Nadeau explained that during his term at St. Joseph's, he never drove the car to which Hinds referred because he was only twenty-three at the time and no member of the order under age twenty-five was allowed to drive. He didn't even have a driver's licence. Furthermore, the keys were kept locked up in the superintendent's office, and anyone wishing to drive the car had to sign it out, state the purpose for needing it, and have the superintendent's assistant co-sign the register.

Nadeau also disputed the location of his room as described by Hinds. In fact, he said, his room was on a different floor and faced a different direction.

In his summation, Murray MacDonald told Mr. Justice Emile Millette that Hinds hadn't travelled to Ottawa on a pleasure trip. He urged the court to remember that his client was a child when the assaults occurred and that there were bound to be gaps and inconsistencies in his story. Hinds was an unsophisticated man with no motive to lie. "What does he have to gain from telling such a detailed story?" MacDonald asked the court. "He has nothing to gain, and, on the other hand, the accused has everything to lose. There can be no doubt that Mr. Nadeau committed the sexual assaults."

In his closing speech, Denis Pommainville argued that Nadeau's credibility outweighed that of Hinds'. He repeatedly slammed the contradictions in Hinds' testimony – the location of the room and the story about being assaulted in the car that Nadeau could not possibly have driven. He also said the former ward grossly exaggerated parts of his testimony. Hinds' flippant remark about Nadeau's "small" penis had come back to haunt him. Pommainville had produced evidence from an urologist, who had examined Nadeau the previous week, to refute Hinds' allegation.

The verdict came down on August 7, 1992. About a dozen people sat in the courtroom, including Nadeau's wife, Mary-Lou, and David McCann. Millette went over a long list of inaccuracies, contradictions, and exaggerations in the complainant's testimony. To illustrate his point, he read aloud, in English, Hinds' description of Hillcrest Reform School at Guelph, where Hinds had been sent after starting a riot at St. Joseph's. "Hillcrest was all bars. It was horrible. . . . It was great." Such a statement, the judge said, defied logic. With that, he acquitted Réjean Nadeau, saying the Crown had failed to prove its case beyond a reasonable doubt.

Pommainville nodded to his client, who was seated in a chair behind him. Nadeau glanced at Mary-Lou, who began to weep out of joy and relief. "Cry now because they will take your picture outside," he said softly to her.

Outside the courtroom, MacDonald brushed aside questions from reporters who demanded to know why he had proceeded with the case when the complainant's credibility was so shaky. "It is up to the judge to test this issue of credibility – not the Crown attorney," he said. "The matter was vigorously prosecuted, and the judge did what he felt he had to do."

Nadeau, holding his wife's hand, expressed great relief at the verdict and suggested Hinds may have made up the story to receive compensation money. He told reporters that it was his understanding that a conviction was necessary to be eligible for compensation.

David McCann, however, was quick to refute Nadeau's statement. Less than 5 per cent of the former wards eligible for compensation were even scheduled to appear in court, he said. Moreover, many of the people who allegedly abused them – a total of seventy-eight Christian Brothers and some civilian employees at the training schools – were dead. While a conviction might bolster a claim, an acquittal did not necessarily negate one.

At the same time, McCann did not quibble with the judge's decision. "The judge didn't say it didn't happen," he said. "He said there was not enough evidence to convict beyond a reasonable doubt.

"The sad part of this is this trial should have gone on twenty-five years ago. It might have been easier to bring evidence into court."

In light of Millette's verdict, the Crown decided in October 1992 to withdraw the two counts of assault against Réjean Nadeau's brother, Gilles. In the meantime, Gerrard Hinds was transferred to a prison psychiatric hospital. Eventually, despite the acquittal, he would receive nearly $40,000 in compensation.

Despite this setback, the Crown was generally satisfied with the way the trials were proceeding, considering the immense hurdles the prosecutors had to overcome. Many cases boiled down to the single issue of credibility, and the judges more often than not were finding the victims credible, despite their often horrendous criminal backgrounds. One judge, a devout Roman Catholic who had been educated by the Christian Brothers, described the case he heard as the most difficult of his career. He sent the Brother to jail.

Each case had its particular challenge or challenges. At one trial, a former ward testified from a hospital where he was bedridden with a herniated disk. After complaining that he was drugged and in too much pain to continue his testimony, the man discharged himself from hospital, purchased street drugs, then bashed in a door of someone's house with his shoulder. The next time the Crown attorney heard from him, he was in police custody.

Not surprisingly, the defence for the accused, a former St. John's Brother, urged that charges levelled by the man be dismissed. The accuser clearly was "an underhanded snake and the best feigning malingerer around," they said. However, the accused, Bernard Recker, a fifty-four-year-old farmer and father of six, was

subsequently convicted on three of the ten assault charges levelled against him by three others, and received a conditional discharge and eighteen months' probation.

While the man described as "a snake" was deemed unreliable
as a witness in the Recker case, his testimony was accepted as the
truth at the trial of another Brother. Five months after Recker's
trial, fifty-two-year-old Stanley Roy Clark, who was known as
Brother Andrew when he served as a choirmaster at St. John's,
pleaded guilty to sexually assaulting him and another boy. He was
sent to jail for a month.

As the trials progressed, the Crown found it was more likely
to be successful when it had several victims alleging abuse by the
same man over a span of decades. Judges could see the same *modus
operandi* from the testimony of victims who had attended the
school at different times, now lived across the country, and had
never met. Looking at the alleged incidents in retrospect, they
could even see a progression in the man's behaviour, with the
accused generally appearing to become bolder and more sexually
adventurous with each new victim. But when a case boiled down
to one man's word against that of a man of God, the result was
predictable.

14

The Hook

———————————— • ————————————

*"I never thought I would see the day when
the Catholic Church would sic drug dealers after me."*
– David McCann, November 11, 1992

WHEN MCCANN decided in March 1990 to begin the campaign to expose the abuse that had occurred in St. Joseph's and St. John's, he knew he was putting his career as a police agent, and possibly his life, at risk. His police handlers had explicitly warned him not to do it. It was just a matter of time, they said, before some of the people he had helped put in jail came calling to settle the score.

In May 1990, two months after the story about the Ontario Christian Brothers broke, a lawyer for a Montreal drug dealer sent out a blizzard of letters to politicians and media attacking McCann as a liar and a scoundrel. "Equity and prudence requires that the news-reading public be aware of the unreliable and untrustworthy source of such serious allegations," Daniel Rock told the *Toronto Star*, enclosing a copy of a two-page letter he had sent on May 17 to then premier David Peterson. The letter accused McCann of theft, possession of stolen goods, false representation, uttering forged documents, dealing in illicit drugs, and importing narcotics. "That yourself [Peterson], your ministers, and the press have not been cautioned by federal law enforcement agencies about this untrustworthy and disreputable character is a disturbing and alarming omission."

In response, McCann had sent a letter to the premier, informing him that Daniel Rock was defence counsel for one Patrick Lee, who was serving a twenty-five-year sentence for drug dealing. McCann acknowledged his involvement in some of the activities cited by Rock. At the same time, he assured the premier of his reliability and invited him to seek references from his previous employers. Over the previous six years, McCann wrote, he had been a paid agent of the RCMP, the U.S. Customs Office, the Metro Toronto Police, the Quebec provincial police, the U.S. Drug Enforcement Administration, the FBI, "and various NATO-member intelligence agencies."

He continued, "My testimony has been accepted by many government committees, grand juries, civil and criminal judges and juries and other panels, and I have never been charged with perjury, nor have I been convicted of giving perjured evidence."

McCann had added, a little boastfully, that Rock had only begun to unravel his career. He urged Peterson to listen not to him, but to the truth, which was to be found in the government's own files and in the hearts of the shattered men who had come forward. What did his activities after leaving St. Joseph's have to do with the abuse suffered by him and other wards at the hands of the Brothers of the Christian Schools? "I might add that the over 200 victims who have come forward to date and the documents from your own archives will speak for themselves," he wrote.

McCann, of course, had become heavily involved in drugs, both as a seller and as a user, in the early 1980s. In July 1983, he was arrested, in Toronto, having crossed the Canadian border with half a kilogram of cocaine. He was subsequently charged with conspiring to import an illegal drug and conspiring to commit an indictable offence, but the charges were stayed when he agreed to co-operate in a DEA–RCMP sting operation designed to nab his Boston connection, Frank Foley.

Daniel Rock's client, Patrick Lee, had a criminal record that included convictions for drug trafficking, possession of firearms, an attempt to corrupt a peace officer, theft, and possession of burglary tools. In March 1986, having gone AWOL while on a one-day pass from Collin's Bay Penitentiary, where he was serving a ten-year term, Lee and his girlfriend contacted McCann. After a series of meetings, they arranged to provide McCann with just over two kilograms of cocaine in exchange for $132,000 and a quantity of chemicals needed to manufacture amphetamine. Unbeknown to the both of them, McCann was working for the RCMP.

Lee and his girlfriend were later arrested and charged with trafficking cocaine and conspiring to traffic in a controlled drug in August 1986. At their trial in Montreal, Rock argued that the pair had not planned to sell narcotics to McCann, but to con him out of the $132,000. To bolster his case, Rock examined McCann's personal history in a deliberate attempt to damage his credibility. He said that McCann had lied, for example, when he said he had attended San Diego State University and Rock said that he could prove it. The jury, however, believed McCann, and Lee was sentenced to fifteen years on top of the ten-year sentence he was already serving.

At the subsequent appeal, the panel of judges rejected Rock's claim that McCann had perjured himself, citing a letter the defence had received in response to a letter of complaint sent to the solicitor general. The letter, dated December 22, 1988, indicated police had investigated Rock's charge.

"The RCMP determined that Mr. McCann had attended this university during the period in question and that this institution gives university degrees," it read. "However, he was enroled under another name that neither Mr. McCann nor other sources want to, nor can, reveal at this time. There would seem to be no proof to support the accusation of perjury if it is based only on your investigator's inability to find the scholastic records of Mr. McCann."

The issue would come up again.

In November 1992, four years after the Patrick Lee affair, McCann was about to be called as a witness against, among others, Lucien Dagenais, also known as Brother Joseph, the Hook. The lawyers for the Crown assumed that McCann's credibility would, once again, be a significant issue. They were also concerned about his ability to withstand cross-examination. During each of the three preliminary hearings at which he testified, he had broken down in the witness box. At a recent Helpline meeting in British Columbia, he had been overcome by tears. Was he up to testifying?

McCann had given the matter a lot of thought. In the weeks leading up to the trial, he had been tormented by memories. At times he became so enraged he thought he would go insane. He suffered from migraine headaches almost daily. He was having difficulty sleeping, and at times he lay in his bed weeping like a child.

But his sense of obligation to the other victims kept him going. He really did not want to see an old man of sixty-six sent to jail. But as chairman of Helpline, with four hundred men counting on him, he felt a responsibility to testify. How could he ask others to do what he could not? To quit now would be seen as a cop-out. But to testify and have the testimony blow up in his face, well, that would be a severe blow to the credibility of the group at the very moment it was trying to implement the all-important reconciliation deal.

At the same time, McCann was well aware that the trial would

attract extensive media attention. As the spokesman for Helpline
and the first victim to come forward, McCann's story and fate
were big news. Other victims had asked that the press be forbidden by the court from publishing their names, but McCann,
as the most visible Helpline member, would be expected to decline
such a ban. He would be exposed and vulnerable to the public
and to all the people he had ever helped convict. Yet, having been
denied the opportunity to testify against Pierre Durocher six
months earlier, he wanted to do this. To hell with the consequences.

Lucien Dagenais symbolized, as vividly as any one of the
Christian Brothers, the terror visited upon the wards of Ontario's
Catholic training schools.

Dagenais arrived at St. Joseph's in December 1953. He was
twenty-seven years old, the youngest child of a poor, illiterate
baker in a village north of Montreal. Weighing 180 pounds and
standing over six feet tall, Brother Joseph cut an impressive figure
with his wavy brown hair and black robe.

What made him even more formidable was his physical deformity. When Dagenais had joined the Brothers of the Christian
Schools at the age of thirteen, he had hoped to become a teacher.
But in the late 1940s, while training in the monastery just up the
road from his family's home in Laval-des-Rapides, he began to
experience severe migraine headaches, accompanied by nausea
and vomiting. Dagenais was unable to write his teaching exams.
As a result, Dagenais, having been groomed to be a member of
an order dedicated to teaching, could not teach. Instead, he was
assigned supervisory responsibilities that had more to do with
babysitting than education.

In 1947, Brother Joseph was a supervisor at one of the order's
elementary schools in Laval, Quebec. While working in the
school's carpentry shop one day, he accidentally placed his left

hand in the path of an electric circular saw; he lost all of his fingers and part of his thumb. Doctors at a Montreal hospital managed to reattach only his index finger, which now stuck like a hook from the blunted knuckles of his hand. Over time, Brother Joseph learned to manipulate these two digits with pincer-like efficiency. Combined with his sturdy frame, his hook could achieve an almost unbreakable grip on any youngster who questioned his authority.

Brother Joseph's first duties at St. Joseph's were as assistant prefect in the junior dormitory (boys under age thirteen). It was a stressful, demanding job. His day started at 6 A.M. and didn't end until 9 P.M., when his charges were supposedly safe in bed. His only vacation was an annual eight-day retreat.

He had no training in the handling of juvenile delinquents. What training he did get was on-the-job. His supervisor, Brother Irenée, seemed to prefer using his fists and his boots to keep the wards in line. Brother Joseph quickly followed his example.

It was Brother Joseph's responsibility to ensure that runaway boys who had been recaptured were discouraged from making a repeat attempt. This was accomplished by strapping them brutally and publicly, in blatant contradiction of departmental regulations that discipline be conducted privately with only "official" witnesses present.

David McCann had his first encounter with Brother Joseph shortly after arriving at St. Joseph's in 1958. McCann was chatting amiably with a fellow ward in a line-up when he felt an excruciating pain on his shoulder. Brother Joseph had grabbed him with his hook. Telling him to shut up, Brother Joseph then whacked the boy on the head with the back of his hand.

The fourteen-year-old Grant Hartley had a memorable run-in with the Hook just after he had been sent to St. Joseph's in 1954. Hartley was standing in the school's recreation room when he saw Brother Joseph pick up a boy about seven years old and proceed to beat him. When the boy fell to the floor, Brother Joseph began to kick him.

An enraged Hartley, astonished that no one had leapt to the boy's rescue, grabbed a pool cue and advanced on the monk. When another ward wrestled the pool cue from his hands, Hartley grabbed a hockey stick and began to flail at the Brother.

Another monk grabbed Hartley from behind and the beating was on. While the other monk held him, Brother Joseph unleashed a flurry of punches to Hartley's face and ribs. When Hartley slumped to the floor, Brother Joseph used his boots. On the verge of losing consciousness, Hartley begged the Brother to end the beating. Instead, Brother Joseph dragged him to the dormitory and lashed his bare buttocks with the strap. Hartley was then thrown, gasping and sobbing, into a solitary confinement cell. Later that night, after the other boys had their dinner, Brother Joseph came back for one last punch-up. Hartley tried to give the Hook a wide berth after that, but his penchant for escapes brought the two back together time and time again.

As prefect, Brother Joseph would supervise most of the activities in the recreation room when the junior boys couldn't go outside because the weather was too cold or wet. Sometimes he played floor hockey with them. Although he towered more than a foot over the tallest of them, this didn't stop some of the braver boys from taking runs at him. Brother Joseph would make them pay with thundering body checks that often left them lying in a heap on the floor.

While monitoring the wards, Brother Joseph would often sit in the school's barber chair, where they received their monthly haircuts. From this comfortable vantage point, he could scrutinize them as they played ping-pong, pool, and other games. Sometimes, he would beckon a ward over, barking "Come here" in French. The Hook would draw the boy close and yank the boy's hand under his black robe, whereupon the boy would have to massage his genitals.

Wards who refused to comply were punished severely. One slow-witted boy, for example, was dragged into a boxing ring and brutally beaten under the pretence of teaching him to box. The sixteen-year-old ward had never been in a boxing ring before and had never struck anyone in anger. He was no match for the Hook.

One punch bloodied the boy's nose. Another split his lips. The other boys watched in horror, but no one intervened. When the boy finally did land a kick on Brother Joseph's knee, the infuriated monk launched a volley of punches that lacerated the skin around the boy's eyes. They were soon swollen almost completely shut. When an exhausted Brother Joseph finally stopped punching him, the boy dragged himself up to the dormitory. He could barely see as he, sobbing, groped his way up the stone stairs.

Brother Joseph's sexual proclivities were well known at St. Joseph's, despite the code of silence that surrounded the Brotherhood. And occasionally they threatened to get him into trouble. In 1958, for example, after a boy complained to his father that the Brother was "playing pig" with him, the Department of Reform Institutions conducted an investigation, but discovered no evidence to back up the ward's accusation. When another boy charged that Brother Joseph had fellated him, a department inspector interviewed the accused. However, Brother Joseph's English was so bad that the interview, while lengthy, revealed nothing incriminating. The inspector later reported that, "Whilst I was not particularly impressed with the Brother's manner or his rather vehement expostulations, there was not sufficient evidence to warrant further investigation, and it appeared indiscreet to continue under the circumstances."

Over time, however, Brother Joseph was accused of so many assaults upon children that his confrères could no longer turn a blind eye. When yet another boy told a kindly, elderly Brother about the Hook's assaults, Brother Joseph was transferred from the training school to a Christian Brothers' construction project near Trois-Rivières, Quebec. He stayed there for two years, at the end of which he was in rough shape. He checked into a Montreal hospital complaining of urinary problems, but it was quickly recognized that he required treatment for anxiety and depression. Alcohol and tranquillizers were now the crutches on which he depended.

Returning to Alfred in June 1965, Brother Joseph was appointed director of the school's sports centre, a position where his access to wards was limited. When the province took over St. Joseph's in 1974 and renamed it Champlain School, Brother Joseph was retained as the school's purchasing officer. This position, too, limited his access to students.

The Brother's sexual fortunes underwent a decided change in 1975 when he met Florence Bourbonnais, a twice-divorced cook who had been hired to work in the school's kitchen. Four years later, after Dagenais received permission to leave the order, the couple were married. Dagenais continued to work at the Alfred school until the early 1980s, when the government closed it.

At the time of his departure, Lucien Dagenais had spent almost a quarter-century of his life working at St. Joseph's, and his behaviour had had a profound impact on the lives of hundreds of boys. As many of these boys struggled, post-St. Joseph's, to make their way in the world, some forgot the name and face of the tall, sturdy Brother with the wavy brown hair. But they never forgot the hook. It would be his undoing.

It was still dark on the morning of November 9, 1992, when David McCann climbed into his big red pickup truck and roared out of the farmyard to start the three-hour drive to L'Orignal. As he pulled out onto the narrow, winding dirt road that led to his farm-house, the sun set the tops of the trees ablaze and the hoar frost on the fields glowed.

McCann strode purposefully into court in L'Orignal wearing a light-blue suit and carrying a leather briefcase. Rather than swear an oath on the Bible, he affirmed he would tell the truth. Like most of the former wards of St. Joseph's and St. John's, he had been unable to separate the acts of the Christian Brothers from the Roman Catholic faith. As soon as he left St. Joseph's, he had turned away from religion.

Melville O'Donohue, general counsel to the Toronto Brothers, sat in the front row of the spectator benches. He had made the long trip from Toronto in anticipation of this moment. Much effort and money had been spent to probe McCann's past, and now it would be seen if it had been worth the price.

A bevy of lawyers were huddled at the defence end of the legal counsel's table. Two lawyers from Toronto, Peter Shoniker and Graham Pinos, had been parachuted in to assist the attorney of record, Gilles Charlebois, and his assistant, Jean Legault, in their attack on McCann's credibility. Shoniker, who was in charge of administrating the defence of the Toronto Brothers, had been appointed to cross-examine McCann. He would be assisted by Pinos, a former federal prosecutor, who had worked previously out of L'Orignal. The defence didn't use this team approach in any other trial.

To the six-man, six-woman jury, the number of lawyers must have seemed a little lopsided in favour of the defence. The Crown's case would be carried solely by thirty-two-year-old Robert Pelletier, who sat at the other end of the table with only OPP Det. Sgt. Bob Carpenter for company. The Montreal-born Pelletier had become an assistant crown attorney at the age of twenty-eight and less than two years later had been appointed to run the judicial district he fondly referred to as Green Acres.

The accused sat hunched over the side of the prisoner's dock, clutching a cane in his right hand. The infamous hook was out of sight. Dagenais was still a big man, almost a Santa Claus figure with his girth and silver-grey hair. However, his long, scraggly white beard and tinted wire-rim glasses gave him a sinister cast.

Life had not treated Dagenais well since he had left the order in 1978. After just three years of marriage, his wife, tiring of his boozing, drug abuse, and erratic mood swings, left him. Arthritis now crippled his legs and back. He had developed a hernia, high blood pressure, and Ménière's disease, which made him prone to bouts of dizziness and deafness. He had been unable to work the entire decade before retirement age. Mostly he just puttered around Sudbury, helping out the Catholic parish, doing volunteer work for several francophone service clubs, befriending children.

McCann sat in the witness box, Dagenais slumped against the side of the prisoner's dock. He wore headphones to listen to McCann's testimony through a French interpreter.

McCann said he did not remember the face of the man in the prisoner's dock because he had changed a great deal in the thirty-four years since he had last seen him. But he remembered the deformed left hand.

McCann delivered his testimony quickly, answering the questions put to him by Pelletier with short, direct answers. He said that within a month of his arrival at St. Joseph's in 1958, Brother Joseph had come to his bed and beckoned him to follow. It was about a half-hour after the dormitory lights were switched off. McCann said he followed the Brother to the dormitory showers. The Brother, he said, told him to remove his pyjama bottoms and then sexually assaulted him. It was over in a couple of minutes.

"Did you say or do anything?" asked Pelletier.

"I don't think so."

"Can you explain why?"

"I was twelve years old."

Mr. Justice Hector Soublière told Pelletier more detail was required to ensure the jury understood the nature of the allegation.

"I know what you said," he explained gently to McCann. "I know what it means. But I want to make sure the jury understands."

"He made me take my clothes off and bend over," McCann said. "He raped me. He stuck his penis in my anus. It hurt for a long time."

In the spectator seating, a woman whose father had also been a ward at St. Joseph's cried quietly and dabbed her eyes with tissue.

"Was there any blood?" continued Pelletier.

"I don't recall. He told me to put my pants back on and go back to bed."

"What was he wearing? Do you recall?"

"I don't recall," said McCann. He testified that if any of the boys in the dormitory had been awake, it was unlikely that they would have noticed anything. All they would have seen was a little boy following a Brother to the washroom. He did not remember crying out.

A second assault several months later was almost identical to the first, McCann said. Other Brothers also abused him sexually during the two terms he spent at the institution, but most of the abuse occurred during his first stay.

McCann described, under Pelletier's gentle guidance, how he had mentioned his ill treatment at St. Joseph's to his mother, only hinting, however, about the sexual abuse, and how she had complained to two police officers, his probation officer, and the parish priest. He said he told no one after that until late 1989.

"As most of the Canadian public was, I started watching the Mount Cashel inquiry in Newfoundland and started listening to the statements made by the kids," he said. "I admired their courage."

McCann explained his role with Helpline and then the Crown's examination was over. It had lasted barely thirty minutes. Now he was in the hands of the defence.

The mid-morning sun was shining brightly through the courtroom's cathedral-style windows. Charlebois, Shoniker, and Pinos huddled briefly before embarking upon their cross-examination of the witness. Shoniker began with a series of questions about McCann's life after he left St. Joseph's, but was soon interrupted by Soublière, who could not understand where the questions were leading. Several times Shoniker resumed his cross-examination only to be interrupted again. The trial deteriorated into a series of starts and stops, with McCann and the jury being excused during each stoppage while the defence and judge, and occasionally Pelletier, bickered over the process. Finally, an exasperated Soublière demanded to know what bearing McCann's post-St. Joseph's activities had upon the allegations against Dagenais.

Shoniker replied that if he couldn't cross-examine McCann on his background, he wouldn't be able to test his credibility. "This man has a very interesting background – very interesting," he assured the judge. "I intend to test his credibility with respect to whether he has done what he has said he has done. Whether he told the truth today."

"Can you be specific?" asked Soublière. "I can't understand why you are hedging on this matter."

"I just want to know where he has worked because I don't think he is telling the truth at this point," responded Shoniker. "I am prepared to prove beyond a doubt that he has already lied about his educational background. His whole life is really a fabrication. To start splitting it up into pieces is really difficult."

"I want to hear why it's relevant," said the judge.

"The case law is very clear," said Shoniker.

"If it is so clear, I wish you would tell me what it is," replied the judge. "Collateral issues are about lies told on previous occasions."

"We'll get to lots of those," replied Shoniker.

The two fenced for several minutes. Shoniker still wouldn't give the judge details about the areas he intended to canvass. Finally, Pelletier rose to his feet and demanded to know just what was behind Shoniker's reluctance. Was the defence concerned the Crown would reveal the defence strategy to McCann? Once McCann was in the witness box, it was illegal for the Crown to advise him.

"I am a little taken aback by counsel's reluctance about placing his cards on the table," he told Soublière. "I find it somewhat offensive. While we do things differently in L'Orignal, we follow court procedure. I'll ask that his concerns be specific and that they be brought forward."

After a brief meeting between the Crown, defence counsel, and the accused in the judge's chambers, during which Shoniker mapped out his strategy, the cross-examination resumed before the judge and jury.

"Have you used any other name than David Richard McCann?"

"When I worked for various law enforcement agencies, I used other names," McCann replied.

"What names?"

"I don't remember them."

"Were there a lot? Were there more than five?"

"Significantly more than five names."

Shoniker then asked McCann, "Do you lie?"

Immediately Pelletier was on his feet, objecting. "I think everybody, at one time or another, has lied," argued Pelletier. "If the answer is yes, it really doesn't help us much." Soublière concurred and ordered McCann not to answer.

Shoniker asked McCann about the stories he fabricated while

working for various police agencies as what McCann called a CI – a co-operating individual.

"Were you good at it?"

"I was considered a good undercover officer," answered McCann.

Shoniker then asked about the offences that resulted in McCann being sent to St. Joseph's – break-ins at a construction company, a flower shop, a coal company, and a photo studio. "You did this in one and half to two weeks?" asked Shoniker. "At the age of twelve, you were into some pretty serious stuff. You were like a one-boy crime wave."

Soublière interjected. "I don't think that is a proper comment and not calculated to get the sympathy of the jury, I don't think."

Shoniker went on to accuse McCann of trying to downplay his involvement in criminal acts when he was interviewed on "The Shirley Show" and "Geraldo" in late 1991. "You said you were sent by juvenile court for being truant and delinquent," he noted. "You always say truant first."

"I was involved in what I was involved in," replied McCann. He sat calmly in the witness box, resting his elbow on the railing. His eyes followed Shoniker as he paced around the room, never leaving him. "[They were] what would be called petty crimes and nuisance offences."

"Six B and Es in one and a half weeks and you call that petty?" challenged Shoniker.

"They weren't bank robberies," responded McCann, his voice rising. "They weren't rapes and they certainly weren't abusing children. They were serious offences, but not as serious as a lot of other offences."

Shoniker moved on to McCann's university career. After receiving instruction from Soublière on how best to proceed, he showed McCann, but not the jury, a copy of McCann's application to McMaster and the transcript of his marks from San Diego State

College, which later became a university. "Who created the document?" he asked.

"I don't know," responded McCann.

Shoniker then produced affidavits signed by the university's directors of academic services and admissions, affidavits that said they had never heard of David Richard McCann. But he didn't get an opportunity to read them aloud. "I hope you are not going to say what those people said," interrupted Soublière. "If you are, we are going to have a little problem. I am very much concerned about what you are going to say."

Again, McCann and the jury were dismissed while the defence, the Crown, and the judge debated evidentiary procedure. Shoniker told the judge, "I am going to suggest he never attended San Diego College and that he fabricated the transcripts which resulted in his introduction to medical school."

Pelletier was concerned about what the jury would think, given that it had seen Shoniker show McCann the documents, but without having an opportunity to know what they said. Would that be more damaging to McCann than having the contents of the letter known? He wasn't sure. He suggested Shoniker be permitted to confront McCann with the allegation. Let him answer the question.

The jury was recalled and Shoniker played his ace. "Is it not a fact that you never attended San Diego State University as a student?" he asked McCann.

"As the attorney general pointed out in the appeal court decision [in the case involving Patrick Lee], I did attend. I attended San Diego State College and graduated."

"You either fabricated or know of the fabrication of the transcripts to McMaster University on your behalf. Is that not true?" pressed Shoniker.

"No."

"Is it not a fact that during the time you were living in the United States, you never attended any facility or institution of continuing education?"

"That's incorrect," replied McCann, indignation colouring his voice.

McCann was answering the questions clearly, without waffling, but on the inside he felt like he was beginning to come apart. A migraine was pounding in his head, and his skin was cold and clammy. During the noon recess he complained of the courtroom being cold, when, in fact, it was hot and stuffy.

Shoniker kept chipping away. He asked McCann how he was able to explain to his drug dealer connections why he wasn't convicted in 1983 of the charge of importing cocaine.

"I just told them I had an extremely brilliant defence counsel like yourself," McCann said.

"I can see you have a sense of humour. Are you serious?"

Shoniker noted that McCann had testified at another trial that he told his hoodlum cronies he was able to beat the charges as a result of his political connections. "It was an awful curious matter to attribute a stay in criminal proceedings to what in essence is political corruption," he remarked to McCann.

An exasperated McCann pointed out that if he had told the truth – that he had negotiated a deal to sting a drug dealer – he would have been killed. "When you're dealing in the drug business and you are operating undercover and you develop your cover in co-operation with the authorities, you work with what you have. I am sorry, but drug dealers – and you probably have represented some of them – think there are crooks in the justice system. There are crooked judges and there are juries who can be bought. People who operate outside the law are aware of that and it's a story that can fly sometimes."

Shoniker wasn't impressed. "I suggest you have one and only

one motive for cooking up a story of political corruption. You know that if you continue doing work for various police agencies, you will continue to be paid by those agencies."

"That's correct," answered McCann.

"That's the same motive that brought you here today," continued Shoniker. "You know there is money. That's why you lied to people and you told them that there were corrupt politicians. It is only because the gravy train would have been cut off if you didn't lie."

McCann glared at Shoniker. He spoke slowly and evenly so his words would not be lost upon the defence lawyer and the jury. "This is not about money," he said. "I never want to see another kid go through what I came through as a child."

Pelletier congratulated McCann as he left the witness box at the end of the day, placing a hand on his shoulder for reassurance. So far, so good. It hadn't been the disaster he had feared. But who knew what the jury was thinking about the exchange over San Diego College?

McCann, his skin pale, walked out of the courtroom with a half smile on his lips. He climbed into his truck and began the drive back home. It was a spectacular evening. The moon was full and the skies were clear. But McCann could see a huge black cloud, illuminated by the moon, on the horizon. It was a nasty piece of work, bound to bring rain or snow. It was a metaphor, he thought, for what might lie ahead.

McCann had a restless evening, starting at every creak in the drafty old house. His cosy study no longer felt like a safe haven. Sitting in his comfortable chair with a newspaper, facing the curtainless windows with the reading light on behind him, he suddenly felt very exposed.

In the middle of the night, his dogs began to bark. Something outside must have disturbed them. McCann padded downstairs to investigate, but there was nothing out there. He climbed back into bed for a few more hours of uneasy sleep.

When McCann arrived at the courthouse the following morning, he was startled to see a man he had helped send to jail for drug trafficking four years earlier standing outside the courtroom with Christian Brothers lawyer Graham Pinos. Gary Provost was talking to William McNeil, a former St. Joseph's ward. McCann knew that McNeil, a bartender with a criminal record for assault, was going to testify for the defence that he, McCann, had counselled him to submit a fraudulent compensation claim to the reconciliation fund. But what was Gary Provost doing here? McCann greeted the pair as if their presence meant nothing to him. "Are you having a nice day?" he asked. "Better than you're going to be having," said Provost with a snarl. McCann nonchalantly made his way into the courthouse, but he was chilled by Provost's menacing glare.

All day, Provost sat in the courtroom, his eyes on McCann as McCann testified. It was quite unnerving. McCann wondered if that was the reason Provost was there. He could not testify himself if he heard others testify. The judge had made the customary order excluding witnesses from sitting in the courtroom.

Shoniker questioned McCann about his drug habit, an alleged arson, and an allegation that McCann had counselled a former ward to commit fraud. McCann denied hiring an arsonist to burn down his farm, and he told the court that the compensation agreement he was helping to negotiate would be designed to weed out false claims. "Why would I counsel somebody after having worked with the other parties to put a mechanism in place to weed out such claims? It would be found to be a bogus claim and rejected."

McCann was repeatedly questioned by Shoniker about his marital status. The previous day, McCann had said he had been married to a Kingston-area woman, but had divorced several years ago. Today, McCann asked the judge if he could add to his testimony. He had been married another time, he said, in California to a woman named Wendy. He had written about her February 1971 death from cancer in an essay he was required to produce for entry into McMaster University's medical school.

It was that document, Shoniker would later concede, that motivated him to want to destroy McCann in the witness box. With his own wife suffering from cancer, it galled Shoniker that McCann might have fabricated a tragic story simply to gain admission into a school. "Any man who lies about how many times he married, about his wife dying of cancer, about being a doctor, I believe an independent mind might ask what is this man not prepared to lie about? And I think the answer is nothing."

As dusk settled over the Ottawa Valley that afternoon, the eve of Remembrance Day, it appeared the cross-examination would go another day. However, since court wouldn't sit on the November 11 holiday, McCann would get a brief respite from the constant questioning.

On Remembrance Day, McCann met with his RCMP handler and Det. Insp. Tim Smith. They were concerned that McCann's unmasking as a police agent in the witness box might have put him in imminent danger. And they were most alarmed about his encounter with Gary Provost outside the courtroom. In addition, an Ottawa reporter had overheard a man remark in the courthouse corridor that he would sooner kill McCann than testify against him. Smith didn't think anyone would make a move while the trial was on, but when Provost's grey Cadillac was spotted on the dirt road near McCann's farm, an OPP officer armed with a shotgun was assigned to guard McCann.

McCann's handler made plans to get him into a witness protection program once he wound up affairs with Helpline. McCann wanted into the program run by the U.S. Marshall's office.

After the police officers left, McCann phoned Roger Tucker. While they talked, a Helpline employee, Tina Lentz, who worked out of McCann's office at the farm, took McCann's dogs for a walk. When she returned, she found the Helpline chairman sitting on a couch, rocking back and forth, tears streaming from his eyes.

"David, what's the matter?" she asked gently.

He didn't hear her and he didn't see her. Lentz became alarmed. When McCann spoke, it was in the voice of a child. "It hurts," he kept sobbing over and over. "It hurts."

Lentz called McCann's doctor and the psychiatrist who had been treating him. About thirty minutes later, McCann seemed to have snapped out of his trance, but he was shaking like a leaf. Sensing that perhaps McCann was afraid to go back to court alone the next day, Lentz offered to accompany him. She had made the offer before, but he had rejected it, fearing that if she was seen with him, she too might become a target. This time, however, he accepted. He didn't want her in the courtroom, but he would appreciate it if she could drive him home after he testified. He didn't think he would be in any shape to drive.

At the L'Orignal courthouse early on November 12, Lentz told Cosette Chafe, the victim-witness program co-ordinator, what had happened the previous day. She felt McCann shouldn't be anywhere near a witness box in his state, but he couldn't be persuaded into discontinuing his testimony.

When McCann sat in the box, the change in him was readily apparent. He sat with eyes downcast, answering questions in soft monosyllables. He had to be asked repeatedly to speak louder.

Shoniker was on the offensive again. He accused McCann of lying in other court proceedings. He grilled him again about the barn fire. He also accused McCann of telling a Belleville couple that he was a doctor and of impersonating a lawyer while visiting an inmate at Millhaven Penitentiary. McCann denied all the allegations.

Later in the day, Shoniker and his entourage, their ammunition spent, returned to Toronto, leaving the attorney of record, Gilles Charlebois, to complete the cross-examination. His was an extremely slow, plodding cross-examination.

Charlebois spent little time dealing with the allegations of assault that had been made against Dagenais. What mattered for him was setting a detailed account of each of the witnesses' lives after St. Joseph's, the extent of their alcohol and drug abuse, their brushes with the law, and their familiarity with the other witnesses and the Helpline organization.

The witnesses had been a little baffled by the approach – wasn't Lucien Dagenais the one on trial? – but they made no attempt to gloss over their problems. Many of them attributed their problems to the treatment they had received at St. Joseph's. Some even volunteered intimate details of their sexual problems before Soublière could cut them off.

Charlebois began meticulously to compare McCann's testimony at the preliminary inquiry to his testimony at the trial, focusing on what he believed were inconsistencies. He asked McCann if he knew that something sexual was about to occur when Brother Joseph took him to the shower the first time. When McCann replied that he didn't, Charlebois referred him to his testimony at the preliminary hearing, in which he said that another Brother had previously taken him to a room and buggered him on a bed "so it was slightly different, but I thought something was going to happen. I wasn't sure what." When the judge interjected, saying he disagreed with the lawyer's interpretation of McCann's evidence at the preliminary, the two became embroiled in a heated procedural argument.

McCann, meanwhile, was falling apart. He felt totally detached, as if he was watching the drama from a ceiling skylight. Then, the courtroom disappeared and he was alone and afraid. Observers noted that McCann's face was getting flushed and tears began streaming down his face. Soublière and Charlebois looked at him in astonishment. The judge quickly called a recess to enable McCann to compose himself, but the jury was barely out of the courtroom when McCann put his head in his hands and began to cry out in anguish.

Pelletier had never seen anything like it. His first instinct was that McCann was bailing out on him. He and Carpenter helped McCann into the courthouse library, gently sat him in a chair, and asked him if he could continue his testimony.

McCann just sat rocking in the chair with a fixed stare. He was rocking rapidly back and forth and breathing heavily.

"Can I take that as a yes?" Pelletier asked, cracking a lame joke, which he immediately regretted. He realized he was not getting through to McCann, who was now starting to mumble in the voice of the little boy that Tina Lentz had heard.

Someone called an ambulance. When the ambulance attendants determined McCann wasn't in any immediate medical danger, Lentz decided to take him back to the farm, and the jury was advised that McCann was not in a position to finish his testimony.

At home, McCann's dissociated state continued for four days. He remembered the names of his cows and the names of his neighbours, but he had no inkling, it seemed, of anything connected with Helpline, or the abuse he had endured as a child. Lentz had difficulty grasping that this was David, her friend of twenty years. He had the same body, the same wrinkles, but now there was a sort of child where there had once been a man. He had a child's openness, trust, and vulnerability.

His psychiatrist, whom McCann did not now recognize, concluded his patient was suffering from post-traumatic stress disorder – a mental state that was widely studied after the Vietnam War when shell-shocked American soldiers who had returned home found themselves reliving their wartime experiences. The psychiatrist told McCann his memory would come back, but it could come back all at once, or a bit at a time. When McCann's memory finally did return, it was not whole. He still could not clearly recall certain things, particularly the sequences of events. It was like reading a page in a newspaper that had been creased on the press before it was printed: most of the story was there, but there were gaps everywhere.

The trial of Lucien Dagenais continued without McCann. It had started one week before McCann arrived to testify and would run four weeks after. Altogether eleven witnesses, including such Helpline stalwarts as Grant Hartley and Gerry Champagne, gave testimony.

One former St. Joseph's ward, fifty-year-old Albert Daigneault of Kirkland Lake, said that when he was eleven, Brother Joseph rammed his hook up the boy's rectum on two separate occasions. When he called police from a pay phone to report the abuse, he was told to get lost. "I am sick and tired of hearing from you little bastards," Daigneault quoted one policeman as saying. "If I get one more call from you I will report you."

On November 22, McCann returned to the witness box. He appeared much stronger, and anger seemed to have replaced the sorrow that had filled him when he was forced to recall the abuse. When Gilles Charlebois intimated that McCann's claim of being raped was inaccurate and that he may have been sexually assaulted with a finger or some other "object," McCann flew into a rage.

"I know what buggery is!" he screamed at the defence attorney. He challenged Dagenais' counsel to drop his drawers and bend over if he required a demonstration.

On December 2, 1992, the key witness for the defence, William "Billy" McNeil, took the stand. McNeil, a Kingston bartender, had been in St. Joseph's between 1958 and 1962, roughly the same time David McCann had been there. McNeil said he had never been abused at the school, except on one occasion when Brother Joseph had pinched him so hard in the area between his shoulder and neck that it made him cry. He had not been sexually abused at the school, he said, and he rather doubted that McCann had been either since the showers where McCann claimed to have been abused were like an echo chamber that would have magnified the sound of the assault through the dormitory. There was also a night watchman on duty when the boys were sleeping, he testified.

"Brother Joseph may have been a lot of things, but he wasn't a child molester," McNeil said, adding that he thought McCann was "out for blood money."

McCann, he said, first telephoned him in the summer of 1990 to ask if he was interested in starting proceedings against the Christian Brothers. McNeil said he initially thought it was a good idea, but later changed his mind. He said he forgot about it until he received mail from Helpline for his deceased brother, Danny, who had never attended St. Joseph's. He said it angered him to think McCann had padded Helpline's membership list with the name of his dead brother. That's when he decided, he said, to meet with Shoniker to expose McCann. "I was angry at McCann for using my brother and I wanted something done about it," he said.

There was no logical explanation for Helpline having sent a letter to McNeil's dead brother, unless it was a mistake. Charlebois had entered as evidence an envelope, addressed to Danny McNeil from McCann's farm. But Pelletier focused his cross-examination on McNeil's actions, rather than what he alleged McCann had done. McNeil said he had talked to police after he was approached by McCann, and, despite his anger with McCann, had not told them about any fraud. Instead, he had contacted a Christian Brothers' lawyer in Toronto. Pelletier suggested that McNeil had not told the police about any fraud because there had been nothing to tell; that McNeil, in fact, had made up a story built around the Helpline letter that had been erroneously sent to his dead brother. "I'm going to suggest to you, sir," Pelletier said to McNeil, "that . . . Mr. McCann did not approach you to make a false complaint."

"No, sir, that's wrong," said McNeil, his hands trembling. "The difference between David McCann and I is I'm not a stool pigeon. He is. And he's admitted that."

"A stool pigeon?"

"Yes, sir."

"Like he gives evidence against people?"

"Yes, sir."

"Like this gentleman back here?" asked Pelletier, gesturing to Gary Provost in the spectator seats.

"Yes, sir."

"Did you travel here with that gentleman back there?" asked Pelletier.

"And Mr. Shoniker. Yes, sir."

"He was in the same car when you came down from Kingston?" asked Pelletier.

"Yes, sir."

"Who is that gentleman I am pointing at?"

"Gary Provost."

"And how did McCann stool on him?"

"I have no idea."

"None at all?"

"I know McCann did cop-out on him. What it was about, I don't know."

McNeil conceded that he and Provost had been at the courthouse when McCann testified, but said that he, McNeil, had stayed outside the building.

"What do you think Mr. McCann did to Mr. Provost [at Provost's trial in 1988] in terms of testifying?" asked Pelletier. "Did he put him in the pen?"

"As far as I know, yeah."

The exchange, in effect, ended McNeil's credibility as a witness for the defence. Pelletier's cross-examination exposed him as the companion of a man who had a motive to seek revenge against McCann for sending him to prison. The exchange also raised the question why a lawyer for the Christian Brothers had brought Gary Provost, a convicted drug dealer, to court when McCann was in the witness box if he was not calling him to testify.

Shoniker, who was educated by the Toronto Brothers and served as chairman of the board of trustees of their De La Salle Academy in Toronto, would later say that he required McNeil at the courthouse when he was cross-examining McCann to back up his allegations, if necessary. McNeil would only agree to come, he said, if Provost, who was still on parole, agreed to drive with him from his Kingston home to the courthouse. "I swear I wasn't trying to intimidate David McCann," said Shoniker. "I intended to take David McCann apart piece by piece as a deceitful person. I didn't need any help from anyone."

On November 30, Lucien Dagenais sat in the box in his own defence, and denied all the allegations. "It's all fabrication," he said, testifying in French before the bilingual jury. He said he would never have committed buggery, indecent assault, and assault causing bodily harm because he respected both the wards and himself too much.

Pelletier had looked forward to cross-examining the legendary Hook, but when the time came, he felt sorry for the man. "I never felt so low in my life," he said later. "He didn't seem to care what was going on. He seemed rather oblivious to it all."

Although Dagenais never contradicted himself, his testimony about a phone call he received from Brother Provincial Jean-Marc Cantin just before the charges were laid was revealing. Brother Jean-Marc had asked him if he had anything "for which he wanted forgiveness." Dagenais had answered no. Yet when Brother Jean-Marc ordered him to Ottawa to meet the police, Dagenais did not even ask what he had been accused of doing. "He never even bothered to ask one of his close associates 'What are they saying I did?'" noted Pelletier. "It seems to me to be something someone would do if they had something to hide."

Eight days later, Dagenais was convicted of fifteen of the eighteen charges against him, including seven counts of indecent assault, six counts of assault causing bodily harm, and two counts of buggery – the last two crimes related directly to McCann. When the jury registered convictions on both buggery charges levelled by McCann, Charlebois stared at the jury foreman in astonishment. Dagenais, for his part, stood as if in a trance. Sentencing was put over until February 1993. In the meantime, Soublière set Dagenais free.

After the trial, Grant Hartley accused the lawyers for the Christian Brothers of character assassination in their four-day grilling of McCann. But McCann, who was back at his farm when the verdict came down, praised the jury for seeing through "the smoke screen" and passing judgement on the allegations that were really the issue. "What happened to me as a child has

nothing to do with what I did or did not do thirty years later,"
he said. "I have been a shitbag part of my life, but I have done
some things that I am proud of. No one is totally evil or totally
good."

Later, in a victim impact statement, McCann wrote, "I do not
feel any sense of revenge or vengeance towards the perpetrators.
In many ways, they are as much victims as I was. They were subjected to a social setting where there were few winners and many
losers. The justice I should have had thirty years ago, I cannot
have today. Justice delayed is justice denied.

"I seek healing and reconciliation for the abuser and the responsible institutions. Brother Joseph should not be sent to jail. He
should be placed in an institution where he can receive proper
medical care and counselling to help him deal with the effects of
his isolation.

"What will we in society gain if we warehouse him in a penitentiary? We need to show compassion. We need to heal him as
well as those he abused."

He urged the judge to be creative in sentencing lest he simply
perpetuate the cycle of abuse. McCann said he had met a priest
who told him that Dagenais had been active on the Sudbury
social planning council and had done some good things in his
later life. "The one thing I have learned is that nothing is cut
and dry. There are black areas and white areas and this huge grey
area in the middle. When a guy gets convicted, nobody sees the
good he has done. We do ourselves such a huge disservice when
we try to make it simple."

David McCann's appeal for mercy for Lucien Dagenais was almost
his last public act. After the December 11 press conference was
called to announce that the reconciliation agreement was going
ahead without the St. John's Brothers, he stepped into a side

room with an Ottawa television reporter and gave her an interview, which, when aired that night, astonished the members of
Helpline who watched it.

McCann told the reporter he would be resigning immediately
from Helpline and would be going underground into a witness
protection program. He had received threats, he said, and would
be assuming a new identity in another location. This manoeu-
vre, he would later tell friends, was something he had been planning to do for a long while, but the recent events had made it
urgent.

One week earlier, McCann had held an auction sale at his
farm. Everything except for a wood stove and the living-room
carpet had been sold. Neighbours had been surprised to see an
OPP officer in a flak jacket stationed just inside the entrance to
the yard. When Gary Provost showed up at the auction, McCann's
old nemesis was escorted off the property by police.

Later, Provost told the *Ottawa Citizen* that if McCann had
received death threats, they weren't from him. "I have a grudge
against McCann, but I don't want to hurt him," he said. "I want
him to go to court. I want him to go through what I did."

Melville O'Donohue suggested in the same newspaper that
McCann had left because he was fleeing prosecution for perjury.
"I think that McCann saw that the game was up and flew the
coop," he said. He boasted, almost gleefully, to the *Toronto Star*
that he had run McCann out of the country. The documents
lawyers produced at Dagenais' trial, which showed that San Diego
State University had no record of a David McCann ever attending there, would, he said, be grounds for the perjury charge.
However, no perjury charges were ever laid.

McCann had barely disappeared when Sean Upton, a reporter
for the *Ottawa Citizen*, wrote a controversial full-page article in
the newspaper's January 30 *Weekend Observer*. Under the headline
"WHO IS THE REAL DAVID MCCANN?," the article expanded upon

many of the accusations the lawyers for the Christian Brothers had made at the Dagenais trial.

"He's just the most compulsive and consummate liar I have ever seen," Peter Shoniker had told Upton. The quote was highlighted in the centre of the page below a photo of a pensive-looking McCann. "I believe he lives in a world of his own, where he creates whatever circumstances he finds convenient."

The character assassination of McCann following Dagenais' trial did not go unnoticed by Ottawa area residents. "After all that has been said about the injustice of putting the character of a rape victim on trial, I was appalled that the *Citizen* dedicated an entire page to doing just that," wrote one *Citizen* reader in a letter to the editor on February 10, 1993. "The intentions of this article are cruel."

Tina Lentz was more perplexed than angry about the Upton article. Even if some of the allegations about McCann's past were true, what did it have to do with the issue of abuse? McCann had initiated the largest sexual abuse investigation in Canadian history and been a principal force behind the creation of a one-of-its-kind model for reconciliation. He had come forward when no other victim had the courage. The man deserved a medal – not ridicule.

The sentencing hearing for Lucien Dagenais took place February 5, 1993. Now, instead of slamming McCann as a liar and a fraud, Dagenais' counsel asked Soublière to heed the wisdom imparted in McCann's victim impact statement. It was an irony that did not go unnoticed by Pelletier when he made his case for a six-year prison term.

Yes, Charlebois conceded, his client was going to jail, but he argued strenuously for a provincial term of two years less a day, rather than a lengthier federal term. An Ottawa criminologist hired by the defence called Dagenais a medical wreck who needed ongoing treatment. He urged Soublière to consider sending Dagenais somewhere to get help for his health problems, his alcohol and drug dependencies, and the sexual deviancy, which Dagenais still refused to admit.

The criminologist expressed concern that because of his age and physical deformity, Dagenais would have a difficult time if sentenced to a federal prison, which is where anyone sentenced to two years or more is placed. At sixty-six, Dagenais was more than twice the age of most inmates in Canada. "This man has already suffered and been disgraced. The media have broadcast his conviction and his activities and that is, I suspect, some form of punishment."

The judge decided to set the case aside for another month while he considered an appropriate sentence. As Dagenais hobbled out of the courthouse back door with his cane clenched firmly in his hand, he told reporters he was not guilty.

On March 19, 1993, Soublière sentenced Dagenais to five years in prison. At the time, it was the stiffest sentence any Christian Brother from St. Joseph's or St. John's had received, although it was "about average" compared to the sentences handed down against members of the Irish Congregation of Christian Brothers from Mount Cashel Orphanage in St. John's, Newfoundland.

In sentencing Dagenais, Soublière declared he was taking into account Dagenais' age and poor health. However, the lack of remorse and the denial on Dagenais' part compelled him to decide in favour of incarceration in a federal prison. Dagenais had abused the trust placed in him by the Church, the government, and the administrators at the training school, he said. "We built walls around that school, not of brick and mortar, but of much stronger material – walls of silence and indifference. I'm even tempted to say, walls of ignorance."

15

An Airtight Case

•

"What happened to me, a dog wouldn't do to another dog.
I thank Claude Larocque I am alive today."
— Armand Jobin, Jr., April 6, 1991

THE TRIAL of Jean-Paul Collin was one of the odder cases
that Crown lawyers had to deal with. The difficulties they
experienced reflected the psychological frailty and uncertain
resolve of many of the witnesses called to testify in these decades-
old abuse cases. Collin was acquitted of all the charges that were
brought against him.

The two main witnesses in the case were former wards who
had actually been brought together again by the public revelations
about the Christian Brothers in the spring of 1989. Both Claude
Larocque and Armand Jobin, Jr., had been wards at St. Joseph's
in the late 1960s. Both had memories of their time in the school
that continued to give them nightmares more than twenty-five
years later. Both had found solace in their friendship when they
were wards, and later, when they found each other again.

The day after the first meeting of the victims in Ottawa, I joined
the pair on a visit to St. Joseph's. Tears streamed down their faces

239

as they walked around the building, through wind-driven snow, pointing out familiar sights. There was the classroom where they learned Latin. There were the shops, the kitchen, the bowling alley, the swimming pool. And there, on the top floor, were the dormitories where they had been beaten, often until they bled.

They stopped briefly in front of the statue of St. Joseph that stood in front of the building. The saint held a child in his arms. The inscription on the pedestal said: "Saint Joseph, *protégez nous*" – Saint Joseph, protect us.

Larocque was by far the larger of the two. At St. Joseph's, the kids had called him Moonhead or Bunny. Despite his size, even then, he had been fast on his feet. He had represented the school in the Olympic torch run for the Montreal Summer Olympic Games. The Brothers had another use for his size and speed: Larocque was ideally suited for the goon squad sent after runaways.

Locals would watch the pursuit from the windows of their houses. Whenever a ward escaped, a Brother would select a handful of boys from the senior division, load them into the back of a truck, and then drop them off, one at a time, at intervals along the distant railway track. They would walk back towards St. Joseph's twenty or so metres apart, searching the tall grass, scrub brush, and cornfields for the frightened boy who lay trembling in anticipation of his capture. Larocque was so good at tracking escapees that often the Brothers sent him after a runaway alone.

"When I caught them and brought them back, the Brothers would ask if I punched them out," he explained. "If I said no, then they would punch me in the mouth."

Larocque was rewarded for his work with small gifts: a half a pack of cigarettes, a lighter, money. Two decades later, it shamed him to think that he had done such a thing. "I chased them and I punched them out," he said, tears welling up in his eyes. "I should have taken the punishment."

Larocque knew all too well how the runners felt. He had

escaped several times himself only to be caught and returned by area farmers. He stopped running away when he realized he had no place to go. His mother and stepfather in Ottawa didn't want him back. For six years, St. Joseph's was home.

Jobin, too, had taken off. Sent to the training school in June 1966 at the age of fourteen for theft of an electric fan, he had been categorized by the Christian Brothers as mentally deficient. (They assessed his I.Q. at 65.) After two suicide attempts in the school – futile and unreported attempts to hang himself in the stairwell – he confided to his father that he was being abused. Armand Jobin, Sr., didn't doubt him for an instant.

The elder Jobin, an Ottawa truck driver, had also spent time as a boy at St. Joseph's, where he had enjoyed almost legendary status. Once he took off during an unusual winter ice storm: he skated down Highway 17 all the way back to Ottawa. He had escaped to avoid punishment for having broken a Brother's nose during a hockey game. While on the lam, he visited the Brother in the hospital to taunt him. It was, he would later tell his son, the only satisfaction he ever got out of the place.

The Brother sent to collect him fared no better. Jobin, Sr., beat him up in the frontyard, astonishing the neighbours who thought it was a priest he had by the throat. Not wishing to tangle with Jobin further, the Brothers had granted him his freedom.

The younger Jobin's escape was not nearly as dramatic. His father had advised him to wangle his way into kitchen duty, where he would not be watched so closely. On the appointed day, the boy took the garbage out the back door of the school and just kept on going. His father was waiting in a car in a lane and they sped off, taking the back roads to Ottawa. Armand, Jr., savoured his freedom, but it wasn't long before the police came to his father's house and took him back to St. Joseph's.

Jobin's experience of abuse by the Brothers began his first night at St. Joseph's. While he was brushing his teeth, he mischievously sprayed another boy he knew from Ottawa with toothpaste. The next thing he knew he was flying headlong into the sink. He had not even seen the Brother coming. He was punished by having to stand perfectly still in front of the clock on the dormitory wall. Even the slightest movement earned him another blow from the Brother supervising the dorm. "When he figured I had learned my lesson, he said, 'Another Brother wants to see you.'"

Jobin said he was taken to a room at the end of a long corridor. As the door opened, he was thrust from behind headlong onto a bed and immediately set upon by two Brothers. One rolled him over on his back, pinned his arms with his knees, and thrust his penis in the direction of Jobin's mouth. Jobin said he yelled and twisted his head violently from side to side while the Brother ejaculated on his face. Jobin said the second Brother, who had been pinning his legs, then rolled him over, removed his boxer shorts, and sodomized him.

Larocque, who was sleeping nearby, recalled that Jobin was sobbing when he crawled into bed. "I asked him what happened. He said, 'The Brothers hurt me. The Brothers hurt me.' In the gym the next day, he came up to me and got it off his chest. Anybody who tried to hurt him after that, I fought them, and I got punished for it. I fought back at the monitors. I fought back at the Brothers."

Jobin credited Larocque with helping him survive St. Joseph's. The two men, and their wives and families, got together frequently after the scandal broke. It was great to have a friend with whom to commiserate.

Two days before the February 10, 1993, trial of Jean-Paul Collin, police investigators were gripped with foreboding. The case against fifty-eight-year-old Collin, who was known as Brother

Daniel during the four years he worked at St. Joseph's, appeared to be unravelling.

Collin had been charged with buggering Armand Jobin, Jr., two counts of assault causing bodily harm, and one count of assault. Jobin seemed to be a believable, albeit an excitable and somewhat inarticulate witness. Moreover, police had, in Claude Larocque, an independent witness who said he had consoled the victim when he went bleeding and sobbing to bed on the night of the assault. Or they thought they did.

But on February 8, 1993, police learned that Claude Larocque had changed his statement. He now claimed it was neither Jobin who had been raped on the evening of June 1, 1966, nor Brother Daniel who had been the rapist.

The OPP was aware that Larocque had been visited by private detectives, hired by lawyers for the Brothers, prior to the Crown's discovery that he intended to change his statement. Larocque, however, told the police he had decided to change his statement long before that meeting. He said he had called an Ottawa city police station earlier to ask how to go about it and was told to tell the Crown attorney of his intention when they met before the trial. Police suspected that Larocque had been induced to retract his story corroborating Jobin's allegation and called him in for questioning.

On February 9, Det. Insp. Tim Smith brought Larocque in to the OPP detachment in Ottawa for a hastily arranged polygraph test. When Larocque passed the test, the police were forced to consider the possibility that Jobin was lying. They were reluctant to accept this. After all, Jobin was the former ward who had hidden a knife in his sock when he first met with police. Although forty years of age, he remained so afraid of his nightmares that he often stayed awake all night. He was a man so psychologically shattered that no one really believed he would ever be able to enjoy a normal life, whether or not he was vindicated in court or benefited from the compensation package. The story Jobin had told police was intricate and they doubted that he had the capacity to invent it.

To complicate matters, Jobin was also a scheduled witness – one of eleven – against Brother André Charbonneau, the Horse. The Crown had a police officer willing to testify at the Horse's trial that Jobin had complained to him as a boy about being sexually abused by Brother André at St. Joseph's. It also had medical evidence showing that Jobin had major intestinal surgery shortly after leaving St. Joseph's to correct a prolapse – a portion of Jobin's intestine had collapsed upon itself, a condition a doctor said could be caused by either worms or sexual abuse.

With Larocque ready to declare his friend a liar, the Crown's cases against both Collin and Charbonneau were in jeopardy. On February 10, assistant Crown attorney Ronald Laliberté asked for a delay in the start of the trial to put Armand Jobin on the polygraph.

Jobin was perplexed by the turn of events. He knew his former friend had changed his story, but he wasn't sure why. He did know that when he asked Larocque to return an air-conditioner he had loaned him, he had been rebuffed. Jobin subsequently filed a police report alleging that Larocque had stolen the appliance, which effectively ended the relationship.

The police were not surprised that Jobin also passed his polygraph test. While Jobin was cheered immensely – he wanted to celebrate with a beer and a cheeseburger – Laliberté was less jubilant. He now had two key Crown witnesses with conflicting stories, both of whom apparently believed they were telling the truth.

The trial of Jean-Paul Collin got off to a slow start. Mr. Justice Jean-Jacques Fleury met briefly in his chambers with Laliberté and Gabriel Lapointe, Collin's counsel, before opening testimony. In this meeting, Lapointe argued vociferously to have the case dismissed in light of the new developments. Repeating his plea in open court, the defence lawyer also told Fleury that Jobin had offered Larocque "a house and a car" if he would support Jobin's story. He said that Larocque was prepared to testify that Jobin had falsely accused the Brother, that the wrong Brother had been charged, and that it was someone else who was raped that night.

By way of counter-argument, Laliberté showed the judge Larocque's 1990 statement supporting Jobin's story. He also pointed out that Larocque had an active criminal record with recent convictions for break-and-enter, fraud, aggravated assault, and obstructing justice.

Fleury read and reread Larocque's short statement, then took a brief adjournment to arrive at a decision. Returning to the courtroom, he announced that it would be premature to dismiss the charges against Collin before the evidence was heard.

Jobin was the first witness called. With his parents sitting in the front row of the spectator gallery, he described how he was molested by Brothers André and Daniel on his first night at Alfred in 1966. He said he remembered Brother Daniel especially well because his features and the dark-framed glasses reminded him of pop singer Buddy Holly.

"When he penetrated his penis in my ass, my rectum, I thought I was going to die," Jobin testified. "I yelled so loud that Brother André grabbed my head and shoved it into a pillow."

Following the attack, he said, the Brothers told him to clean himself up and get back to his bed. But before he left, they warned him not to say anything about the incident to anyone.

Jobin testified that as he made his way to the dormitory, he felt that he was having diarrhoea. But when he wiped himself, there was only blood on the tissue.

"I was sobbing," he said. "I heard a voice as I got to my bed. There was a young man by the name of Claude Larocque. At the time, I didn't know his name. He asked what was wrong. I told him in French, 'The Brothers hurt me.' Mr. Larocque told me, he said, 'Don't say anything to anyone because if you do, you are going to get a beating.'"

The next morning, Jobin said, he was awakened by a booming voice ordering the boys to get up. He noticed all the other boys were standing beside their beds so he stood up beside his. "I was standing up and I heard Claude go, 'Psst.' He gave me a movement to put my hands behind my back and bow my head, so I did. I saw Brother Daniel walking into the dorm.

"After coming to my bed, he seen the sheets full of blood. He took the sheets. He rolled them over. He told me to take my shorts off. They were full of blood. Claude Larocque was right beside me. He is the only one that knows."

Jobin said Brother Daniel gave him clean shorts to wear and took his blood-stained sheets and shorts to the laundry. When he came back from showering, he had clean bedding. After breakfast, when the boys were having a gym class, he told Larocque precisely what the Brothers had done to him.

Collin, a Montrealer, who had retired from the Christian Brothers in 1968, watched the proceedings intently from the prisoner's dock. He sometimes squeezed his bottom lip between his thumb and index finger, but he showed little emotion during Jobin's testimony.

Jobin further testified that Brother Daniel struck him in the head once after catching him masturbating in the washroom. The blow drove him into a wall and he cut his lip, he said. "He started slapping me. I tripped and he started kicking me in the stomach."

Under cross-examination by Lapointe, Jobin said he always

thought he had been sent to St. Joseph's for stealing a colouring book, but after he requested his ward files from the government, he learned he had been sent to the school for stealing an electric fan from a dairy. Asked why he had never mentioned the sexual abuse when he visited the school's doctor or nurse, Jobin replied, "I was too ashamed. I felt too dirty."

However, when his parents came to visit and saw the scars on his face and back, they asked how he'd gotten them and he told them. Jobin said his father had immediately confronted the school superintendent, Brother Maurice-Jacques. "My father went crazy. He said, 'I want an explanation of what you are doing to my son.' Brother Maurice-Jacques said, 'Mr. Jobin, can't you see he just wants to go home?'"

It was shortly after this episode, Jobin said, that his father started to plan his son's escape, which resulted in Jobin's absence from St. Joseph's for several months.

Lapointe started to expose the contradictions among Jobin's first statement to police, his preliminary hearing testimony, and his testimony at the trial. It quickly became apparent that Jobin had substituted Brother Daniel's name for Brother André's on occasion and had mixed up the incidents of physical abuse. As Lapointe pointed out the errors, Jobin grew increasingly frustrated. They were, he said, honest mistakes. He was trying to remember the events of more than twenty years ago as best he could.

Jobin initially had said that Brother Daniel had punched him in the face, driving his tooth through his cheek and creating a hole large enough to stick his finger through. Now, he told the court, it was another Brother, not Brother Daniel, who had punched him. He was nervous and confused when he gave the first statement, he said, and made mistakes. "There's a lot of things I do know and a lot of things I forgot," he told Lapointe. "I am not a mastermind. I am trying my best, Mr. Lapointe. I know what Brother André did to me and I know what Brother Daniel did to me."

Jobin told Lapointe that he and Larocque met "about eight times" after Larocque read about him in an *Ottawa Sun* story about abuses at St. Joseph's. "He was the only friend I had in Alfred. He used to protect me. Sometimes if Brother André hit me, he would even put himself in front so he wouldn't hit me again. He was something like a big brother to me."

Jobin said he never discussed the issue of compensation with Larocque. Still, he hoped to receive money for the horrific abuse he had endured at the training school. "I don't want to be a millionaire," he said. "I said, '$300,000 would be nice.'"

Laliberté cringed at this. Jobin pointed out that he didn't expect to receive money for testifying against the Brothers, but for the pain and suffering he endured at their hands so many years ago. He added that Helpline was not formed to win compensation for the victims, but to help them get justice.

As he was excused from the courtroom, he bowed to the judge.

The next morning a flaxen-haired man in a maroon shirt sat in the witness box. With his dimpled cheeks and slicked-back hair, he looked rather like an older Jimmy Dean. This was the man that Larocque now believed had been raped that night twenty-seven years ago at St. Joseph's, not Jobin. The OPP had located him the previous day in Winnipeg and flown him in to testify at the trial.

Nick Lee (not his real name) testified that there was much he had forgotten of his stay at St. Joseph's, but he still remembered Larocque, whom he had not seen in nearly three decades. "We called him Bunny – Bunny Larocque after the hockey player," Lee said. "The only friend I had when I was at St. Joseph's was Bunny Larocque."

Lee acknowledged he had twice been sexually abused at

St. Joseph's, but he testified it did not happen in a Brother's bedroom. The rapes, he said, occurred while he was in solitary confinement. "It was dark," he recalled. "There was a steel bed, a tiny little mattress. I was blindfolded. I was told to bend over and I did and a penis went into my body. It hurt me. I can't identify the individual who did it."

Lee said it was a large man who assaulted him, someone weighing between 180 and 220 pounds. After the assault, he said, he was sent to his bed in the dormitory. He remembered lying there, desperate for a drink of water, but he was too terrified to get out of bed. Eventually, he fell asleep and woke up, soaking wet, the next morning. "I thought I had peed myself or by accident I had diarrhoea, but when I checked my backside, it was all bloody. The blood was on the sheets. Also on the mattress." Lee and the other boys in the dormitory were sent to the showers, and when they returned, Lee noticed the bloodied sheets and mattress had been removed.

Under cross-examination by Lapointe, Lee said he had never told anyone about the incident.

Once Lee was excused from court, Claude Larocque's long-awaited testimony began. A ward of St. Joseph's from 1963 to 1969, Larocque said he was reunited with Armand Jobin, Jr., in the spring of 1990. Together they shared many of their memories of St. Joseph's.

"Did you witness anything that happened to Armand Jobin," asked Laliberté.

"I thought I did," said Larocque. "I thought I saw blood on a boy's underwear the morning after he woke up from crying and sobbing."

Larocque said he remembered telling a boy during the night to shut up and he remembered pointing out the blood on that boy's underwear the next day. He also remembered returning

from the washroom in the morning and noticing the boy's bedding
was gone.

"I thought it was Armand Jobin," he testified. "My evidence
today is that it was not him."

He recalled a boy being summoned to Brother André's room
that evening, he said, and he remembered thinking about what
would happen behind the closed door. "I knew because I seen
Brother André so many times on the junior side doing it to so
many kids. In a few minutes another Brother comes from upstairs
and he went into the room with Brother André. I turned around
and tried to fall asleep."

Larocque said he never discussed the incident with the boy he
thought had been molested, but he did vaguely recall discussing
it with Jobin the next day in the gymnasium. What he could not
be certain about was whether he and Jobin discussed a sexual
assault on Jobin or on Lee.

Laliberté asked Larocque if he remembered Jobin describing
how the Brother attempted to put his penis in his mouth. "You
remember Jobin telling you something about this?"

"Yes."

"What you don't remember is if it happened to him or
someone else?"

"That's right."

"The conversation in the gym, you don't remember if he said
it happened to him or someone else?"

"That's right."

"So you recall asking him if it was Brother Daniel?"

"Yes. I asked him if the other Brother was Brother Daniel. He
said it was the tall one who screwed him up the ass."

Larocque said Jobin had talked to him before he gave his statement to police and convinced him he was the victim.

"He said, 'That happened to me. Remember? Remember?' I

thought I could have made a mistake. I do not remember saying that it was Brother Daniel twenty-seven years ago, but I wrote it [in my statement to police in 1990]."

"Do you remember telling him [that night] to keep quiet for his own good?" asked Laliberté, referring again to Larocque's first statement. Larocque said he did not recall saying that, but put it in his statement because Jobin had told him in 1990 that was what he had said to him that night. He said he was angry and confused when he wrote his statement to police, and he wanted to get even with the Christian Brothers for the abuse he suffered over those six long years of his childhood. "When I wrote this," he said, referring to the statement Laliberté placed before him, "I was screwed up badly. I wanted revenge."

Later, after his friendship with Jobin had broken up and Larocque had time to think about what Jobin had claimed, he said he began to suspect Jobin was lying. "The things Jobin was saying didn't make sense. He said it was one rape. When money came into the [Helpline] group, he said it happened two or three times a week. I knew then he lied."

He said he had concluded that Jobin had tricked him into thinking it had been him who was abused. "He convinced me it was him. He played with my mind."

The only other witness to testify against Jean-Paul Collin was Wilfrid Marion, who had spent four years at St. Joseph's in the 1960s and 1970s. He alleged that, at age ten, he was savagely beaten by Brother Daniel after he tried to escape from St. Joseph's with another ward. "I was struck on the back, the thighs, the arms, the back of the head. I was bruised on the thighs, the arms, and the back. All I know is both of us were crying."

In cross-examination, Lapointe went over Marion's lengthy criminal record, which included a conviction for armed robbery and a number of drug charges. He then began to point out contradictions in Marion's statements. Was he struck with an open hand or a fist? "We have three statements from you, Mr. Marion. The first one, May 8, 1990, your testimony at the preliminary hearing November, 25, 1990, and your testimony today. Which is the true statement?"

"They both left bruises and welts on my body," Marion replied. "Maybe I am wrong on the punches, but I am not wrong about the man who abused me."

The next day, Collin pointedly denied all the allegations. He said he would not have and could not have committed the crimes. The records, Collin said, show that he was working in another dormitory on June 1, 1966, when Jobin claimed he was raped. Moreover, he hadn't become a supervisor in Jobin's dormitory until December, six months after the alleged incident.

On February 16, Fleury acquitted Collin on all four charges. Accusing Jobin of perjury, the judge said the former ward likely adopted another boy's true story of rape as his own for financial gain. He said Jobin had no credibility and was "manipulative and dishonest."

What was most disturbing about the entire case, said Fleury, was the fact that a boy indeed had been raped, yet no one had been charged with the offence.

Outside the courtroom, Collin told reporters he bore no grudge against the former wards who testified against him. "I forgive them," he said softly. "I'm glad it's over. I have no animosity. We forget and we continue on."

But Jobin could not forget. When he heard the verdict, he became suicidal. He checked into a psychiatric hospital and made an attempt to slash his wrists. The Crown subsequently decided not to call Jobin to testify against André Charbonneau after a psychiatrist warned that he might not survive the trauma of, again, not being believed. Also, police were uneasy because Jobin had threatened to kill Charbonneau with his bare hands if the man was also acquitted. During Charbonneau's sentencing hearing on February 4, 1994, an OPP officer was assigned to sit beside Jobin as a precautionary measure. But, throughout the hearing, Jobin remained calm.

The same could not be said of his father, Armand, Sr. During a break in the proceedings, he sidled over to Charbonneau and, after introducing himself, said, "You are going to burn in hell."

After pleading guilty to twenty-two counts of buggery, assault, and assault causing bodily harm, Charbonneau received the longest sentence of any of the thirty Christian Brothers thus far brought to trial: six years. Armand Jobin, Jr., was satisfied with that.

The Boys of St. Vincent

•

"The accused have a right to a fair trial, of course, but in this case we should be wondering if there's a distinction between rights and righteousness."
– Greg Quill, *Toronto Star*, December 8, 1992

THE FILM *The Boys of St. Vincent*, directed and co-written by John N. Smith of Montreal, told the story of an orphanage in Newfoundland run by a Catholic religious order. As described by a reviewer in *The New Yorker*, "from the outside, St. Vincent is Boys Town; on the inside, it's a Dickensian hell in which trapped boys burn for their elder's sins."

Smith had been in Newfoundland in the late 1980s shooting another film when Father James Hickey and the other Roman Catholic priests were charged with having abused boys. Smith had met Father Hickey while he was shooting a documentary on Tamil refugees coming to Canada.

Like most Canadians, Smith was shocked when Father Hickey was charged. As the scandal grew, he was increasingly perplexed by the reaction of the Roman Catholic Church and the government. He began to draft a story which, while taking its initial inspiration from the orphanage tragedy, he insisted was fiction.

The completed four-hour film was scheduled to run as a two-part miniseries on CBC-TV on December 6 and 7, 1992. Aware that the scandals at St. Joseph's and St. John's had some resonance with the events depicted in *The Boys of St. Vincent*, the National Film Board (NFB) and the CBC invited members of Helpline to an advance screening of the miniseries on December 1 at the External Affairs Department conference room on Ottawa's Sussex Drive. David McCann, in turn, extended invitations to others, including Ronald Caza, the Ottawa Brothers' lawyer.

McCann had developed some respect for Caza, who, he felt, had been "very creative" in moving the mediation process forward. Caza had close contacts with McCann and Helpline because he was the man who, on behalf of the Church, signed the cheques that kept the group afloat. McCann jokingly referred to him as "God's banker." The cheques usually came late, and McCann was often left to carry the bills on his credit cards, but he generally made light of it. He would prod Caza for the funds. "Could you please let me know if the mutual agreement we have has changed, or is there simply a bureaucratic delay that lawyers are famous for?" he asked Caza after a number of cheques got waylaid in the system. "Do lawyers have to take special aptitude tests to ascertain whether or not they can actively promote the bureaucracy, or is it simply a genetic trait that needs no assessment, but is obvious to the bar when they take their bar examination?"

Caza, too, had come to admire McCann and appreciated the former ward's contribution to the reconciliation talks.

At the advance screening, the former St. Joseph's wards who attended found *The Boys of St. Vincent* to be a powerful film. Many of the scenes of child abuse were so vivid the former wards could not bear to watch. McCann was just one of many who cried as they viewed the children being victimized and betrayed by the Church and the government as they had been.

Caza was moved, too, but in a different way. Three days after the advance screening, lawyers for the Ottawa and Toronto Christian Brothers were in court asking a judge to ban the film

from being aired in Ontario until after the jury trials of Lucien
Dagenais and a number of other Brothers in L'Orignal and
Whitby had been completed. The lawyers for the case relied
heavily on an affidavit, filed by Caza, describing the content and
the plot of the production. Caza complained about graphic scenes
of naked young boys involved in sexual activity with Brothers in
the first part of the film and the portrayal of lawyers for the
Brothers as cruel and insensitive in the second part.

"Because the audience has witnessed all of the actual physical
and sexual assaults, the contentions of the lawyers seem ridiculous and misleading," he noted. "The audience is left with the
feeling that the victims, no matter what problems there may be
with their testimony, should be believed because all of their problems are due to the abuse inflicted upon them by the Brothers."

On December 4, just three days before the first segment of the
show was to air, Madam Justice Lorraine Gotlib of the Ontario
Court, general division, banned not only the broadcast, but also
prohibited the media from reporting on the ban as well as the
reasons for her decision.

McCann was shocked by Caza's actions and angrily confronted
him at the next mediation meeting. "I felt he had betrayed the
trust I had placed in him," he explained later. "It was probably
foolish on my part to have invited him in the first place. I was
literally disgusted that again the Church wanted to slap a blanket
of silence over what I considered to be a very important work of
fiction."

At the *Star,* the *Globe and Mail,* and other newspapers, editors
grappled to save their already printed television guides from the
scrap heap. Both the *Star* and the *Globe* were featuring *The Boys of
St. Vincent* as their TV guide cover story for the week. After considerable discussion with its lawyers, the *Star* decided to distrib-
ute the guide in its Saturday newspaper, while the *Globe* held its
magazine back.

The decision to stop a broadcast of a fictional account of child sexual abuse by monks on the basis that it could impede fair trials surprised many in the legal community. How could a fictional account interfere with an accused's right to a fair trial? Surely a jury knew the difference between fact and fiction?

Clayton Ruby, a prominent Toronto lawyer, said it was one thing to "inconvenience" twelve jurors by telling them they have to put something they have seen out of their mind while they decide the case on its merits. It is an entirely different matter to tell ten million people they have no right to discuss the issue.

The *Globe* struggled to find a way to explain to its readers what had happened to the missing edition of its weekly television magazine. It ran a three-paragraph article on the front page of its national edition: "Somewhere in Canada yesterday, a group requested a court ban on the publication/broadcast of a certain work for certain reasons. The court granted a ban on the publication/broadcast and, in addition, imposed a ban on reporting the fact of the ban. This has required *The Globe and Mail* to withhold *Broadcast Week* magazine. . . . *The Globe and Mail*, with certain other parties, has mounted a legal challenge against the ban on reporting the ban on the grounds that it interferes with freedom of expression and freedom of the press and other media of communication, which is guaranteed in the Charter of Rights."

The appeal was argued on December 5, a Saturday – which constituted a rare emergency sitting of the Court of Appeal – and the result was even more astonishing. While the three justices of the Ontario Court of Appeal struck down the prohibition imposed by Justice Gotlib on reporting the ban, it upheld the injunction against airing the movie until the last of four upcoming Christian Brothers trials, scheduled for July 1993, had concluded. The ban applied to CBC-TV stations across all of Ontario and in Montreal.

Unfortunately for the *Globe*, which doesn't publish on Sundays, its readers were left in the dark until Monday, December 7. Turning on their TV sets to CBC on Saturday night, they expected to see a powerful movie about sexual abuse. Instead they found a rerun of *Justice Denied: The Donald Marshall Story*.

The CBC, not surprisingly, was also aghast at the ban on reporting the ban. "If Friday's ban had been allowed to stand, a film would have disappeared off the face of the earth without any reasons given," remarked Ivan Fecan, then the CBC's vice-president of entertainment programming. "It's hard to fathom that happening in a country like Canada."

John Smith was upset that none of the judges – neither the trial judge nor the three members of the Court of Appeal – had taken the time to view the film before making the ruling. An NFB spokesman expressed fears the production could be banned from broadcast for ten years because of the likelihood of future trials in similar cases. Indeed, at the time, police were still investigating a further three hundred allegations against the Christian Brothers in Ontario, and allegations against clergy were being raised across the country with increasing frequency.

"What you are saying is that if there is a murder of a pawnbroker, then you take *Crime and Punishment* off the shelves," lamented the NFB spokesman.

To the victims of St. Joseph's and St. John's, the ban was just another example of the awesome power of the Church. They had seen it firsthand decades ago and they were seeing it again. This time, the Christian Brothers were preventing millions of people from seeing a movie that wasn't even based on the tragedies of St. Joseph's and St. John's.

In December 1993, as the CBC prepared to finally broadcast *The Boys of St. Vincent* in Ontario, lawyers for the Toronto Christian Brothers struck again. Two weeks earlier, police had laid additional charges against five former Brothers and employees who had worked at St. John's, four of whom had also been charged initially in 1991. Once again, the order argued that airing the show would jeopardize the men's right to a fair trial.

This time the CBC's lawyers were ready. Dan Henry said the circumstances were dramatically different than when the court imposed the initial ban, which the CBC was now appealing to the Supreme Court of Canada. Because the Christian Brothers had only just been charged, considerable time would elapse between the airing of the show and their trials.

Clayton Ruby again slammed the application. "I don't think there is any realistic risk that Ontario jurors will be rendered partial by a work of fiction," he said.

Filmmaker James Cullingham, a graduate of the Christian Brothers' De La Salle Academy in Toronto, appealed to Brother Provincial Francis McCrea to drop the application. "In my opinion, your stated concern for a fair trial for those charged at the Uxbridge reformatory is actually a transparent attempt to suppress a film that raises legitimate and disturbing questions about the potential for the abuse of power by a Church official in even a fictional way," he said.

Smith was devastated that his film, which had been named the best dramatic series at the 1993 Cannes Television Festival and had won the grand prize at the Banff Television Festival, might be blocked a second time. "Everywhere this was shown in the world – Australia, Spain, Switzerland – it has caused a national debate about the subject in their own country," he said. "That needs to happen in Ontario."

However, that debate seemed to be precisely what the Christian Brothers were attempting to avoid.

Arguing that it would lose $600,000 in advertising revenue if the miniseries didn't air as scheduled, the CBC pressed the court to rule quickly on the injunction to enable it, if required, to appeal the court's decision before the scheduled broadcast. There was, however, no need for that. After viewing the film, Madam

Justice Sandra Chapnik of the Ontario Court, general division, rejected the application for the injunction on December 1, 1993. She said she found *The Boys of St. Vincent* to be "a responsible and effective film on a matter of public concern" and had every confidence that an unbiased jury could be found to try the accused Christian Brothers.

When the two-part miniseries was finally aired on the Sunday and Monday following the hearing, it had a profound effect on many viewers. More than one thousand people called a Kids Help Line that was monitored by counsellors after the broadcasts. Most of the callers were middle-aged men recalling incidents of abuse in their childhoods. The case, which the CBC argued all the way to the Supreme Court of Canada, prompted a landmark ruling that limited the future use of publication bans against what the court called "remote and speculative dangers." The Dagenais case, as it becomes known, recognized that the public's right to know was just as important as the right to a fair trial. It became an integral part of media arguments against subsequent bans in criminal cases across the country.

The attempts by the Christian Brothers to block the CBC broadcast astonished and saddened many Roman Catholics, who now wondered whether the money they were putting in the collection plate on Sunday was winding up in the pockets of lawyers for the Brothers on Monday.

17

The Final Analysis

•

"I don't think I will ever get over it. They can have a public inquiry.
They can throw the whole Brotherhood in jail and
it is not going to do me any good."
— Gerry Sirois, former St. Joseph's ward, September 13, 1992

IN JUNE 1993, the first compensation awards, fourteen in total, were granted to former wards by a panel seconded from Ontario's Criminal Injuries Compensation Board. During the trials, defence attorneys for the accused Christian Brothers made much of the notion that former wards were fabricating stories of abuse to win hundreds of thousands of dollars in compensation. But when the actual dollar figures were announced, almost everyone was stunned.

One man who had been raped received $10,000. Another rape victim got $12,000. One man got nothing. Worst off were victims of physical beatings: their awards ranged from $2,000 to $3,000. The average payout was $6,200, little more than half of what had been promised in the agreement.

The victims were incensed. Unlike the Christian Brothers' lawyers, they had not expected large amounts, but they had expected the average amount set out in the December 1992 deal. They had been extremely reluctant in the first place to put their trust back in the government and the Church, and now they felt betrayed.

"This is hard to swallow," said Michael Watters, now a member of the Helpline executive. "It's a slap in the face. It is like saying, 'We don't believe you again.'"

The former wards had already been disappointed by the meagre amounts of money they had been awarded for their unpaid labour at the training schools. While the order and the Church had acknowledged that the wards were entitled to wages for their work on the farm and in the shops, the payments, when they came through, were token.

Archie Villeneuvre, aged seventy-three, who was among the first wards sent to St. Joseph's, was flabbergasted to receive a $750 cheque for his three years of work in the institution's tailor shop in the mid-1930s. "I got that cheque and I said to myself, 'If I wasn't obligated on the government to live, I would send that fucking cheque back,'" he said. "But I needed it like any other guy." Villeneuvre, who said he had been sexually abused by two Brothers, both of whom were now dead, later received a second cheque for $1,579.13. At 3 per cent interest over fifty-five years, it worked out to four cents an hour.

Much to the chagrin of the Helpline executive, David McCann called me at the *Toronto Star* to express his displeasure with the awards. He had been among the first recipients, receiving, he said, $10,000 as compensation for fifteen sexual assaults and six beatings from seven Brothers. "When I see the most severe cases – and not just my own – coming in at what the average is supposed to be, I have a real problem with the deal," he complained.

Had he been conned, he wondered, by the government and Church negotiators? He warned other victims not to allow themselves to be abused again and recommended they demand a public inquiry "into the entire mess." McCann said he was mad enough to drop out of the witness protection program and return to

Ontario to lead a demonstration march to Queen's Park and to St. Michael's Cathedral in Toronto.

Not surprisingly, McCann's comments poured fuel on a fire the executive and Douglas Roche, now chairman of the implementation committee, were anxious to contain. All parties to the agreement were concerned about the low range of the awards, but no one really knew what could be done, short of reopening the agreement. As it stood, the implementation committee simply screened the applications for compensation and passed those it deemed worthy of compensation on to the panel from the Criminal Injuries Compensation Board. Unfortunately, no appeal process had been negotiated. The implementation committee could only try to persuade the independent panel members to bump up the awards.

On June 30, 1993, Roche sent a letter to all the victims listing the awards, and demonstrating that when topped up by various other funds, those in $2,000 to $12,000 range would actually be worth from $5,200 to $31,200. He also reminded them that each award was accompanied by a benefits package, worth an estimated $10,000 per ward, which provided opportunities for educational upgrading, job training, medical and dental treatment, and counselling. "I can only hope as this process continues to develop, that the intent of the participants around the table to effect this reconciliation will be attained," Roche said. "I don't think it is in anybody's interest to have 685 unhappy individuals."

The Ottawa Brothers remained hopeful that the negotiated deal would satisfy the victims. "When everything is said and done, I am quite confident that all parties involved, including Helpline, will be satisfied with the process," said Ronald Caza, the order's lawyer. "It is not the perfect process, but I think it will accomplish a lot of good."

The next batch of twenty-five cases went before the assessment panel in July 1993. The Helpline executive, anticipating more controversy, embarked on a series of trans-Canada meetings to cool the emotional temperature among their members. The fate of the deal hung in the balance. If the awards weren't higher, no one wanted to even think about the consequences.

Fortunately, the news this time was better. The average award for the second group was $10,360, making the average award for the thirty-nine cases assessed overall $8,969.

Although the second compensation round went a long way to defusing the anger, it didn't appease everyone. Some former wards wondered why they didn't all just receive an equal lump sum. "Abuse is abuse," one new Helpline member snapped at Grant Hartley at a membership meeting in Toronto. "What's fair about telling someone they're worth $25,000 and telling someone else they are only worth $3,000? We're talking about a group of men who are fucked for life – not about dollars."

Roger Tucker explained that the other parties insisted that each case be assessed on its own merits and each victim's suffering be compensated on its own merits. "Given that we had to go with individual assessments, we picked the most victim-sensitive body we could find, which was the Criminal Injuries Compensation Board. We tried to get the decisions made by people with as much experience as we could find. The board hears 2,000 cases a year; 1,500 deal with child abuse. I must say I am fairly comfortable with the decision. It was the best possible choice."

The fact that victims were still coming forward had required a further restructuring of the December 1992 deal, which had foreseen only four hundred victims in total. The number of former wards who had contacted Helpline or contacted police had now climbed well over seven hundred, and a second stage had to be built into the agreement to accommodate them. The Ottawa Brothers and the government bolstered the reconciliation fund by another $10 million, raising the pot to $23 million. If the Toronto Brothers decided to contribute, it would now cost them $8 million. But still the Toronto Brothers remained aloof.

As a result of the order's steadfast refusal to assist the victims of abuse at St. John's voluntarily, Tucker was exploring the possibility of bringing a lawsuit against them. It was not his preferred strategy, he said, and not one he would have pursued back in 1990 or 1991. "If we had gone in litigation after the Ottawa and Toronto Brothers and the government and the two archdioceses, we would be sitting here with nothing. If I spent my lifetime designing an organization that would be impossible to sue, I couldn't do any better than the Catholic Church."

It appeared, however, that a lawsuit could no longer be avoided. The former wards were angry that the Toronto Brothers had turned their back on them and were determined to make them pay. Their refusal to participate in the deal had reduced the awards to 80 per cent of what had been envisioned when it was negotiated. Helpline members were willing to contribute another $600 each, on average, to fund the civil litigation.

Tucker put four lawyers at his Ottawa firm to work on the suit. The legal situation had changed considerably since the first victims came forward in 1990. Class-action suits were now legal in Ontario, and the Supreme Court of Canada had ruled that there was no statute of limitations on sexual abuse cases. Moreover when a jury awarded $275,000 to a nineteen-year-old B.C. woman who had been sexually abused as a child by her father, it appeared there was no ceiling on what compensation could be awarded.

Any civil suit would be a nasty, long, drawn-out, and expensive procedure. Helpline's preferred approach was to keep the pressure on the Toronto Brothers to join the agreement. Perhaps, they thought, the Toronto Brothers were refusing to participate only while trials against members of its order were being held. But an article in the September 1993 edition of *Lasallian Signum Fidei* showed the Brothers' real reasons. The article, signed by Brother Provincial Francis J. McCrea, belittled the police investigation, claiming that in the vast majority of allegations, the police and the attorney general could not proceed with charges because of the witnesses' lack of credibility or the lack of evidence of wrongdoing.

Downplaying the fact that five of nine accused former staff members at St. John's had been convicted, Brother Francis focused on three acquittals and one withdrawal. "The failure of these prosecutions speaks for itself," he wrote. "Moreover, the failure of the police investigation to find any evidence of large scale abuse vindicates the Brothers' belief that St. John's Training School was a well-run institution. Unfortunately, the attorney general and solicitor general have directed the police to investigate and consider further prosecution of elderly Brothers and former Brothers. They, too, have now become victims of abuse – the abuse of an investigation which no longer serves a useful purpose."

The Toronto Brothers, he wrote, decided not to participate in the agreement for several reasons. One was that David McCann was the founder of Helpline, the organization "through which some of the money for the alleged victims was to be funnelled," and was "an admitted cocaine importer and an admitted persuasive liar."

Another reason Brother Francis offered for non-participation was his view that the reconciliation model appeared to be in conflict with the most fundamental principles of natural justice because the Brothers accused of abuse were not called to give evidence. The process implied guilt even before the accused went to trial.

It also was flawed, he argued, because a committee made up of a representative of each of the signatories to the 1992 agreement, rather than a qualified and impartial panel of adjudicators, screened the claims. Money, wrote the Brother Provincial, not reconciliation, not healing, was the primary motivation of numerous alleged victims, as their trials showed.

The animosity directed at McCann personally by individuals speaking on behalf of the Toronto Brothers was astonishing in its intensity. Melville O'Donohue, the Toronto Brothers counsel, said David McCann was the real villain of the piece. According to O'Donohue, every step the order took to stop McCann from carrying out his conspiracy to defraud the Church was justified. O'Donohue maintained that McCann was a con artist who was trying to blackmail the Church, and "we don't pay blackmail." The Christian Brothers' other general counsel, Peter Shoniker, said he considered McCann to be of worse character than any of the murderers he had ever encountered. Although both lawyers conceded there were legitimate victims of abuse at St. John's – often allowing that "even one case is too many" – they continued to use McCann as the reason they could not participate in reconciliation with the victims in Helpline. They maintained this position even after McCann had departed from the scene.

Since McCann had never been sent to St. John's, he wondered why the Toronto Brothers were so caught up in haranguing him. Several hundred former St. John's wards had come forward of their own volition to complain about abuse there, and McCann believed O'Donohue should begin to deal with them. Sure, he conceded, he had done some things in his life of which he was not proud, but why should the Toronto Brothers' animosity towards him cause them to turn their backs on the men the courts had already found to be legitimate victims of abuse? "I am not asking them to like me. I am asking them to do something that is very Christian."

O'Donohue replied that the order's own investigation had established that these claims were phoney. "These people saw and read about the horrible things that happened in Newfoundland and decided they would make some money by coming here and alleging that happened to them, even though it didn't happen."

Roger Tucker was furious with O'Donohue. Where was the Christian Brothers' compassion? The Toronto Brothers had yet to offer a single apology or help one victim of genuine abuse at St. John's. "The membership and executive of Helpline are amazed and shocked that the Toronto Brothers are able to spend literally hundreds of thousands of dollars or more on defending criminal actions, yet cannot spend a penny on helping a single victim. The door is still open. Why are they afraid to walk through it?"

The reconciliation deal didn't guarantee any victims any money, he insisted. Each former ward had to make his case to independent arbitrators who made an assessment of damages based on the balance of probabilities that the abuse had occurred – the same standard of proof required in civil litigation.

Moreover the compensation hearings were rigorous. It would take more than two years – until early 1995 – to assess the claims of the first 375 victims. Hearings for hundreds of men who came forward after the 1992 deal was signed were optimistically scheduled to be completed by the end of 1995. Those in this second group – ostensibly because they had not come forward until a compensation deal had been announced – would be subject to cross-examination by lawyers for the Christian Brothers.

The thought of having to wait so long was extremely disconcerting to some wards, who were anxious for some resolution that would enable them to put their suffering behind them. For some, just attending the meetings triggered nightmares from their days in the school.

Fortunately, at every Helpline meeting, someone like Clem Gagnon would stand up to remind everyone why they were there. Gagnon had been physically and sexually abused at St. Joseph's during his one-year stay in the mid-1960s. When he left in 1964, he had led a life, in a manner typical of many former wards, of alcohol and drug abuse, suicide attempts, crime. A mining injury had damaged his spine, and he now shuffled around with his back permanently stooped.

Gagnon said he probably wouldn't have survived the last three years without the counselling he had received through Helpline. The assessment panel had awarded him just $8,000 for the beatings, the anal sex, the forced fellatio. He wasn't happy with the amount, but he was not going to go through the rest of his life complaining about it. "It's $8,000 more than I had before and at least I get to share it with someone who loves me. The only thing I want to see is that one day – whether it's against boys or girls – this abuse has got to stop."

Gagnon wanted Helpline to lobby the government to establish residential treatment centres for male victims of abuse. "I think it's time they recognize that violence against men also exists," he said. "Let's not have the kids go through what we've been through."

In the meantime, Helpline was reaching out to other victims in need. As they hoped their agreement would be a model for other victims of institutional abuse, they offered support to the men and women who had been abused as children in Church-run Indian residential schools and elsewhere.

Roger Tucker encouraged the membership to hold together and praised them for what together they had already accomplished. "People are listening," he told them at one meeting. "You have made it socially acceptable to talk about child abuse. Society is changing. They were ready to hear you. If a guy on the street sees someone abusing a kid, he won't turn his head. He will call police."

Meanwhile, the police investigations and the court proceedings continued through 1995. Only a handful of accused won outright acquittals, but three cases – against Pierre Durocher, Jean Ravacley, and Jean-Paul Monfils – were stayed because the accused were deemed too ill to defend themselves. Another, against Étienne Fortin, was stayed as a result of the Crown's failure to disclose evidence to the defence. When, on February 11, 1984, André Charbonneau was sentenced to six years' imprisonment, it marked the conclusion of the cases against the twenty former and present St. Joseph's Christian Brothers first charged in 1991. Of the twenty, eleven either pleaded guilty or were convicted.

Only three of the most brutal Brothers from St. Joseph's – Lucien "the Hook" Dagenais, Léo "Puss Eyes" Monette, and André "the Horse" Charbonneau – were sentenced to federal prisons. It was expected that, because of their ages, they would be released at the earliest possible parole date. But for a time, all three, including eighty-three-year-old Monette, shared a wing at Kingston Penitentiary and were often observed shuffling down the prison hallways together. Dagenais had initially appealed his conviction, but he eventually dropped the appeal and served his time.

Aimé Bergeron, the St. Joseph's plumber, and Camille Huot, the monk who raped Lawrence Siple at his parent's cottage, both sentenced to two years less a day, were immediately released on temporary absence programs. Huot appealed his conviction, but lost at both the Court of Appeal and the Supreme Court of Canada.

Since almost as many former wards came forward after the reconciliation package was announced as before, the OPP continued its probes, pushing the total cost of the investigation close to $3 million. However, since most of the new complaints were against Brothers who are dead, jailed, or whose cases had already been stayed because of ill health, police focused upon only a small group of Brothers.

On November 23, 1993, the OPP laid twenty charges against five former St. John's employees. An investigation into a sixth man, who had earlier been acquitted, was aborted when the man suffered a heart attack and died. All but one of the men charged had been previously tried on charges laid in 1991, and three had been convicted and sentenced. The new charges were serious: buggery, gross indecency, and indecent assault.

One of the former St. John's Brothers facing new charges was a Roman Catholic priest named Father Robert Morrissey, who was known as Brother Frederick when he worked at St. John's in the early 1960s. Morrissey, convicted in October 1992 on charges of attempted buggery, indecent assault, and assault, now faced new charges of buggery, gross indecency, and three counts of indecent assault. He successfully appealed and was granted a new trial. The outcome was the quashing of the convictions on all sexual charges and a reduced sentence for the assault.

Although described in 1960 by his superiors as "weak, insincere and nervous," the nineteen-year-old Brother Frederick had been put in charge of a dormitory full of troubled youngsters and assigned to teach Grade 8 – for which he was manifestly unqualified. At his first trial, witnesses testified that he quickly acquired a reputation for roughness and "queering." Boys complained that he grabbed at their chests and buttocks. He was transferred to Montreal after two years. He resigned from the order but was subsequently reaccepted, only to resign again in order to enter the priesthood.

One man testified at Brother Frederick's first trial that when he was in his teens, the monk had plied him with cigarettes and candy to persuade him to have sex with him in his bedroom. After Brother Frederick was found guilty of all the charges and sentenced to prison for eighteen months, Bishop John Sherlock of London, Ontario, who had ordained Morrissey, complained to his congregation that the court had made a mistake. After a public outcry, the bishop apologized for stating his personal views publicly.

The new charges against Bernard Monaghan of Harrow, Ontario; Lawrence Lessard of Scarborough; Bernard McGrath of Brampton; and James Clarke of British Columbia did nothing to persuade the Toronto Brothers to accept what had happened at St. John's. As the Christian Brothers' lawyers in Toronto earmarked more money for a defence budget that had climbed to over $2 million, the Toronto order continued to argue that there had only ever been isolated incidents of abuse at St. John's. In all, the defence of the Christian Brothers accused of these supposedly isolated incidents was estimated, by one lawyer, at well over $6 million. Meanwhile, the Ottawa Brothers spent more than $16 million in legal fees for both the civil process and the criminal defence of the twenty accused monks from that branch of the order.

On September 2, 1994, Roger Tucker filed documents in an Ottawa court on behalf of twenty-eight former wards of St. John's. The 115-page statement of claim alleged a variety of abuse had been committed by sixty-four Christian Brothers and civilian employees at the institution between 1944 and 1979. Each ward was seeking damages of $1.4 million. The suit was the first of a series of claims for damages expected to reach nearly $300 million.

18

Boys Don't Cry

•

"Some of the boys are beyond hope and there's nothing anyone can do for them. Their lives are ruined. Some are dead and some are in jail, and some should be dead or should be in jail."
— Gerry Sirois, former St. Joseph's ward, March 21, 1993

THE MEN who came together in Helpline were a motley lot. Many had nervous mannerisms and missing teeth. Most could not read or write beyond elementary school level. Many were unemployed, and those who did work were stuck in menial or semi-skilled jobs.

The pain and suffering they endured as boys at St. Joseph's and St. John's could be neither outgrown nor easily forgotten. Paul Bennett, a Toronto therapist who counselled male sexual abuse victims, likened many of the survivors to shell-shocked war veterans. "We're not talking about people with minor psychological problems here. The damage is profoundly deep. None of these guys will ever be cured, and they probably will spend the rest of their lives trying to recover," he explained.

Some of the former wards exhibited post-traumatic stress disorders that triggered psychotic episodes. Insomnia was commonplace. Even those who could sleep suffered recurring nightmares. After leaving St. Joseph's, many found it difficult to find steady work and drifted from temporary job to temporary job, only to end up on social assistance. Those who worked earned annual incomes just above the poverty line. "They are just façades walking around and the only thing behind that façade is pain and confusion and anger," said Merlin Kobsa, another counsellor. "They are barely making it."

Some had turned to crime. Explained Bennett, "Their treatment in the schools set them up to be sociopaths. Many of them carry tremendous rage, anger, confusion, guilt, and shame."

For some of these victims, sympathy was hard to come by. Douglas Lawrence McCaul, for instance, had been sent to St. John's in 1967, when he was fourteen. During his two years there, he was sexually abused by a civilian employee. Six years after his release, he attacked and killed a Toronto woman. The circumstances of her death were so horrible that McCaul's three-day trial was closed to the media and the public "in the interests of maintaining public morals."

Bernard Jordan, who spent five years at St. Joseph's, became a biker and, between stints in jail, earned his living as a debt collector for drug dealers. Hurting people didn't bother him. Whenever he found himself thinking about the sexual and physical abuse he experienced at St. Joseph's, he either resorted to drugs and alcohol or started a fight.

Jordan was not the only ward who turned to drugs and alcohol. Many former wards used them. It was usually only when they sought treatment for their addiction that there was any recognition or acknowledgement of the underlying problem. One man said, "I quit drinking, or started to deal with my alcoholism, at age twenty-seven. Up to this point I thought my problem was alcohol, and I accepted responsibility for my behaviour and the consequences of my drinking. So the solution seemed simple: quit drinking and I would have no problems – only after eight years of complete sobriety, I found myself contemplating suicide."

Many went beyond just contemplating suicide. Nelson Trudel, a St. John's ward in the 1960s, tried to kill himself at least five times before he finally succeeded with a drug overdose in January 1993. "When he wasn't overcome by his past, he was a great father, a caring husband," said Jituska Smahel, his common-law wife. "He would help at food banks. But when his past would come back to him, he would have bouts with the bottle and talk in circles about his childhood and get extremely bitter and suicidal. I have always wondered what would have become of him had he not been haunted by the demons that plagued his soul."

Trudel killed himself after a family friend informed police and the Children's Aid Society that Trudel was abusing one of his daughters. The daughters were interviewed and no charges laid, but Trudel was devastated. In the suicide note to his wife, he wrote, "Hello and Goodbye. Honey, I can't tell you enough how you are my first true love. The Church, once again, has succeeded in stealing my soul. I have been accused by a friend of a crime so heinous, well – child molestation. Just imagine how I feel."

Trudel's horror and revulsion at being accused of committing child abuse was shared by many former wards. The scientific literature on the correlation between victimization and future abuse is not definitive: some psychiatrists and psychologists estimate that 30 per cent of those who abuse children were abused themselves. Many wards, however, believed most victims were seen to be abusers and were terrified that if they spoke out about having been abused, Children's Aid would swoop down and snatch their children away to protect them from similar abuse.

Some, at least, did become abusers. One forty-year-old former ward, who had been sexually abused by both staff and fellow wards during his three-year stay at St. John's in the late 1960s, was twice convicted of child molestation after leaving the school. "I can now see both sides of the coin," he said. "I can see that these Brothers took out their years of isolation and the anger on those who were vulnerable. I don't agree with it, but I can understand it now."

For his last offence, touching a five-year-old for a sexual purpose in Edmonton in 1991, he was sentenced to one year in jail and received treatment at Alberta Hospital, near Edmonton. "I don't try to make excuses for what I have done. There's a part of me that wants to go back to jail and stay there for life, but I don't want to be in a place where I could be abused again."

One British Columbia man, who had been abused while at St. John's in 1948, said eight of his ten adult children "are all confused and on welfare." Thrice-married, the man calls it a chain reaction. "I have passed it on to my children and I see it going on to their children. There is sexual abuse. I see their children having the same problem."

Sexual confusion and dysfunction were not uncommon among the wards who often asked themselves am I straight? Am I gay? Was there something about me that triggered that sexual response from the Brothers? One former St. John's ward worked as a male prostitute after he left the school, then decided he was heterosexual, found a "straight" job, married, and raised a family. Another former St. John's ward wanted to have sex with virtually every woman he met just to prove he wasn't gay. Others adopted a code of silence, coupled with a "more-macho-than-thou" stance. Any sexual intercourse, especially fellatio, became something "dirty" for others: one former St. Joseph's ward punched his wife in the face, breaking her nose, after she attempted playfully to perform oral sex on him as he slept. He thought he was back at the training school.

Another man, molested by two Brothers at St. Joseph's, spent many of his thirty years of marriage sleeping behind a locked door in a room separate from his wife's. Diagnosed as obsessive, compulsive, and narcissistic, he was revolted by sniffing, coughing, snoring, gurgling, and barking. The sight of people chewing gum or eating popcorn could bring on a cold sweat, cramps, and nausea.

Few former wards ever achieved success. Most were so encumbered with problems from their childhood experiences that they fell into ruin along the way.

Benjamin Chee Chee was an Ojibwa from Temagami, Ontario, one of many Indians at St. Joseph's. At any one time, North American Indians made up a third of the St. Joseph's ward population. Chee Chee's life mirrored the lives of hundreds of other wards. The only difference was his remarkable artistic talent and his perseverance in bringing it out.

Chee Chee was twelve years old when, in 1956, a judge decided an evening of joyriding in a stolen car deserved a period of indefinite incarceration at St. Joseph's. He was a ward there for four years. Chee Chee was a runner. Every chance he had, he would make a dash, usually short-lived, for freedom.

Then came the strap and solitary confinement. But once the handcuffs came off and the welts had begun to heal, he was off again. Where Chee Chee thought he was going, no one really knew. He was five hundred kilometres from home and there was little for him there. It was more than his mother could do to look after him, and his father was dead.

Chee Chee was a quiet boy who kept to himself, but the other wards could not fail to notice his talent for whittling and sketching. He would sit on a bench in front of the wooden lockers in the basement recreation room and draw while the other boys played floor hockey. He loved to draw birds, and began to nurse a quiet ambition to be an artist.

Released in 1960 with a Grade 8 education, Chee Chee moved in with his mother in North Bay and began to attend high school. But he soon lost interest in academics and wandered back to Temagami and places beyond, doing odd jobs, getting drunk, getting into fights.

He was encouraged by friends in Montreal to put his artistic talents to use, and by 1965, he was painting billboards and exteriors for a living. He helped paint the British Pavilion at Expo 67, strutting his talent on the high scaffolding where few dared go. In 1973, he moved to Ottawa and a lawyer friend there helped to arrange his first exhibition, a collection of colourful abstracts in painted beadwork patterns on graphic backgrounds. Chee Chee joked he was selling beads back to the white man.

The twenty-nine-year-old could scarcely believe that people would pay money for his work. He used the canvas to express his life: his sadness, joy, and humour. One painting showed a group of birds "hot-footing" across a lake on take-off. Another, purchased by the Royal Ontario Museum, featured the seemingly aimless tracks of wandering caribou. One depicted a herd of buffalo sheltering in the haze of a prairie dust storm. The National Indian Brotherhood, the forerunner of the Assembly of First Nations, commissioned a painting of a buffalo for a calendar in 1977. But he was best known for his colourful acrylics of flying birds. They were his obsession.

Sadly, his success in the art world did not spill over into his personal life. He was a moody man, prone to drinking binges and fits of rage. Sometimes his marathon painting sessions would end abruptly with him destroying a nearly finished work or throwing cans of paint against the wall of his apartment. He often joked that he could sell his wall and carpet as a Chee Chee original.

Art critics said Chee Chee painted in the style of the second generation of Woodland Indian Painters, but unlike its founder, Norval Morrisseau, and his contemporaries, Chee Chee's work had an abstract flair. Bright colours. Bold strokes. *Kitchener-Waterloo Record* art critic Liane Heller found his paintings of birds to be "dark, almost stark, communicating both the loneliness and the ecstasy of freedom in flight." For his part, Chee Chee denied that he was an Indian painter. He was a painter who just happened to be Indian.

Sometimes he had difficulty accepting the acclaim that was heaped upon him. He often felt that people liked his work, but not him. He worked hard, then he partied hard. He would slave away in his apartment for weeks, cooking and eating from a single pot, until he had enough work to sell. Then it would be the best hotels and restaurants and bars until the money was gone. Although he could sell a single painting for $450, he once had to borrow $150 to go to Toronto to see one of his own exhibits.

"His life was marked by unhappy and haphazard events," a friend would write in 1975. "He was convinced that only death could bring him peace, and he is said to have been near dead already five times."

Chee Chee attended Alcoholics Anonymous meetings with his mother, but he couldn't seem to overcome the addiction. After one exhibition, in Vancouver in January 1977, Chee Chee was arrested for drunkenness. A few months later, back in Ottawa, he went on another binge. On March 12, 1977, he was arrested for causing a disturbance outside an Ottawa restaurant and placed in a cell for difficult prisoners on the fourth floor of police headquarters.

Fifteen minutes after he was placed in his cell, he was found hanging by his shirt from the bars. Death came two days later, just twelve days before what would have been his thirty-third birthday. Police said he had a blood alcohol content of .337 milligrams – about the equivalent of drinking fifteen bottles of beer, more than four times the legal limit.

"It was a tragic end to a tragic life," said Pierre Gaignery, who owned the gallery where Chee Chee held his first exhibition. "Benjie was a very sad, lonely man."

He died a pauper, leaving his friends to solicit donations to pay for his funeral. Except for his brief embrace with fame, he could have been any one of the men who would later claim to have been abused as children at St. Joseph's and St. John's.

It's a tenet of the therapeutic professions that the uncovering of forgotten, painful experiences locked in our unconscious is a good thing. Once these memories are brought to consciousness, they can be talked about, understood, modified, and, over time, made to loosen their hold on us. Hysterical misery, in Freud's words, can be transformed into "common unhappiness."

However, for some of the former wards of Ontario's training schools, the revelations of the spring of 1990 were hardly therapeutic. Their lives, after all, had been built on coping, surviving, denial. Their fragile worlds were maintained by a combination of drugs, alcohol, and long-suffering spouses. When the news broke, they were faced with a choice of either confronting the demons they had tried to keep at bay and joining forces with fellow sufferers, or keeping the lid on and stay at home. More and more chose to come forward. While some would confess to their wives that they had been sexually abused at the training school, that was as far as the catharsis went. No amount of potential financial compensation nor the satisfaction of seeing justice done could make them change their minds. While they could freely admit to having been physically beaten, they balked at talking openly about sexual abuse.

The wives of other former wards have seen their husbands disappear for months at a time, provoke fights in bars, or pack up the whole family and move three times in a month. One woman's husband broke her nose on two occasions. The closer she tried

to get to him, the harder he would push her away. She has lost
track of the number of times he has left her, but he has always
come back. "To be blunt, our lives have been hell. When we met,
I honestly don't think he knew how to love, nor how to accept
love from someone. I have been chastised by my friends and my
family for sticking by him, and I don't regret it, although it has
been hard."

Many of the wives had coddled their husbands all their married
lives, acting as both mother and lover. They frequently had to
assume full responsibility for taking care of the family and their
husbands. Joan Hartley said that in the early years of her marriage to Grant, he would often have nightmares and thrash around
in bed. He would go drinking and disappear for days at a time.
She felt he was unreasonably harsh with the four children,
although he rarely struck them. None of the four have finished
school. All have had difficulties in their relationships and problems with drugs.

But she has seen a new side of her husband emerge as he began
to deal with the experiences of his childhood. "As each day goes
on, Grant grows and is more and more willing to show his humane
side, to reach out for help when he needs it. He has come to the
realization that not everyone is out to get him and that he is not
alone."

Susie Costello, a co-ordinator with the Ottawa Rape Crisis
Centre, said it is not unusual that the men stayed quiet about
their pain for so long. "We're not very kind to abuse victims,"
she said. "There is a strong tendency to minimize their pain and
blame them for what happened." While the women's movement
gave women the courage to speak out against rape, men have not
yet come that far. "It's even more difficult for them to talk about
abuse, especially sexual abuse. Men are expected to be strong and
look after themselves."

No one can say for certain what the abuse of so many children had cost society, but police and social workers pegged it in the billions. "I am sure the cost has been astronomical," said therapist Paul Bennett. "Most of these individuals ended up in society's safety net – the mental health system, the criminal justice system, drug and alcohol treatment programs, and family counselling."

As the abuse they had kept silent about all their lives became public, most again needed help. But many could not afford the cost of bus fare to see a therapist, let alone the $75 an hour fee for counselling. On April 17, 1990, the province began providing counselling to the former wards of St. Joseph's through the Ottawa-Carleton Family Services Centre. The centre provided one-on-one counselling and group therapy to former wards, their spouses, and their families. Victims from other regions of the province were able to choose their own therapist and have the fees paid by the province through the Ottawa-Carleton centre, which took on the responsibility of administering the province-wide program.

Some former wards were already in therapy, but the new clients who flooded the centre were in a volatile state when they came through the door. All the therapists could do was try to contain the crisis.

Former wards in the Ottawa area would meet for group counselling each Tuesday evening in a starkly furnished, smoky, bare-walled basement room. At first the meetings, which often lasted four hours, were full-blown "ragefests," with men pounding their fists on tables and shouting to be heard. Bitter arguments often broke out among them, and they often blasted their therapists. It was as if they were openly challenging the counsellors to betray them. Each mention of the case in the media or the revelation of a new horror story would set the victims off, making it virtually impossible for counsellors to embark on a treatment program. It was all they could do to keep the victims from taking matters into their own hands.

One ward said he dreamed of killing the Brothers with rat poison. Another threatened to burn down their churches and homes. Another was intercepted by police headed to St. John's with a loaded handgun.

Counsellor Frank Landino said, "They were so stuck in their rage and anger that for a long time the work was maintenance – just helping them to manage their anger. I must say I never expected in my life to ever encounter something like this. I never realized there could be such sadism. I have heard some terrible things. It is hard to comprehend."

Landino found himself caught up in the victims' pain and often wept at their stories of abuse and degradation. He saw men whose development had been radically stunted. They weren't just uneducated, they were arrested emotionally, cognitively, and intellectually. Most seemed to lack basic life skills, making it difficult to relate to them.

"The abuse twisted their ability to connect in any meaningful way with the outside world," Landino noted. "If anyone looked at them on the street, they punched them out. They carried knives. Many of them had guns. They were mad at the world. My own honest opinion is that if they [hadn't] come to counselling, a lot of them would have gone out and committed suicide, or robbed a bank, or hurt somebody else out there. There are quite a few who have attempted suicide, either by trying to hang themselves or taking overdoses."

Almost two-thirds of the former wards who came forward did take advantage of some form of counselling program, as did many members of their families.

David McCann has little doubt where he would be without the therapy he has received through the deal. "I would not have survived the last six years," he said. "I would have killed myself. Counselling has permitted me to openly reach out and embrace those who love me."

Former St. John's ward Paul Goulet said his therapy sessions have given him a greater sense of self-esteem and a positive outlook on life. "I don't think of myself as an evil, worthless person anymore."

Many former wards fear that their problems will remain long after the funding for counselling has run out, but most have learned coping skills they hope will help them survive that day.

Epilogue

Throughout 1994 and 1995, there were many heartwarming stories of lives changed as a result of the reconciliation agreement. Although the compensation payments the victims received were not large, for many it was the most money they had seen in a lump sum in their lives. For some, it was enough to put a down payment on a house, or buy a car, or take a trip.

Patrick Healey, who had been struck in the head with a crutch at St. Joseph's, took his thirteen-year-old son, Sean, to Disney World. Another former ward, who had spent time at both St. Joseph's and St. John's, used his settlement to purchase the best available photographic equipment. Armed with a contract to "shoot" a prison chaplain's conference in Toronto, he resumed his discontinued career as a professional photographer.

After two police officers attended Armand Jobin's compensation board hearing and testified on his behalf, he received one of the largest settlements the board designates awarded. The detectives told the panel they were convinced Jobin was the victim of brutal sexual assaults at St. Joseph's, but that he lacked the communication skills to present his allegations adequately in court. Police believed that Claude Larocque may actually have witnessed attacks on both his friends at St. Joseph's and confused them in his mind.

The board, which makes its rulings based on the civil court standard – the balance of probabilities, rather than proof beyond a reasonable doubt – awarded Jobin $25,000, which when added to contributions from the Christian Brothers and the Catholic archdioceses, topped $50,000. It was far below the $300,000 he had hoped for, but he believed in the end that he had been treated fairly. Although Jobin used some of the award to purchase a vehicle and tucked some away for a trip to Disney World, he said he would trade it all away to escape the nightmares that still haunted him.

"The money they gave me made a difference because before I had nothing," he said. "I got the maximum, but that doesn't keep away the nightmares. It doesn't stop me from urinating and defecating in bed. It doesn't stop that." He and his wife split up shortly after he received his award.

After testifying in court at the trials of Aimé Bergeron and Lucien Dagenais, Gerry Belecque pulled up stakes in North Bay and moved to a remote community farther north. His testimony against the Brothers, he said, had alienated him from his staunch Roman Catholic parents and made him feel like an outcast in his own community. He was still looking for that inner peace that David McCann talked so much about.

Gerry Sirois, whose wife Hélène had once described him as a man "trapped inside a wall," was eventually divorced. He gave his award to his two daughters to attend college – one to study nursing, the other, accounting – and they invested some in the stock market. When the implementation committee refused his application for $3,000 from the opportunity fund, he threatened to go to small claims court. He eventually received the money.

Gerrard Hinds, the rapist who was accused of lying to gain compensation at Réjean Nadeau's trial, received nearly $40,000.

For some former wards, the public airing of the shameful secret of their abuse was therapeutic; for others, it was not. Daniel Joanisse, who had been incarcerated in Penetanguishene's Oak Ridge maximum-security psychiatric hospital for twenty-two years, used his award and a seven-day pass to carry out a vengeful attack against St. John's.

In the summer of 1994, Joanisse tried unsuccessfully to set the main building ablaze. He finally managed to set a vehicle in the parking lot on fire. When he returned two days later, armed with a hunting knife and a pair of binoculars, police were waiting and took him into custody.

Joanisse, who had been found not criminally responsible for the attempted murder of a childhood friend when he was just a teen, said later his intention was to "hurt the people who hurt me. It is not like I went to a corner store and did this. This was a place where I was abused. I wanted to get back at them. I don't regret what I did." His lawyer called his actions "a cry for help. He is hurting. He is like a lost soul."

Joanisse was sentenced to six months in a provincial reformatory, where he could receive counselling for sexual abuse. The penal hospital where he had spent most of his life was more adept at treating abusers than victims.

He had been angry that the school had not been closed or taken over by the Ontario government. But this has not been for lack of trying. Officials in Ontario's Ministry of Community and Social Services have been involved in two years of futile negotiations to purchase or lease St. John's from the Toronto Brothers.

By the summer of 1995, the independent panel had paid out more than $9 million to more than 350 former wards of the two training schools, but the process was so filled with snags that at times it seemed it was barely moving.

Patrick Healey, who had taken over the leadership of Helpline, said he could not recommend the process to anyone else unless "there was a big turnaround in the way it was run." He added, "It needs to be refined so there are less delays. It needs to acknowledge that it is dealing not with numbers but with human beings who have been hurt and traumatized and who have carried this pain silently most of their lives."

The financial problems that plagued Helpline throughout the reconciliation negotiations had continued through the implementation stage. Healey said the executive frequently had to go to the Church and government with hat in hand, begging for enough funding to keep the phone lines and advocacy office open. "We were like little birds following a trail of crumbs, and in the end, we weren't even getting crumbs anymore. Victims should certainly not have to be beggars," he said.

The financial difficulties, coupled with the stress of dealing daily with the tremendous needs of the victims and the endless bureaucracy, led Tina Lentz to resign her job as Helpline coordinator on May 26, 1994. She suffered a heart attack soon after. In her letter of resignation to Douglas Roche, she expressed her strong objections to the manner in which the agreement was being implemented. One former ward, Ralph Jackson, had already killed himself after his claim stalled somewhere in the system. "He believed he would never see compensation," she said. "He felt he had been abandoned. There are too many hoops, too many forms, too many delays." She said it was proving too much for the former wards, many of whom had barely a Grade 4 education.

Lentz also had harsh words for the Church and the Ottawa Brothers. She said they appeared to take no real responsibility for the victims, and although they talked about reaching out to the victims, their words were really only window dressing. "In actual fact, [their] actions show that the Christian Brothers give as little as possible, drag it out as long as possible, and treat it like an insurance claim. This would appear to be an attempt to discourage the victims and make them go away."

In the wake of these criticisms, all the representatives met to draft a strategic plan to address what Roche called "irritants" in the agreement. They established a schedule of funding for Helpline and the process until the end of 1995 and set out what key principles should be followed in order to foster trust and respect among the parties.

But all Roche's deft masonry came crashing down on August 15, 1994, with news of the suicide of former St. John's ward Bernardo Bafaro. The forty-seven-year-old Toronto man overdosed on heroin after telling his sister he could not cope with the delays in the compensation process. Bafaro claimed he had been told that his application for compensation had been bumped from the first group of victims to the second group, delaying his settlement by at least a year. "He was really frustrated that nothing was going right," his sister said. "He was angry and yelling and screaming."

When news of Bafaro's death reached Roche, he arranged for the family to receive $3,000 for funeral expenses. Ironically, that was the amount Bafaro was eligible to claim as a grant under the agreement's "opportunity" fund.

Healey called Bafaro's death "a tragic failure. Sometimes it seems like we're running a gauntlet and every once in a while somebody gets struck with a fatal blow." The other parties in the deal, he said, were obsessed by the cost of the process and seemed to have forgotten what it was all about. "It is not like we are manufacturing cars here or fixing washing machines."

When David McCann learned of Bafaro's death, he was devastated. "I am angry as hell over this, and my nightmares have returned," he roared over the telephone to me. "We entered this process to avoid tragedies like this."

Roche tried to control the damage and keep the process on track, but this time he was infuriated by Healey's comments, which were published in the *Toronto Star*. He sent out a fax to all parties in the agreement demanding a conference call, after which he would submit his resignation unless the criticisms of the process were immediately withdrawn. "With all its problems, this historic process is worthwhile – but not at the cost of unchallenged falsehoods," he stated.

When Healey and Michael Watters advised Roche through their lawyer that they would not be available to take the conference call, he postponed it until the next day. But Helpline had concluded that Roche had ceased to be a neutral member of the reconciliation process, and again they advised him they would not be available. Roche's neutral position had become compromised by his participation in attempts to implement a reconciliation agreement between Chippewa natives on the Bruce Peninsula, three hundred kilometres north of Toronto, and the Jesuit order. Roche had been hired as a negotiator for the Jesuits. While he maintained he was not in a conflict of interest, former wards wondered how he could be neutral one day and on the side of the Church the next.

Nevertheless, Healey and Watters did write a letter to the editor of the *Toronto Star* on September 1, 1994, clarifying their statements and endorsing the reconciliation agreement. Roche would later concede that the implementation of the reconciliation agreement was being attempted in what was at times "a toxic environment." And the most controversial aspects of the agreement, the apologies to the victims from the Church and the legislature of Ontario, had yet to happen. After Bob Rae's government was swept from power in June 1995, it was unclear if they ever would.

Meanwhile police continued to investigate a seemingly endless stream of complaints. By the spring of 1995, more than a thousand former wards had come forward with allegations of abuse, including more than one hundred since Roger Tucker announced the lawsuit against St. John's.

Det. Insp. Tim Smith expected to lay even more charges as new victims came forward. "I don't think it is ever going to completely stop," he said. While some victims claimed not to have been aware of the investigation prior to the lawsuit announcement, many indicated they had been grappling with the idea of coming forward for some time. It was not an easy decision to make, particularly for those who had been sexually abused.

The cases of the five St. John's employees charged in November 1993 with twenty sexual offences were slowly making their way through the courts in Oshawa and Whitby. All five were remanded to trial. (One, James Clarke, pleaded guilty in 1995 and was sentenced to nine additional months in jail.) By spring 1995, Roger Tucker's firm had filed six lawsuits on behalf of 160 former St. John's victims, claiming more than $225 million in damages against the Toronto Brothers and St. John's. The firm was working on six additional claims involving a similar number of victims when it was replaced by another firm in April. Meanwhile, lawyers for the Toronto Brothers finally began making overtures to settle with the St. John's victims in a procedure separate from the reconciliation agreement. Peter Shoniker, general counsel for the order, suggested the creation of a panel consisting of a former St. John's ward, a former Metro Toronto police chief, and the former head of the provincial Criminal Injuries Compensation Board to hear the claims. Panellists would vote either to accept or reject the claim, and the majority would rule. However, if a claim was rejected on the basis that the panellists did not believe the applicant, the victim would still have the option of taking a lie detector test.

David McCann was still angry that the Toronto Brothers had ignored the St. John's victims for nearly five years while the other parties struggled to reconcile their differences, but he hoped they would now move to implement a fair and just proposal.

As the Toronto Brothers opened discussions, in Newfoundland the Irish Christian Brothers and the provincial government conceded that they were, in fact, liable for the damages claimed by the victims of Mount Cashel Orphanage. The amount of compensation due to the victims, however, remained at issue.

McCann saw the reconvergence of the two tragedies as a sign that attitudes were indeed changing within the Church and government and hoped that the victims both on the East Coast and in Ontario would at last take the final steps in their journey towards healing.

David McCann remained in hiding, although his health was poor and he longed to return home to his friends and family. From time to time, he contacted trusted friends and followed the latest developments in the implementation of the deal he negotiated, but for the most part he refrained from commenting on the issues publicly. He deferred to the new leadership now, men he trusted and respected. The executive still read his letters aloud at meetings, never forgetting that he was their leader, if now only in spirit.

His own mortality preoccupied McCann now. In 1993, he was diagnosed as being HIV positive, and soon he could not help but wonder if Helpline would be his last achievement. There was still so much he wanted to do, so much he had not done.

He prayed that the reconciliation agreement he had helped negotiate would work and that the dying would stop, but he knew full well that Bernie Bafaro's untimely death would not be the last.

Afterword by David McCann

Should I have made that phone call to Darcy Henton? Would someone else eventually have called another reporter if I hadn't? Has it been worth all the anguish and pain? I know there are no real answers to these questions. Perhaps it is a futile exercise at this point, but I can't stop wondering about it all. So much has happened since I was inspired by the courage of the boys of Mount Cashel to speak out. Every now and then I have to stop and be still for a moment and ponder how my life has changed.

In my heart, I know what I did was an achievement. It was more than worth it in the sense that it was the right thing to do. It had a tremendous impact on a lot of people's lives, and will continue to do so.

But for me personally, it was a disaster. I'll never regain what I lost: the simple pleasures of a quiet country life, the neighbours who always had an extra plate at their table and a chuckle for some of the outrageous stories I told. There was always the shadow world, but it was separate from my private life.

I'm very melancholy and homesick and lonelier than I have ever been. I still smile and laugh, enjoy the beauty around me, but my pleasure is tinged with a sadness at what might have been.

Could I have made something more out of my life? How would my life have been different if I had never been sent to St. Joseph's?

There is not much I can change in the time I have left. Many of my friends have already died of AIDS. I watched them fade away, some with dignity and many without it. None lived more than six years after they tested positive. Not much time, is it?

I dreamed of accomplishing something far greater than the deal that was negotiated, but I guess it's true that reality always intrudes into the affairs of men. By speaking out, I turned my world and the world of hundreds of others upside down. I walked away broke, burned out, and knowing I would probably spend the rest of my life alone. Now I wonder if there is any point in me staying underground when I already have a death sentence hanging over me.

It amused me to see the lawyers, private detectives, and journalists trying to figure me out, trying to define me as this person or that person. No one is all bad and no one is all good. I am so full of contradictions that even I don't understand myself. I have so many competing values that I find it impossible to reconcile them. Take me for what I am.

The first fourteen decisions of the Criminal Injuries Compensation Board designates wounded me deeply. While I do not envy them the job of putting a price on a man's pain, their awards were insulting. I will survive the revictimization, but what about the others? What about the man who got nothing because he would not admit he was mistaken about the dates he was abused?

I had to fight to get my medical and dental benefits, and I had to fight for counselling, both of which were to have been provided under the agreement. Then I had to fight for my apology. It made me realize that negotiating the deal was one thing and making it work is another. I now know that, unfortunately, the victims will have to battle every step of the way, and if they let up their guard for an instant, the other parties in the deal will walk over them – intentionally or not. This was to be, supposedly, a kinder, gentler way.

To this day I still don't think the other parties really understood why we did what we did. We were simply looking for peace and dignity. We only wanted to be treated fairly.

We wanted to spare children the horror we suffered. I still hope that in some small way, we have given male victims of child abuse the courage to speak out, to realize that in today's society, boys do cry.

Acknowledgements

I could not have undertaken this project without the mandate I received from David McCann, who gave me the story, and James Adams, who gave me the opportunity to tell it. Both provided immeasurable help during the five-year project, David as a walking source and James as the first of my three editors at McClelland & Stewart. This was to have been a story told by David and myself about the other victims, but circumstances changed all that.

I am also greatly indebted to the dozens of victims who bared their souls to me, telling me about horrific experiences they had told no one else. Early in the development of this story, I was asked by a colleague how I knew the former wards were telling the truth. When grown men crumble before your very eyes, you tend to believe what they say. Many tears have been wept over the past five years; some of them were mine. I applaud the survivors of St. John's and St. Joseph's for their courage, and their stamina, and I apologize for making their lives hell.

I am especially indebted to Ed Armstrong, Gerry Belecque, Gerry Champagne, Armand Jobin, Jr., Norman Godin, Grant Hartley, Patrick Healey, Jacques Pacquette, Lawrence Siple, Gerry Sirois, Gary Sullivan, Roger Tucker, Michael Watters, and Archie Villeneuvre for their insights.

A great deal of assistance was required to put this book together, particularly since it involved coverage of more than thirty criminal trials, most of which were in French. To that end I thank Gerry Sirois, Cosette Chafe, Ronald Laliberté, Robert Pelletier, and Claudette MacFarlane for helping me see the light.

There were a legion of researchers and colleagues who backed me up in every way, so I must graciously thank Jason Berry, Phil Bingley, Hazel Blythe, Paul Cantin, Lou Clancy, Sandro Contenta, Steve Fisher, Dave Gamble, Daniel Girard, Jeannie Harrison, Chris Van Krieken, Helena Kranjec, Vivian Macdonald, Brian McAndrew, Phil Mascoll, Judy Masdorp, Lisa Priest, Don Reimer, Wayne Rempel, Nick Van Rijn, Dan Smith, Judy Steed, and Sean Upton.

I am forever indebted to lawyers Stuart Robertson and Peggie Ainsley for going to bat for me and for freedom of the press when I was refused access to public court exhibits by the attorney general.

I was astonished by the courtesy and the professionalism of the detectives involved in the case, particularly Tim Smith, who, from the outset, asked what he could do for me rather than the other way around.

Many of the photographs in this book were provided by, or with the assistance of, Dominic Battaglia, Ron Bull, Grant Hartley, Patrick Healey, David McCann, Kevin Omura, Jim Rankin, Wayne Rempel, and the Uxbridge–Scott Museum. I thank them all.

Lastly, I must thank the three special women in my life, Joanne Bosch, Esther Henton, and Debbie Weismiller, for guidance, assistance, advice, and much, much more.

— Darcy Henton

I find it sad that Christian Brothers who toiled all their lives in the service of their Church and who dedicated themselves to helping others have had their work diminished by the misdeeds of a few. They deserve better than the public legacy of abuse which now casts a shadow over the order. These good men have earned our respect and gratitude.

However, this book is not about them and their good deeds;

it is about the abusers of thousands of children and those who failed to stop their reign of terror.

I could not have led Helpline for three years without the overwhelming support of its members. They and their families were always there with encouragement as we tried to peel away the shroud of silence that cloaked our terrible secrets. The executive was, and still is, a group of wonderful, caring, and dedicated men who rose to the occasion.

As we lifted the veil, OPP Det. Insp. Tim Smith and his team of investigators treated us with respect, earned our trust, and exposed the truth. The Crown attorneys and court witness-victim co-ordinators helped us through the trials. Thank you.

Perly-Robertson, Panet, Hill & McDougall gave us more support than I ever could have hoped for or expected. Roger Tucker's tireless work resulted in the empowerment of the victims. The effect of his guiding hand cannot be measured, only marvelled at, and his caring touched my heart.

Peter Kormos, Brother Provincial Jean-Marc Cantin, and Archbishop Marcel Gervais earned my respect. I believe they truly understood that we were searching for reconciliation and healing.

My neighbours and friends, old and new, rallied round and supported me. I am sorry that I never really thanked them – I noticed but the whirlwind of events didn't always afford the time to express my thanks properly.

Tina Lentz, Joli Manson, Gus Mackey, and Debbie Weismiller welcomed me into their homes. It meant more to me than they will ever know.

To the boys in Newfoundland: Thank you for your courage and for leading the way.

Darcy, you trusted me enough to search for the truth. Thank you, my friend.

– David R. McCann

Christian Brothers Trial Synopsis

As of June 1995

Aimé Bergeron, aged eighty, (Brother Gabriel): Two counts of indecent assault and one count of buggery. Convicted in April 1992 and sentenced September 1992 to two years less a day.

Pierre Durocher, aged seventy-seven, (Brother Pierre): Three counts of indecent assault and one each of buggery and indecent assault. Charges stayed June 1992 for medical reasons.

Sylvio Valade, aged fifty-five, (Brother Sylvio): Pleaded guilty to one count of indecent assault in June 1992. Suspended sentence and thirty days' probation. He apologized to his victim.

Jean-Louis Jeaurond, aged fifty-six, (Brother Remi): Pleaded guilty in September 1992 to three counts of indecent assault. Four months.

Camille Huot, aged seventy-eight, (Brother Camille): Charged with two counts of indecent assault and one count of buggery. Sentenced in October 1992 to two years less a day. Appeal denied.

Réjean Nadeau, aged forty-nine, (Brother Rhéal or Réjean): Acquitted in August 1992 of indecent assault and buggery.

Étienne Fortin, aged seventy-four, (Brother Étienne): One charge of assault causing bodily harm. Stayed in October 1992 on a technicality.

Gilles Nadeau, aged fifty-two, (Brother Gilles): Two charges of assault causing bodily harm. Withdrawn in October 1992.

Timothy V. O'Donnell, aged sixty-one, (Brother Sean): Acquitted of assault charges in November 1992.

Bernard Recker, aged fifty-four, (Brother Mark): Convicted in December 1992 on three of ten assault charges. Suspended sentence.

Jean Ravacley, aged seventy-eight, (Brother Jean): Buggery, assault causing bodily harm, and two charges of indecent assault. Stayed in November 1992 for medical reasons.

Bernard McGrath, aged fifty-five, (Brother Hugh): Pleaded guilty to a charge of assault. Conditional discharge and one year's probation. Faces new charges of buggery, gross indecency, and indecent assault.

Jean-Paul Collin, aged sixty, (Brother Daniel): Acquitted of buggery and assault causing bodily harm in February 1993.

Jean-Claude Provencher, aged sixty-one, (Brother Pierre): Convicted in May 1993 on two of three counts of indecent assault. Two years less a day.

Robert Morrissey, aged fifty-four, (Brother Frederick/Father Bob): Convicted on five of seven counts of indecent assault and attempted buggery. Sentenced in February 1993 to eighteen months. Appeal court quashed convictions on all sexual offences and ordered a new trial. Appeal court dismissed appeal on assault causing bodily harm but reduced sentence.

Lucien Dagenais, aged sixty-eight, (Brother Joseph): Convicted in December 1992 on fifteen of eighteen counts, including buggery, assault causing bodily harm, and indecent assault. Sentenced in March 1993 to five years. Appealed, but abandoned his appeal.

Léopold Monette, aged eighty-three, (Brother Léo): Convicted on eleven of twenty-seven charges, including indecent assault, assault causing bodily harm, and buggery. Sentenced in May 1993 to five years. Under appeal.

Lawrence Lessard, aged fifty-eight, (Brother Albert): Acquitted in March 1993 on a buggery charge, but faces new charges of gross indecency and three counts of indecent assault.

James Clarke, aged fifty-seven, a civilian: Pleaded guilty in March 1993 to buggery, indecent assault, and assault causing bodily harm. Two years less a day. He also pleaded guilty in January 1995 to additional charges of buggery, gross indecency, and indecent assault and received another nine months.

André St. Jean, aged fifty-six, (Brother Andrew): Acquitted of assault causing bodily harm in March 1992. Convicted of indecent assault. Sentenced in November 1992 to one year. New trial ordered.

Robert Radford, aged sixty-four, (Brother Michael): Two counts of assault causing bodily harm. Withdrawn in April 1993.

Jean Clement, aged seventy-four, (Brother Pierre): Acquitted in July 1993 of charges of indecent assault and assault causing bodily harm.

Maurice Perrault, aged sixty-seven, (Brother Gérald): Convicted on two charges of assault causing bodily harm. $2,000 fine, two years' probation, and two hundred hours of community service.

Stanley Clark, aged fifty-one, (Brother Andrew): Pleaded guilty to two counts of indecent assault. Sentenced in July 1993 to thirty days. He is currently facing additional charges relating to his activities after leaving the order.

Joseph Dugas, aged sixty, (Brother Basil): Acquitted of indecent assault and assault causing bodily harm in May and June 1993. Deceased 1994.

Jean-Guy Pagé, aged sixty-two, (Brother Yves): Convicted in August 1993 on four counts of indecent assault. Four months jail, eighteen months' probation.

André Charbonneau, aged sixty-three, (Brother André): Pleaded guilty on seventeen charges. Sentenced in February 1994 to six years in prison.

Jean-Paul Monfils, aged eighty-one, (Brother Irenée): Seven charges of assault causing bodily harm. Stayed for medical reasons. Deceased 1994.

André Desjardins, aged fifty, (Brother André): Acquitted in October 1993 of charges of buggery and indecent assault.

Bernard Monaghan, aged sixty-four, (Brother Stanislas): Buggery and indecent assault. No determination.

Sources

Research for this book began in 1989, fifteen years after the province took over control of St. Joseph's Training School in Alfred. The genesis for *Boys Don't Cry* was material obtained from the Archives of Ontario under provincial access to information legislation, augmented by more than one hundred interviews with former wards and provincial officials and information – news reports, transcripts, and exhibits – from more than thirty criminal proceedings. Detailed information about individual wards was obtained from lengthy and often painful interviews backed up with data from their own ward files, their statements to police, and their testimony at preliminary hearings and trials. I have also relied a great deal upon my colleagues in the media, particularly Paul Cantin, Dave Gamble, and Sean Upton, whose blanket coverage of twenty trials and hundreds of days of court proceedings in Ottawa and L'Orignal was of enormous assistance. Much of the history of the Christian Brothers was provided through the research of Helena Kranjec. Following is a list of the major sources of information:

CHAPTER 1

Ward files of David McCann. Letters of correspondence between the Ontario Department of Reform Institutions and St. Joseph's Training School for Boys. Correspondence between Marie McCann and the Christian Brothers. Inspection reports, 1948 to 1958.

CHAPTER 2

Archdiocese of Toronto, et al. *Walking the Less Travelled Road: A History of Religious Communities Within the Archdiocese of Toronto, 1841-1991*. Toronto: Mission Press, 1993. Fitzpatrick, Edward A. *La Salle: Patron of All Teachers.* Milwaukee: Brace Publishing Company, 1951. Flynn, L. J. *The Story of Catholic Education in Kingston District, Kingston: The Frontenac, Lennox and Addington County Roman Catholic Separate School Board* (Tercentenary Project),

1973. Gabriel, Brother Angelus. *The Christian Brothers in the United States, 1848 to 1948: A Century of Catholic Education.* New York: Little & Ives, 1948. Powers, Brother Cyril, "St. John's School (1893 to 1957) at Scarborough." *Scarborough Historical Notes & Comments,* vol. 4 no. 3, Sept. 1980. Walker, Franklin A. *Catholic Education and Politics in Ontario.* Thomas Nelson & Sons (Canada) Ltd. 1964. Wilson, Donald J., Stamp, Robert M., and Audet, Louis-Philippe, editors. *Canadian Education: A History, Scarborough.* Toronto: Prentice Hall of Canada Ltd.

CHAPTER 3

Archives of Ontario: Department of Reform Institutions memos, ward files, medical records, committal reports, and correspondence, March 5 to 29, 1957; Aug. 8, 1960. Duckett, R. L., coroner, and jury. Investigation into the cause and circumstances of the death of Albert Bruno at Westmount on July 20, 1948, Montreal,Coroner's Court, July 22, 1948. Interviews with Glen Bowmaster, OPP, and former St. Joseph's ward Oscar Fredericks. Charles Lewis. *The Ottawa Citizen,* May 15 and 16, 1990; April 18, 1990. Documents from the Archives of Ontario: Nov. 11, 22, and 28, 1957; Nov. 21, 1958. Preliminary hearing transcripts: *Regina v. Robert Radford,* testimony of Doris Height (née Watters), Michael Watters, Fred Oliver. Ward files, statement to police, and interviews with Michael Watters and Fred Oliver. Thomas, Gwyn. *Toronto Star,* Aug. 22, 1959. Johnston, Monroe. *Toronto Star,* Sept. 3, 1959. Berton, Pierre. *Toronto Star,* Dec. 1958.

CHAPTER 4

Archives of Ontario: Ontario Department of Reform Institutions memos, Feb. 18 and 26, 1960; March 3 and 15, 1960; June 24 and 28, 1960; July 4, 7, 14, 15, and 28, 1960; Aug. 10, 11, 15, 24, and 25, 1960; Sept. 11, 13, and 27, 1960; March 29, 1961. Interviews with Donald Sinclair and Maurice Egan. *Regina v. Bernard Recker,* trial, Nov. 4, 1992. *Toronto Star,* March 28 and 29, 1960. Toronto *Telegram,* March 28, 1960.

CHAPTER 5

Agenda, conference on community participation in juvenile corrections, Carleton University, May 16 and 17, 1975. Apps, Syl. *Ontario Hansard,* Oct. 18, 1973. Archives of Ontario: Ontario Department of Reform

Institutions memos, reports, and correspondence: March 29, 1961; April 18, 1963; May 2, 14, 21, and 24, 1963; Oct. 16, 1964; March 10 and 25, 1969; April 14, 1969; May 10, 1969; July 22, 1969, Aug. 12, 1969; Dec. 18, 1969; June 29, 1970; June 2, 1971. Chronology of Events: Oct. 18, 20, 26, and 29, 1971; Nov. 18, 1971; Jan. 6, 23, and 31, 1973; Feb. 16, 1973; March 12, 1973; April 6, 1973; Feb. 6, 14, and 28, 1975; March 19, 1975; May 9, 1975; April 2, 1993; May 5, 1993. Committee for the Abolition of Training Schools, position paper. Interviews with Wilfrid Marion, *Regina v. Jean-Paul Collin*, trial. Carter, Glen. Ontario position paper regarding the committee for the abolition of training schools. Committee For the Abolition of Training Schools, newsletter, no. 1, July 1975. Finlayson, Jane. *Ottawa Citizen*, March 22, 1975. Green, Bernard. "Trumpets, Justice and Federalism: An Analysis of the Ontario Training Schools Act of 1965." *Canadian Journal of Corrections*, vol. 8, no. 4, Oct. 1966. Grygier, Tadeusz. "A Minor Note on the Trumpet." *Canadian Journal of Corrections*, vol. 8, no. 4, Oct. 1966. McGrath, W. T., editor. *Crime and Its Treatment in Canada*. Toronto: MacMillan of Canada, New York: St. Martins Press, 1966. Noel, E. E. "The Young Adult Offender." *Canadian Journal of Corrections*, vol. 12, no. 3, July 1970. Oliver, Peter. *Unlikely Tory: The Life and Politics of Allan Grossman*, Toronto: Lester & Orpen Dennys, 1985. Shulman, Morton. *Ontario Hansard*, questions in the Legislature of Ontario, June 1, 1970. Sinclair, Donald. "In Service Training and the Goals of Institutional Treatment." *Canadian Journal of Corrections*, vol. 5, no. 2, April 1963. "Changing Concepts in the Institutional Care of Juveniles." *Canadian Journal of Corrections*, The Canadian Corrections Association, vol. 3, no. 3, July 1961. "The Development of Human Resources in the Correctional Field." *Canadian Journal of Corrections*, vol. 12, no. 3. *Toronto Star*, June 20, 1975. Wardrope, George C. "Recent Developments in Ontario's Correctional Services." *Canadian Journal of Corrections*, vol. 3, no. 3, July 1961.

CHAPTER 6

Barstow, Anne Llewellyn. *Married Priests and the Reforming Papacy*. New York: The Edwin Mellen Press, 1982. Berry, Jason. *Lead Us Not Into Temptation: Catholic Priests and the Sexual Abuse of Children*. Doubleday, 1992. The Canadian Press, Dec. 24, 1992; April 22, 1992; June 8, 1993. *Catholic New Times*, July 5, 1992. "From Pain to Hope," report of the *ad hoc* committee on child sexual abuse, Canadian Conference of Catholic Bishops, June 1992. *Commonweal*, Nov. 20, 1992; Jan. 15, 1993. Cunningham, Richard C. *The Tridentine Concept of Sacerdotal Celibacy*. Rome: Tipografia di Patrizio Graziani, 1972. Greeley, Andrew M. *America*, March 20 and 27, 1993. Harkx, Peter. *The Fathers on Celibacy*. De Pere, Wisconsin: St. Norbert Abby Press, 1968. Harris, Michael. *Unholy Orders: Tragedy at Mount Cashel*. Toronto: Penguin Books, 1991. Kertzer, David I., and Saller, Richard P. *The Family in Italy*. New Haven: Yale University Press, 1991. Reuter, May 8, 1992. Wilkes, Paul. "Unholy Acts." *New Yorker*, June 7, 1993. Lipovenko, Dorothy. *Globe and Mail*, March 26, 1988. Loftus, John Allan. "Sexual Abuse in the Church." Emmanuel Convalescent Foundation, 1989. McAteer, Michael. *Toronto Star*, Feb. 14, 1993; March 1, 1993. McKenzie, Robert. *Toronto Star*, March 12, 1993. Murphy, Anne. *The London Free Press*, Jan. 4, 1993. *Owen Sound Sun Times*, Aug. 31, 1992. Rogers, Rix. "Reaching for Solutions." The Report of the Special Advisor to the Minister of Health and Welfare on child sexual abuse in Canada, June 1990. Spears, John. *Toronto Star*, July 18 and 19, 1990. Small, Peter. *Toronto Star*, Dec. 17, 1992. *Whig-Standard* (Kingston), Nov. 11, 1992; Dec. 16, 1992. Picard, Andre. *Globe and Mail*, Sept. 12, 1992. Larrabee, John, and Edmonds, Patricia. *USA Today*, Jan. 27, 1993. Winter, Gordon A. "Report of the Archdiocesan Commission of Enquiry into the Sexual Abuse of Children by Members of the Clergy." Archdiocese of St. John's, 1990. York, Geoffrey. *Globe and Mail*, June 1992. Zerbisias, Antonia. *Toronto Star*, Aug. 15, 1992.

CHAPTER 7

Richardson, Mark. *Ottawa Citizen*, April 2, 1990. Interviews with David McCann, Gerry Belecque, Maurice Egan, Ruth Jenkins, Judi Richter-Jacobs, Tim Smith, Ron Wilson, Claude Larocque, Gerry Sirois. Notes of David Day from "Betrayal of Trust, A Working Conference on Male Child Abuse."

CHAPTER 8

Arts West, vol. 5, no. 7, Nov./Dec. 1988. Blanchfield, Mike. *Ottawa Citizen*, May 2, 1990. Dhooma, Rashida. *Toronto Sun*, Aug. 13, 1990. Ferguson, Derek. *Toronto Star*, May 15, 1990. Manning, Joanna. *Toronto Star*,

April 25, 1990. Maychak, Matt. *Toronto Star*, May 1 and 3, 1990. Murray, Maureen. *Toronto Star*, Aug. 13, 1990. Richardson, Mark. *Ottawa Citizen*, Aug. 3, 1990. *Ottawa Sun*, Aug. 26, 1990. *Ottawa Citizen*, Aug. 26, 1990. *Toronto Star*, April 10, 1990. *Toronto Star*, editorials, April 11 and 24, 1990. *Toronto Star*, April 11 and 12, 1990; May 4 and 13, 1990. Walkom, Thomas. *Toronto Star*, April 11, 1990. Review of Safeguards in Children's Residential Programs, December 1990. Interviews with Roger Tucker, David McCann, Grant Hartley, Harold Graham, Joanne Campbell, and Joanna Manning. Cantin, Paul. *Ottawa Sun*, April 6, 1990. Walkom, Thomas. *Toronto Star*, April 11, 1990. Interviews with Armand Jobin, Jr., Armand Jobin, Sr., Claude Larocque, Normand Mallette, Bernie Lacoste, Eddie Graveline, Gerry Belecque. Peter Kormos, press conference, Sept. 11, 1990. Notes of April 5, 1990, victims' meeting. CBC Radio report of April 5, 1990, meeting.

CHAPTER 9
Interviews with Tim Smith, Armand Jobin, Jr., Mel Proteau, Bob Carpenter, Robert Pelletier, David McCann.

CHAPTER 10
Archives of Ontario: inspector's report, June 25, 1958. Yeager, Matthew G. *Report of Criminologist, Regina v. Lucien Joseph Simeon Dagenais*. Ontario Court, general division, Feb. 5, 1993. Interviews, testimony, ward files, and police statements of Grant Hartley, Gerry Champagne, David McCann, Gerry Sirois, Albert Daigneault, and others whose names are protected by a court ordered publication ban. Gamble, David. *Ottawa Sun*, Feb. 13, 1994. Gonczol, David. *Ottawa Sun*, Feb. 18, 1991. Notes of OPP press conference to announce charges against St. Joseph's Brothers and press conference to announce charges against St. John's Brothers. *Regina v. Étienne Fortin*, decision of Mr. Justice Jean A. Forget, Oct. 22, 1992. *Regina v. André Charbonneau*, preliminary hearing, Nov. 4, 1991. Interviews with Cosette Chafe, Wib Craig, Robert Doyle, Paul Gagnon, Sylvio Goulet, David McCann, Denis Pommainville, Nick Sapusak, Tim Smith, and Ron Wilson.

CHAPTER II
Roche, Douglas and Hoffman, Ben. "The Vision to Reconcile: Process
Report on the Helpline Reconciliation Model Agreement, 1993, Fund
for Dispute Resolution." Interviews with participants and correspondence, reports, speaking notes, and minutes.

CHAPTER 12
Barnes, Alan. *Toronto Star*, Nov. 12, 1992. Belanger, Joe. *North Bay Nugget*,
Aug. 15, 1992. Blanchfield, Mike. *Ottawa Citizen*, Aug. 13, 1992. Canadian
Press, Sept. 30, 1992. Hoffman, Deborah, and Anthony, Liz. "Survey
Team Report," an assessment of brief clinical analysis of the members
and their responses, Feb. 25, 1992. Robertson, Ian, and Ruryk, Zen.
Toronto Sun, Sept. 30, 1992. Upton, Sean. *Ottawa Citizen*, Dec. 12, 1992.
Interviews with David McCann, Roger Tucker, Melville O'Donohue,
Douglas Roche. Minutes of meetings, correspondence, notes from
press conference to announce tentative deal.

CHAPTER 13
Regina v. Aimé Bergeron, preliminary hearing and trial, Sept. 4, 1991; April
13 to 15, 1992. Yeager, Matthew. Criminologists Report, *Regina v. Bergeron*,
Aug. 6, 1992. Blanchfield, Mike. *Ottawa Citizen*, April 14, 1992. *Ottawa
Citizen*, June 23, 1992. Cantin, Paul. *Ottawa Sun*, June 23, 1992. Gamble,
David. *Ottawa Sun*, April 14, 22, 23, and 24, 1992. *Ottawa Sun*, editorial,
April 27, 1992. Payne, Elizabeth. *Ottawa Citizen*, April 13 and 24, 1992.
Upton, Sean. *Ottawa Citizen*, April 15, 18, 22, 23, and 24, 1992; May 5,
1992; June 24 and 25, 1992; Aug. 8, 1992; Sept. 12, 1992. *Le Devoir*, April
14 and 24, 1992; June 25, 1992; Aug. 26, 1992; Sept. 5, 1992. Interviews
with Gerry Belecque, Ronald Laliberté, Denis Oiseau, Matthew Yeager.

CHAPTER 14
Gamble, David. *Ottawa Sun*, Nov. 5, 1992; Dec. 9, 1992. MacLeod, Ian.
Ottawa Citizen, Dec. 3, 1992. Marchildon, Lynn. *Ottawa Sun*, Nov. 10, 11,
and 13, 1992. Millar, Cal. *Toronto Star*, Nov. 10 and 11, 1992. Upton, Sean.
Ottawa Citizen, Nov. 4, 10, 13, and 24, 1992; Dec. 1, 1992; Jan. 5 and 30,
1993; March 20, 1993. Interviews with David McCann, Tim Smith, Tina
Lentz, Robert Pelletier, Peter Shoniker, Melville O'Donohue, Matthew
Yeager, Gerry Sirois, Cosette Chafe, Albert Daigneault. Transcripts and

notes of portions of the preliminary hearing and trial of *Regina v. Lucien Dagenais*. Yeager, Matthew. Report of Criminologist, *Regina v. Dagenais*, Feb. 5, 1993. May 17, 1990, letter to David Peterson from Daniel Rock. May 25 letter from McCann to Peterson. Canadian Criminal Cases, *Regina v. Lee*.

CHAPTER 15

Cantin, Paul. *Ottawa Sun*, Feb. 12, 1993. The Canadian Press, (*Toronto Star*) Feb. 17, 1993. The Canadian Press (*Kitchener-Waterloo Record*) Sept. 17, 1993. Gamble, David. *Ottawa Sun*, Sept. 14 and 17, 1993. Thompson, Chris. *Ottawa Sun*, Sept. 15, 1993. Upton, Sean. *Ottawa Citizen*, Feb. 12 and 16, 1993; Sept. 17, 1993. Interviews with Armand Jobin, Jr., Armand Jobin, Sr., Elaine Jobin, Claude Larocque, Ronald Laliberté, Tim Smith, Wilfrid Marion, Mike Fagan, Bob Carpenter. *Regina v. Jean-Paul Collins*, notes and transcripts of preliminary hearing and trial.

CHAPTER 16

Cobb, Chris. *Ottawa Citizen*, Dec. 14, 1992. Cuff, John Haslett. *Globe and Mail*, Dec. 7, 1992. The Canadian Press, (*Peterborough Examiner*) Jan. 18, 1993. Harris, Christopher. *Globe and Mail*, Dec. 7, 1992. Hall, Joseph. *Toronto Star*, Dec. 8, 1992. Hurst, Lynda. *Toronto Star*, Dec. 5, 1992. *Globe and Mail*, Dec. 5, 1992. Oakes, Gary. *Toronto Star*, Dec. 2, 1993. Quill, Greg. *Toronto Star*, Dec. 8 and 10, 1992; Nov. 30, 1993; Dec. 8, 1993. Welsh, Moira. *Toronto Star*, Dec. 6, 1992. Interview with John N. Smith, Clayton Ruby, Dan Henry, David McCann. Affidavits of Ronald Caza, Laura McKinstray, and Angelo Callegari. Notice of application, Ontario Court of Justice, *Lucien Dagenais, Léopold Monette, Joseph Dugas and Robert Radford v. CBC*, Dec. 3, 1992. Nov. 30, 1993, letter from James Cullingham to Brother Provincial Francis McCrea.

CHAPTER 17

McCrea, Brother Provincial Francis J. Report on trials and our non-participation in agreement, *The Lasallian Signum Fidei*, Sept. 1993. Ritchie, James. Letter of response, Oct. 18, 1993. *Watters, Michael et al v. Brothers of the Christian Schools of Ontario and St. John's Training School for Boys*, Ontario Court, general division, statement of claim, Sept. 2, 1994. Roche, Douglas, letter to Helpline Members, June 30, 1993. Notes of Aug. 1993

Helpline meeting, YMCA, Toronto. Letters to the editor: Bob Henning, *Toronto Star*, Jan. 1, 1993; David McCann, *Whig-Standard* (Kingston), Sept. 12, 1992. Interviews with Michael Watters, Douglas Roche, David McCann, Archie Villeneuvre, Patrick Healey, Melville O'Donohue, Roger Tucker, and Clem Gagnon.

CHAPTER 18

Bies, Ernest. *Ben Chee Chee: In His Own Words, His Life Was A Wild Ride*, unpublished manuscript. Blanchfield, Mike. *Ottawa Citizen*, April 29, 1990. Blanchfield, Mike, and Maloney, Careen. *Ottawa Citizen*, May 3, 1990. Hunter, Mic. *Abused Boys, The Neglected Victims of Sexual Abuse*. New York: Fawcett Columbine, 1990. Dimock, Peter. "Male Sexual Abuse: An Underreported Problem." *Journal of Interpersonal Violence*, Sage Publications Inc., June 1988. *New York Times*, Dec. 21, 1990. Jutras, Catherine. *Ottawa Citizen*, Nov. 1973. *Globe and Mail*, March 17, 1977. Lewis, Charles, and Blanchfield, Mike. *Ottawa Citizen*, April 14, 1990. Hoffman, Ben. An analysis of St. Joseph's and St. John's Survivors of Child Abuse Survey and Assessment of Needs. Concorde Inc., The Dispute Resolution Professionals, Feb. 25, 1992. Hoffman, Deborah, and Anthony, Elizabeth. Survey of Helpline membership, Feb. 1992. Odowa Friendship Centre bulletin, March 15, 1977. *Ottawa Journal*, May 11, 1979; June 10, 1979. Oakes, Gary. *Toronto Star*, April 25, 1990. Interviews with Nelson Trudel, Jituska Smahel, Frank Landino, Grant Hartley, Gerry Belecque, Mel Proteau, Wayne Rempel, Gerry and Hélène Sirois, Tina Lentz, Bernard Jordan, Jerry Hills, Lydia Mason, Archie Villeneuvre, Ed Armstrong, Harold Graham, Yvon Guindon, Mike Baroni, Robert Gregson, Armand Jobin, Jr., David Harrigan, Jacques Paquette, Lionel Paquette, Albert Daigneault, Bob Lacasse, Gary Sullivan, Lawrence Siple, Paul Bennett, Marvin Kobsa, Doug McCaul. *Regina v. Robert Morrissey*, trial testimony of Drs. Ian Collins, John Bradford, and Grant Fair.

Index